# Intelligence and Law Enforcement in the 21st Century

Eugene de Silva
*Virginia Research Institute, USA*

Asanga Abeyagoonesekera
*Parliament of Sri Lanka, Sri Lanka*

A volume in the Advances in Digital Crime, Forensics, and Cyber Terrorism (ADCFCT) Book Series

IGI Global
PUBLISHER of TIMELY KNOWLEDGE

Published in the United States of America by
IGI Global
Information Science Reference (an imprint of IGI Global)
701 E. Chocolate Avenue
Hershey PA, USA 17033
Tel: 717-533-8845
Fax: 717-533-8661
E-mail: cust@igi-global.com
Web site: http://www.igi-global.com



Library of Congress Cataloging-in-Publication Data

Names: De Silva, Eugene editor. | Abeyagoonesekera, Asanga, DATE- editor.
Title: Intelligence and law enforcement in the 21st century /
Eugene de Silva, Asanga Abeyagoonesekera, editors.
Description: Hershey, PA : Information Science Reference, [2022] | Includes bibliographical references and index. | Summary: "This book provides a detailed discussion on the ways in which education and science can be applied to the improvement of security focusing on the necessary blend of education, science, and intelligence activities through the relevant application of educational concepts and scientific approaches"-- Provided by publisher.
Identifiers: LCCN 2021027678 (print) | LCCN 2021027679 (ebook) | ISBN 9781799879046 (hardcover) | ISBN 9781799879053 (paperback) | ISBN 9781799879060 (ebook)
Subjects: LCSH: Intelligence service--History--21st century. | National security--History--21st century. | Law enforcement--History--21st century.
Classification: LCC JF1525.I6 I574 2022 (print) | LCC JF1525.I6 (ebook) | DDC 327.12--dc23
LC record available at https://lccn.loc.gov/2021027678
LC ebook record available at https://lccn.loc.gov/2021027679

This book is published in the IGI Global book series Advances in Digital Crime, Forensics, and Cyber Terrorism (ADCFCT) (ISSN: 2327-0381; eISSN: 2327-0373)

British Cataloguing in Publication Data
A Cataloguing in Publication record for this book is available from the British Library.

All work contributed to this book is new, previously-unpublished material.
The views expressed in this book are those of the authors, but not necessarily of the publisher.

For electronic access to this publication, please contact: eresources@igi-global.com.

# Advances in Digital Crime, Forensics, and Cyber Terrorism (ADCFCT) Book Series

ISSN:2327-0381
EISSN:2327-0373

Editor-in-Chief: Bryan Christiansen Global Research Society, LLC, USA Agnieszka Piekarz Independent Researcher, Poland

## MISSION

The digital revolution has allowed for greater global connectivity and has improved the way we share and present information. With this new ease of communication and access also come many new challenges and threats as cyber crime and digital perpetrators are constantly developing new ways to attack systems and gain access to private information.

The **Advances in Digital Crime, Forensics, and Cyber Terrorism (ADCFCT) Book Series** seeks to publish the latest research in diverse fields pertaining to crime, warfare, terrorism and forensics in the digital sphere. By advancing research available in these fields, the **ADCFCT** aims to present researchers, academicians, and students with the most current available knowledge and assist security and law enforcement professionals with a better understanding of the current tools, applications, and methodologies being implemented and discussed in the field.

## COVERAGE

- Information Warfare
- Global Threat Intelligence
- Vulnerability
- Malicious Codes
- Watermarking
- Telecommunications Fraud
- Malware
- Cryptography
- Cyber Terrorism
- Digital surveillance

IGI Global is currently accepting manuscripts for publication within this series. To submit a proposal for a volume in this series, please contact our Acquisition Editors at Acquisitions@igi-global.com or visit: http://www.igi-global.com/publish/.

The Advances in Digital Crime, Forensics, and Cyber Terrorism (ADCFCT) Book Series (ISSN 2327-0381) is published by IGI Global, 701 E. Chocolate Avenue, Hershey, PA 17033-1240, USA, www.igi-global.com. This series is composed of titles available for purchase individually; each title is edited to be contextually exclusive from any other title within the series. For pricing and ordering information please visit http://www.igi-global.com/book-series/advances-digital-crime-forensics-cyber/73676. Postmaster: Send all address changes to above address. 

## Titles in this Series

*For a list of additional titles in this series, please visit:*
*www.igi-global.com/book-series/advances-digital-crime-forensics-cyber/73676*

***Social Engineering and Information Warfare Operations Emerging Research and Opportunities***
Rhonda L. Johnson (Upper Iowa University, USA)
Information Science Reference • © 2021 • 150pp • H/C (ISBN: 9781799842705) • US $145.00

***Evaluating Emerging Threats and New Research Opportunities in Digital Crime and Forensics***
Rhonda Johnson (Upper Iowa University, USA)
Information Science Reference • © 2021 • 350pp • H/C (ISBN: 9781799822288) • US $195.00

***Confluence of AI, Machine, and Deep Learning in Cyber Forensics***
Sanjay Misra (Covenant University, Nigeria) Chamundeswari Arumugam (Sri Sivasubramaniya Nadar College of Engineering, India) Suresh Jaganathan (Sri Sivasubramaniya Nadar College of Engineering, India) and Saraswathi S. (Sri Sivasubramaniya Nadar College of Engineering, India)
Information Science Reference • © 2021 • 248pp • H/C (ISBN: 9781799849001) • US $225.00

***Cyber Security Auditing, Assurance, and Awareness Through CSAM and CATRAM***
Regner Sabillon (Universitat Oberta de Catalunya, Spain)
Information Science Reference • © 2021 • 260pp • H/C (ISBN: 9781799841623) • US $195.00

***Critical Concepts, Standards, and Techniques in Cyber Forensics***
Mohammad Shahid Husain (Ministry of Higher Education, Oman) and Mohammad Zunnun Khan (Integral University, India)
Information Science Reference • © 2020 • 292pp • H/C (ISBN: 9781799815587) • US $225.00

*For an entire list of titles in this series, please visit:*
*www.igi-global.com/book-series/advances-digital-crime-forensics-cyber/73676*

IGI Global
PUBLISHER of TIMELY KNOWLEDGE

701 East Chocolate Avenue, Hershey, PA 17033, USA
Tel: 717-533-8845 x100 • Fax: 717-533-8661
E-Mail: cust@igi-global.com • www.igi-global.com

*To my father Angelo L. de Silva (February 4, 1939 – July 8, 2019) for generating my interest in intelligence and security at a very young age.*

# Table of Contents

# Detailed Table of Contents



The politicization of intelligence and how it leads to failures in intelligence have been recognized for many years. Those who lead the intelligence community have also been staunch advocates against politicization. Nevertheless, the intelligence community has always been influenced by policymakers at various stages of the intelligence cycle. This chapter discusses politicization and presents a model to determine the degree of politicization qualitatively/quantitatively. The recognition of five factors related to politicization and the use of a simple scale would enable the intelligence team to determine the extent of politicization and insulate each stage of the intelligence cycle. This chapter also applies the new model to two instances where politicization has occurred.



Intelligence gathering by law enforcement officers has been used in the conviction of criminals for many years in the United States. Law enforcement officers must ensure that the information gathered and seized does not violate the Fourth Amendment of the United States Constitution. However, officers, even though acting in the spirit of the law, may not be in legal compliance. This chapter identifies and discusses the requirements of a search warrant, the legally accepted exceptions to the search warrant requirements in the United States, and reviews several historical and modern United States Supreme Court cases on the gathering of intelligence by officers.



The purpose of this work is to examine interagency cooperation within the United States (US) Intelligence Community (IC). To elucidate the importance of interagency interoperability, two cases wherein IC agencies failed to appropriately collaborate are presented: 1) the September 11th attacks of 2001 and 2) the failed bombing by Umar Farouk Abdulmutallab, also referred to as the underwear bomber. This work begins with a brief review of how interagency issues have quite deep roots in the IC. Then, readers are presented with a review of the two cases that is followed by an in-depth analysis of the factors that were common to both failures. Ultimately, the variations in modus operandi (MO), a lack of clear guidelines, and bureaucracy were identified as the three primary factors of failure in both of the cases. Therefore, the work concludes by recommending improved training and educational opportunities for those in the IC in addition to the establishment of an independent entity that would be responsible for overseeing and guiding interagency activities.



The aim of this work is to provide a discussion of radicalization, especially as it has been presented in existing literature. This chapter begins with a focus on how radicalization is defined and how debates surrounding the definition of the term could have pragmatic and theoretical consequences. Further, this work highlights current discourse on the radicalization process. The work also includes a review of the risk factors that may typically lead one to radicalization. To do this, the three main overarching themes, including push, pull, and personal factors, are spotlighted. Finally, the work concludes with a three-pronged course of action (COA) to prevent the radicalization process, mitigate the violence carried by those who have already been radicalized, and also rehabilitate those who have undergone the radicalization process.

## Section 2



Overly complex interdependencies develop systemic risks and flow into our international system. A lesson from the pandemic is the importance of managing systemic risks due to globalization. The entire world is facing a trust recession due to the rise of populist politics and protectionist sentiments. We should regain trust and strengthen economic globalization and promote multilateral agenda. There are four factors identified for the widening trust deficit. If the trust is restored, there will be definite positive outcomes such as strong intra-regional trade, developed economy, and cross-border security. The pandemic exacerbated domestic nationalist viewpoints in many nations; taking this opportunity, pandemic nations like Sri Lanka had parliamentary elections and amended the constitution, shifting power to the president. The present ultra-nationalism and populist policies would further fuel and instill domestic malign mercantilism.



The COVID-19 pandemic has swept the world uprooting people from their livelihoods and toppling the economy of the world. Thus, to everyone's interest, producing a vaccine became the priority to gain at least half the normalcy in day-to-day activities of the world. With over a year passing, several states have come to the front in producing vaccines, having completed tedious processes of research and clinical trials. The next mammoth task at hand is distribution and administration in countries. However, with only a few countries gaining the advantage of production, they are seen to exercise power politics in purchasing and distribution of the vaccine. Developing countries have succumbed to a difficult predicament amidst balancing the great powers and the financial inability to obtain the vaccination. Therefore, the chapter explores the political dimension to vaccine distribution and the plight of developing nations in obtaining the vaccine. Further, the chapter observes the global initiatives taken to address the issue and the impact of distribution on health security.

Most of the existing discussions of the nuclear ambitions of states have neglected hidden ideational factors of nuclearisation. This chapter attempts to fill this gap by analyzing prevailing literature on the Indo-Pakistan nuclear rivalry. India and Pakistan have had a history of conflict with each other since the partition in 1947. The conflict is based on divisions of two religious groups, Hindus and Muslims, and extended to an identity crisis which later turned to a bilateral conflict between two nations. The nuclear test in 1974 diverted the conflict into a novel dimension. The study conceptualizes the factors of nuclear ambitions (material and ideational) of two nations using the model of the iceberg. A constructive psychological theory to analyze the moral orders of social actions and duties of participants to act in certain issues is given. Constructivism is used as the foundation of the proposed ideational framework.

**Section 3**



The authors were presented with the task of reviewing a product by Zipato, which has a sizable user base (20,000 households by Zipato according to an article from TechCrunch). The Cyber-Living team is assessing products in the smart home and cybersecurity realms to help consumers make more informed choices. This is the first part of their risk assessment series on Zipato's smart home solutions. It also expands upon existing reporting by other security researchers. Two articles were found most informative out of what is out there for similar products by Zipato. Some of these articles have appeared multiple times because they were picked up by news sites. They often refer themselves to other researchers' discoveries. Part 2 and 3 are for education and research particularly focusing on firmware update vulnerabilities and possibilities of man-in-the-middle attacks that exploit devices. That will be the authors' contribution to the work. They will review other teams in this first part.

With the advent of IoT (internet of things), our homes are becoming more dependent on technological devices to perform everything from basic to advanced tasks. In this paper, cyber living delves into the realm of home security and the use of Raspberry Pi compute devices to secure our homes. Raspberry Pi is an educational 'system on a chip' that sells for anywhere from $30 and up. Companies have been taking these basic devices, rebranding them, and turning them into the computers that drive a home security system. They operate everything from digital locks, cameras, thermostats, fire and CO2 alarms, and more. The authors take a deep dive and look under the cover at the security and viability of Raspberry Pi as a controlling device for home security.



Reaffirming America's role as the global engine of scientific discovery and technological innovation has never been more critical. Challenges like climate change, pandemic disease, and resource scarcity demand innovation. Meanwhile, the nation that leads the world in building a clean energy economy that will enjoy a substantial economic and security advantage. That is why the administration is investing heavily in research, improving education in science and math, promoting developments in energy, and expanding international cooperation. This chapter is aimed to provide the introduction of the significant role of STEM education for national security. The chapter will provide an introduction to integrating the awareness training of national security into higher education with the demonstration of the practice of our education module of DHS CFATS in the chemical engineering course of plant safety and security.

# Preface

In the twenty-first century, intelligence and law enforcement have undergone and continue to undergo rapid changes. To address the challenges that intelligence and law enforcement now face, researchers and practitioners must adopt novel approaches that are in alignment with the unique dynamics of this time period. Through the contribution of new theory and strategies to address security concerns, academics and researchers are able to ensure that national security is upheld.

Accordingly, this book is a valuable contribution to the field of security as it offers insight to a range of topics, such as the politicization of intelligence, the improvement of intra-agency cooperation, pre- and post-pandemic regionalism, and even the significance of STEM education in national security. The variety of topics offered within this book shed light on the multi-faceted nature of intelligence and law enforcement in the twenty-first century. Practitioners and researchers within the field are faced with challenges that stem from the cyber security arena, human intelligence efforts, and now global health concerns that directly affect the political domain. Recent years have resulted in an abundance of new, unique concerns that must be resolved through forward-thinking strategies.

The chapter authors within this book have judiciously analyzed their individual topics and presented distinctive opinions and insight. The first chapter provides readers with a newly proposed model to measure the politicization of intelligence. The issue of politicization is one that has persisted for many years within the field of intelligence. It is understandable that the complete elimination of the politicization of intelligence may be difficult. Nonetheless, as is presented within this chapter, a measurement of the extent to which intelligence reports are influenced could provide the necessary guidance to make more informed decisions. This author includes examples of the real-life application of the proposed model by reviewing past incidences of the politicization of intelligence.

The next chapter allow readers to further examine the intelligence field, especially by focusing on intelligence gathering practices. The authors of this chapter present readers with a thorough review of the collection of intelligence by the law enforcement officers in the United States, and how these practices should be carefully crafted to avoid any violations of the Fourth Amendment of the United States' Constitution. As such, this chapter presents a clear discussion of the requirements of search warrants and prevailing exceptions to the standard requirements.

The next chapter continues the discussion of the intelligence field with an emphasis on the United States Intelligence Community (IC). The author presents a discussion of the barriers to interagency cooperation within the IC that have persisted within the nation. This chapter also introduces two historical cases of intra-agency interoperability failure to allow readers to more clearly recognize how and why such issues continue to exist within the field. The chapter concludes with a clear strategy to mitigate, if not completely resolve, these issues within the IC.

The fourth chapter breaks away from directly discussing the inner-workings of the intelligence field by focusing on the issue of radicalization and how it can be addressed by those within the security arena. The chapter begins with a discussion of how radicalization can be perceived as a linear or non-linear process, and how this perception can affect how one deals with the issue. The author then closely examines the process of radicalization and how it could be countered through a three-pronged approach via prevention, management, and rehabilitation.

The first four chapters are useful to those readers who seek to gain an understanding of the multi-dimensional nature of the intelligence arena. The authors touch upon many subjects that all contribute to an enhanced awareness of the variety of issues that afflict the field. The next set of chapters allow readers to understand regional security and health security around the globe.

The fifth chapter introduces the readers to the topics of South Asian regionalism, globalization, and systemic risks when shifting from an inward political focus (pre-COVID-19) to an outward approach (post-COVID-19). The author's review of the situation offers readers with novel insight to pre- and post-pandemic issues. Additionally, the chapter presents four novel factors to strengthen regional security.

The sixth chapter also ties into the discussion of COVID-19 by focusing on the distribution of the COVID-19 vaccine. The author of this chapter examines the role that has been played by political leaders and how it has affected health security. As such, this chapter includes a review of regional issues in the provision of vaccines, the plight of developing countries, and overall health security.

The seventh chapter explores security concerns for South Asia by reviewing the nuclear ambitions between India and Pakistan. The author conceptualizes the issue through an iceberg model, and uses constructive psychological theory to analyze the moral orders of social action within specific situations.

Chapters 5-7, therefore, place a strong focus on South Asia and on-going security concerns, such as COVID-19. These three chapters are written by authors who have sought to not only contribute theoretical discussions, but also pragmatic solutions. The chapters will benefit readers with an avid interest in the South Asian region, along with those who desire to learn more about regional security and health security. The final set of chapters place a spotlight on the STEM side of security.

The eighth chapter provides a detailed analysis of Zipato's smart home solutions. The authors provide a review of a product in the cyber security realm. In addition to presenting in-depth insight to the standards of the product, the authors shed light on how practitioners within security must remain aware of the importance of maintaining appropriate standards when dealing with cyber security products.

The ninth chapter continues along the same line as chapter eight by presenting an evaluation of the effectiveness of Raspberry Pi as a security software. The authors explicate how such systems make it possible for hackers to discover and take control of one's devices. The chapter provides readers with the necessary information to make informed decisions related to computing solutions and security.

The last chapter of this book offers a detailed examination of the important contribution of STEM education to national security. The author provides an examination of how critical thinking can be cultivated via the studying of STEM subjects, which is used to clarify how and why STEM should be integrated into security studies. This chapter is a clear example of how inter-disciplinarity is vital within the security arena.

The diversity of the book chapters is one of the strengths of this book. This collection of articles positively contributes to the existing body of literature within the fields of security, intelligence, and law enforcement.

I would like to take this opportunity to thank my co-editor, Asanaga Abeyagoonasekera, reviewers, Dr. Emmanuel Essuman and Dr. Eugenie de Silva, and all chapter contributors. Their individual contributions made this book possible.

I also want to thank Ms. Lindsay Wertman, the Managing Director at IGI Global, and her team for all the support they offered.

Let our individual efforts collectively make a positive impact on the future of the security of our world.

*Eugene de Silva*
*Virginia Research Institute, USA*

# Section 1

# Chapter 1
# Measuring the Degree of Politicization of Intelligence Data:
## A Basic Qualitative/Quantitative Model

**Eugene de Silva**
*Virginia Research Institute, USA*

## ABSTRACT

*The politicization of intelligence and how it leads to failures in intelligence have been recognized for many years. Those who lead the intelligence community have also been staunch advocates against politicization. Nevertheless, the intelligence community has always been influenced by policymakers at various stages of the intelligence cycle. This chapter discusses politicization and presents a model to determine the degree of politicization qualitatively/quantitatively. The recognition of five factors related to politicization and the use of a simple scale would enable the intelligence team to determine the extent of politicization and insulate each stage of the intelligence cycle. This chapter also applies the new model to two instances where politicization has occurred.*

## INTRODUCTION

The politicization of Intelligence is one of the challenges faced by the Intelligence Community (IC). Gates (2006) in his message to analysts acknowledged that "The problem of politicization is as old as the intelligence business." He further confirmed that "Politicization can manifest itself in many ways, but in each case, it boils down to

DOI: 10.4018/978-1-7998-7904-6.ch001

the same essential elements: "Almost all agree that it involves deliberately distorting analysis or judgments to favor a preferred line of thinking irrespective of evidence. Most consider `classic' politicization to be only that which occurs if products are forced to conform to policymakers' views. A number believe politicization also results from management pressures to define and drive certain lines of analysis and substantive viewpoints. Still, others believe that changes in tone or emphasis made during the normal review or coordination process, and limited means for expressing alternative viewpoints, also constitute forms of politicization. (Gates, 2006).

Further, Sherman Kent, who is recognized as the founding father who defined the intelligence profession, explicated the importance of coordinated intelligence-driven policy, while highlighting the difficulty of synchronizing intelligence and policy that is free of bias. He stated that ". . . it is hard enough to develop the kinds of confidence between producers and consumers that alone make possible the completeness, timeliness, and applicability of the product." (Kent, 1949). His view is "that the relationship between intelligence producers and intelligence consumers has been uneven; that intelligence often finds it impossible to get the sort of guidance which it must have to make its product useful; and that one of the places where this lack of guidance produces its most disastrous results" (Kent, 1949). Here he refers to the instance where the problem is analyzed, prior to the collection of intelligence. Nevertheless, this is also one of the common places when politicization could happen effectively. Kent (1949) describes the politicization clearly when he states, "Proper relationship between intelligence producers and consumers is one of utmost delicacy. Intelligence must be close enough to policy, plans, and operations to have the greatest amount of guidance, and must not be so close that it loses its objectivity and integrity of judgment."

Whilst both scholars and the practitioners have recognized the importance of completely ending the politicization of intelligence (Hegemann 2018; Seo, 2018; Davies 2019; Betts, 2003), hitherto actions have not been able to achieve complete freedom from politicization. Therefore, this paper presents a model to measure the degree of politicization at each stage of the intelligence cycle. It is hoped that this quantitative/qualitative model would enable to reduce the politicization to a minimum level, through the recognition of the degree of politicization.

## BACKGROUND

The politicization of intelligence has been observed in almost all countries, whilst the extent to which the politicization happens varies. The work by Hegemann (2018) focuses on how parliaments can be sites for the politicization of intelligence and security and brings examples from the German federal parliament. Seo (2018) studied the politicization of intelligence in South Korea and President Moon's attempts to be transparent in government work. Bar-Joseph (2013) examined the politicization of intelligence in the US, Britain, and Israel. Davies (2019) detailed the problems of politicization in Malaysia.

The inception of modern intelligence in the United States of America (USA) followed as a result of the National Security Act of 1947 after the Second World War. According to James Motley (1987), the former Director of National Security Studies, "First and foremost [...] the role of [...] intelligence [...] within a democratic [...] government is to provide the impartial information and analysis upon which knowledgeable policy decisions can be made in protection of U.S. national interests."

Eisenfeld (2016) relates the importance of maintaining the relationship between policy-making and strategic intelligence. She states that "In the political area, intelligence connotes power; proximity to policymakers implies influence; and influence, relative to intelligence, leads to claims of politicization–a word with many interpretations." In Eisenfeld's paper (2016), she recognizes that while most observers recognize the traditional forms of politicization, there are other external influences from, "Individual citizens, organizations that provide policy research and advice (think tanks), the media (both traditional and new), and lobbyists."

Johnson (2003) defines politicization as "putting a spin on or 'cooking' intelligence to serve the political needs or beliefs of an intelligence manager or policy official." Rovner (2011) describes politicization as "the attempt to manipulate intelligence so that it reflects policy preference." Gannon (2008) states politicization as "the willful distortion of analysis to satisfy the demands of intelligence bosses and policymakers." Ransom (1987) in his chapter titled, "Politicization of Intelligence," brings about several terms to describe politicization. Among those terms, the "intelligence to please" term seems to be the most suitable to describe when intelligence influences policy. Handel (1989) explains politicization as "interference in the intelligence process by leaders and their close aides." Treverton (2008) expands his definition of politicization to the following five forms:

- Direct pressure from senior policy officials to come to particular intelligence conclusions, usually ones that accord with those officials' policies or policy preferences.
- A house line on a particular subject, which shifts the focus of the bias from policy to intelligence. Here, a particular analytic office has a defined view of an issue, and analysts or analyses that suggest heresy are suppressed or ignored.
- Cherry-picking (and sometimes growing some cherries), in which senior officials, usually policy officials, pick their favorites out of a range of assessments.

- Question asking, where, as in other areas of inquiry, the nature of the question takes the analysis a good way if not to the answer, then to the frame in which the answer will lie. A related version of this form occurs when policymakers ask a reasonable question but continue to ask it repeatedly, which distorts analysis—by depriving it of time and effort to work on other questions—even if it does not directly politicize.
- A shared mindset, whereby intelligence and policy share strong presumptions. This is perhaps the limiting case; if it is politicization, it is more self-imposed than policymaker imposed.

Based on the above five forms, Treverton (2008) concludes politicization of intelligence as "commitments to perspectives and conclusions, in the process of intelligence analysis or interaction with policy, that suppress other evidence or views, or blind[s] people to them." Treverton's (2008) description also highlights soft and hard forms of politicization, which is based on the extent to which politicization influences intelligence. Betts (2003) describes politicization from the point of view of its origin. Along this line, he describes three types:

- *Top-down influence* by policymakers dictating intelligence finalizations.
- *Bottom-up influence* by unconscious biases by the analysts.
- *Editorial* influence by the supervisors of the analysts.

The above three types also highlight how proximity is a factor in politicization.

## MAIN FOCUS OF THE CHAPTER

The main focus of this chapter is the development of a qualitative/quantitative model to measure the degree of politicization. There are several theories already developed or accepted in the politicization of intelligence. This work has considered previous models and theories in producing this quantitative/qualitative model to be applied at different stages of the intelligence cycle. According to the theory by Rovner (2011), politicization is recognized as direct and indirect manipulation:

Direct – Policymakers directly apply pressure to change the intelligence directly or appoint analysts who share their opinions. This is also hard politicization.

Indirect – Policymakers imply their expected conclusion of the analysis and at times combine this with rewards and threats. This may fall under soft politicization depending on the extent of influence.

Rovner (2011) provides three types of options for policymakers:

1. Accept the intelligence in good faith.
2. Ignore the intelligence completely.
3. Politicize intelligence by pressuring agencies.

Rovner (2011) mentions both the benefits and problems associated with the policy-centric approach in producing intelligence. He emphasizes the importance of having a receptive consumer for intelligence products.

The work described in this chapter concentrates on recognizing the instances of politicization and quantifying them before the final product is released. The stages of politicization and the degree of influence on intelligence at each stage will be noted and records of changes are maintained to produce an overall map that would display the true value of the final product.

Marrin's (2007) theory extends the proximity through quantification. Hanni (2016) in his work states Marrin's theory as proximity dilemma, "'Intelligence agencies that are close to policymakers tend to produce analysis that is useful for improving decision making but potentially distorted due to the incorporation of policy biases and preferences, while intelligence agencies that are distant from policymakers tend to produce "objective" analysis containing little distortion, but of little use in improving policymaker judgment."

Irrespective of the type of politicization, whether it is proximity (personal or organizational) influenced (Kent, 1949), based on organizational interest (Prados, 1986), or a combination of personal, bureaucratic, and political influence (Bar-Joseph, 2013), the purpose of this work is to identify the politicization at each stage of the intelligence cycle by the factors and players identified by previous work and then quantify it to display the extent to which deviation from the true data has occurred.

## Intelligence Model

The intelligence models given below (Figure 1) are the most known cycle within the intelligence community. According to Hulnick (2013), these models ignore the two most important aspects of intelligence operations. "I am especially concerned that in all their various forms, the Intelligence Cycle models leave out two key functions in intelligence, those of Counterintelligence and Covert Action" (Hulnick (2013, p.151). Nevertheless, the test model presented in this paper can be used in differing settings; therefore, the changes to the intelligence cycle will not alter the effectiveness of the model.

De Silva (2003) suggested a modification to the standard intelligence cycle with quality assurance at each stage (Figure 2). Whilst this quality assurance at each state included various actions to be taken to maintain the integrity of intelligence, politicization would invariably continue to seep into intelligence. Therefore, this model is suggested as one of those quality-assurance actions necessary to determine the politicization factor of intelligence.

*Figure 1. Standard intelligence model*

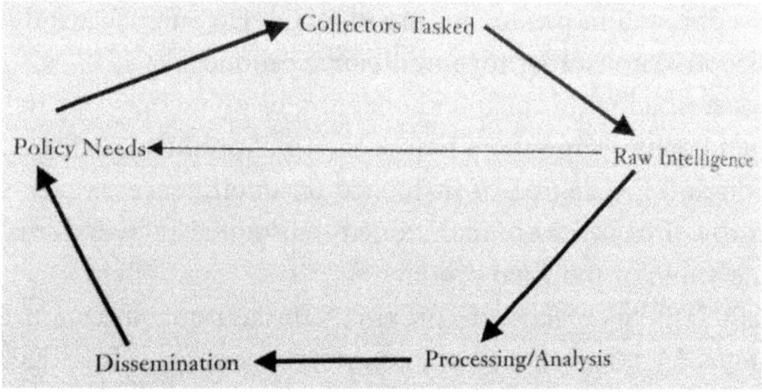


*Figure 2. Quality Assured Intelligence Cycle – A simple modification to the standard intelligence cycle. The circles in the middle of the arrows depict the need for a quality assured review process at each stage.*

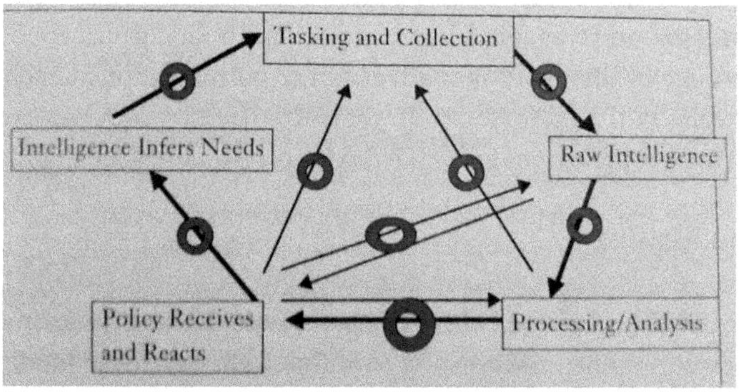


According to Pillar (2010), there are two basic forms of politicization, "the public use of intelligence by the policymakers in bolstering support for their policies and the influence of political or policy preferences on the judgments of intelligence services and intelligence officers." Nevertheless, it should be recognized that the skewing of intelligence could also be made by the intelligence officers who would use it for their own advantages within the agency. These advantages may include prospects of promotions, obtaining an edge on turf-war situations, and/or external favors.

The steps taken within the intelligence agencies to date to insulate intelligence data from politicization have been mainly procedural and not quantitatively measurable or quantitatively determinable. The lacuna in this field necessitates a model that can be applied simply and efficiently to detect any possible politicization, which can then be used to inform the leadership to take the necessary procedural changes. The absence of such a quantitative model leads to the current situation where high subjectivity leads to the politicization of intelligence data.

## The Model– STARR

This model titled STARR is an acronym for the five facets that have been recognized in this work. The letters stand for,

S = System, T = Timeline, A = Access, R = Resources, R = Re-evaluation

The application of this model will produce quantitative values that will enable intelligence officers to confidently declare if the produced intelligence is free of politicization or if it is biased and then the degree of biasness. This detection will allow the leadership within the intelligence field to take the necessary managerial decisions to re-organize the structure and functions within intelligence agencies.

The model was developed to answer the following three main questions?

1. Can the politicization of intelligence be recognized before the release of final intelligence reports?
2. Can the degree of politicization of intelligence be measured quantitatively or qualitatively?
3. Can the above model be applied to past, confirmed instances of politicization of intelligence to verify the model?

In order to answer the above questions, it was decided to first determine the main ways in which this politicization is forced upon the intelligence community.

The first step in the development of this model was to understand how politicization work and to determine what facets are altered or used to politicize intelligence. In this work, five major facets were recognized.

### STARR Model - Facets

The STARR© model presented here was initially developed in 2017 (de Silva) as a direct answer to determine and diminish the politicization of intelligence data. The model presented in this chapter is an improvement to the previous model.

This new, modified model titled STARR© could be used to quantify the degree of politicization at an organizational level and/or at an intelligence cycle level. Whilst the types of politicization can be different, the types of influence could be grouped under the following five major facets:

### *Facet 1 - System*

The system refers to the unit in charge of the intelligence process for a particular task. Everything else should be considered the surroundings of the system. The system includes the personnel, apparatus used, operations implemented, etc. It is expected that the system is insulated against the surroundings, which also include the policymakers, the public, media, etc. in an absolute non-politicized scenario. The proximity between the policymakers and the intelligence personnel involved in the project would determine the degree of politicization. It is imperative that the policymakers do not have any contact with the intelligence personnel and not see the report until it has gone through the entire cycle of quality assurance. Depending on how close the policymakers are to the intelligence personnel and data would determine if soft or hard politicization has occurred.

### *Facet 2 - Timeline*

The timeline is the next factor recognized. The timeline refers to the total period from the inception of the intelligence process to the final report and evaluation stage. This period should be free of influence or politicization. Also, this time period should not be overextended or made very short. In both extremes, the intelligence gathering, processing, and interpretation will be affected either due to insufficient time where the process is rushed to obtain the desired result, or the process is dragged for a longer period of time to dilute the efficacy of the gathered intelligence data. In either scenario, depending on the degree of influence, soft or hard politicization will occur.

### *Facet 3 - Access*

Access refers to the extent to which intelligence personnel is provided with access to operational activities, information gathering, personnel, necessary apparatus, etc. In politicization, these restrictions are visible and play an immense role in controlling the intelligence process, thus hindering access to the facts. When access is restricted, the distortion of intelligence becomes easier. Therefore, this is an important factor to consider when reviewing politicization.

### *Facet 4 - Resources*

The resources refer to the total resources used by the intelligence personnel throughout the intelligence cycle until the completion of the task. This is different to access; here the focus is on actual resources provided to the team to conduct a thorough intelligence gathering, processing, and interpretation of data. When politicization is present, the intelligence personnel not provided with the necessary resources such as money, manpower, apparatus, or in some instances clear directions. It is important to consider the directions and other guidelines provided by the management under this factor. The management that shares the same interest as policymakers may either provide biased directions or vague or misdirection to influence the final findings. It is important that the intelligence personnel are left to explore all possibilities when collecting intelligence data. This could only be achieved by providing all possible resources.

### *Facet 5 - Re-evaluation*

This is the period when the produced reports are reevaluated for accuracy and any errors. This final re-evaluation is one of the crucial steps in the intelligence cycle that takes place just before the dissemination of data. Whilst the quality assured model proposed by de Silva (2003) advocates re-evaluation at each stage, the final re-evaluation is more important since this is when the politicization attempts its final influence on the produced intelligence report. If the quality assured model is followed and re-evaluations are carried out at each stage, major changes to the gathered data should not occur at this final stage. Nevertheless, the management may influence the final report to be altered, reduced, or not disseminated depending on the extent to which the politicization has occurred. This would determine the soft or hard politicization.

## Simple Measuring Scale

Whilst in the previous section the facets where politicization occurs have been discussed, it was necessary to quantify the politicization to understand the degree of politicization for comparison, mitigation, and finally elimination. This is possible only by providing a value to the facet at each stage. After several applications, it was determined to use a simple scale to quantify politicization. Consequently, a range of -2, -1, 0, 1, 2 was proposed as an ideal, simple scale. On this scale, zero was considered a neutral, non-politicized situation. All negative values would display politicization away from the objectives of the policymaker and all positive values would display the politicization supporting the objectives of the policymaker. Scale 2 was considered as hard politicization and scale 1 as soft politicization.

It is hereby noted that this scale could be extended to derive a more accurate understanding of politicization. It is also important to understand that the given number indicated any existing politicization within each facet. The values do not indicate if the final intelligence report prepared is favoring the objectives of the policymaker or not. The scale only indicates that within a given facet if there has been any politicization and if so, if this politicization is towards or against the policymaker's objectives.

The total politicization is achieved through the summation of all the values given under each facet. According to the range used in this project, if all facets show extreme politicization, then the total value would be +10, indicating extreme politicization toward the objectives of the policymaker and -10 would indicate extreme politicization against the objectives of the policymaker. Whilst a total zero should be the ultimate goal, any summation closer to zero should be the most pragmatic expectation.

It is relevant to mention that the assigning of the scores under each facet is completed by three intelligence officers who were not part of the project being evaluated for politicization. None of these intelligence officers should hold any managerial positions. This is to make the evaluation free of biases. It is also important to select these intelligence offices to possess fewer years of experience as possible. Finally, the ratings of all three will be presented as the total sum value. According to the scale explained previously, the two extremes of values would be +30 and – 30 for and against the policymaker's objectives, respectively.

Whilst this scale can be simply applied as it stands, there is a percentage requirement under each facet to be satisfied to justify the issuance of a particular scale number. This assessment training that is necessary to be an evaluator of politicization and apply this model successfully is not included for copyrights and security reasons.

## TESTING THE MODEL

In order to test this model through a simple application of the scale, the following two scenarios where politicization happened in the USA were selected.

1. Vietnam Estimates in 1963
2. Intelligence Reports on Weapons of Mass Destruction in Iraq in 2003

### Scenario 1: Vietnam Estimates in 1963

It has been widely reported that the National Intelligence Estimates (NIE), submitted with the approval of then DCI John McCone in April 1963 (NIE 53 – 63), were quite different from the actual NIE prepared in February of 1963. This shift of NIE supported the view of the then Secretary of Defence Robert McNamara. When DCI McCone stated his original pessimistic view in 1962, he was directed to produce a more promising report stating the weakening of Viet Cong activities and the increase of support of the people for South Vietnam's military operations.[1] This report was the result of hard politicization. (Hastedt, 2013)

## Actual Politicization Points

1. The direct influence by Defence Secretary McNamara to DCI McCone through criticism.
2. Changes from Feb. 1963 Report to April 1963 report.
3. The request that only completed and finished reports (meaning that only the reports approved by the head of the intelligence community who is under the influence of the politicization process) be sent to Washington. This avoided any contradictory information being provided in the final report.
4. Junior officers or officers with contradicting information were forced to change their views.
5. Overruling of NIE drafters' views against the politicized report.
6. Suppression of true information by relating to the previous failures or mistakes of estimates.
7. Existence of hard politicization where intelligence estimates were forced to change to conform to army estimates (who were distorting the reports to show its winning edge).
8. Soft politicization where disagreeing officials were asked to get on board with the politicized view.

## Scenario 2: Intelligence Reports FavoringIraq War in 2003

The September 9, 2001 attacks by Al Qaeda on the US World Trade Center initiated several military operations aimed at eliminating the terrorist groups. After the attack on Afghanistan, the Bush administration was determined to end the reign of Saddam Hussein's domination in Iraq. The pathway to declaring war on Iraq was another classic case of politicization of intelligence. The politicization of intelligence in this scenario was used to win the support of the majority, both in the US and amongst its allies. The intelligence reports on uranium enrichment or the reimplementation of Iraq's nuclear program, which was terminated in the 1991 Gulf War, and the possible links to Al Qaeda were politicized to receive support for the Iraq war (Hastedt, 2013).

## Actual Politicization Points

1. A separate intelligence unit was established directly in the Pentagon to collect intelligence on Iraq.
2. The intelligence cycle was not quality assured or supervised with identifiable assessment points.
3. There was no room for dissent or the evaluation of gathered intelligence.
4. Soft politicization was used via the separate intelligence unit.
5. Hard politicization was used via inaccurate reports on the uranium enrichment program and media reports.
6. A connection between Al Qaeda and Iraq was established through clouding the evidence.
7. Removal of any doubts about the existence of links with Al Qaeda or Iraq's uranium enrichment program in the public version of the white paper.
8. Absence of clear consensus between policymakers and analysts.

*Table 1. Scenario 1 - Vietnam Estimates in 1963*

| Facet | Scale | Reason |
|---|---|---|
| System | +1 | Those who disagreed were forced to align with the politicized decisions. |
| Timeline | +2 | Sec. of Defense request for the second report |
| Access | +1 | The access was limited to the final report to the policymakers |
| Resources | 0 | The access to the resources was not controlled in this instance. |
| Re-evaluation | +1 | There was no actual, fact-based re-evaluation. |
| Total Value | +5 | Highly politicized intelligence data. |

*Table 2. Scenario 2 - Intelligence Reports Favoring Iraq War in 2003*

| Facet | Scale | Reason |
|---|---|---|
| System | +2 | A special intelligence unit was established within Pentagon. A highly politicized situation. |
| Timeline | +1 | A rapid search for evidence to support the case. |
| Access | +2 | Limited to the personnel supportive of the objectives of the policymaker. |
| Resources | +2 | Mostly limited to the personnel supporting the policymaker's objectives. |
| Re-evaluation | +1 | No re-evaluation was requested. |
| Total Value | +8 | This is a massively politicized situation. |

## APPLICATION AND DISCUSSION

The application of the STARR model to the two scenarios has clearly displayed the simplicity and the convenience of the model to recognize the politicization. As mentioned previously, this paper has not discussed how the scores are applied after assessing the satisfactory application according to a percentage requirement. Nevertheless, as shown in this chapter, the scale could also be directly applied as an acid test. For the best results, in addition to applying the percentage requirements, the analyses must be conducted by a three-person committee of intelligence officers (non-managerial and with experience less than 5 years), where an agreement is first made on the signs, the range (in the event an extended range is warranted), and the collection of evidence supporting each stage of the intelligence cycle. Whilst moving from one stage to the next stage of the intelligence cycle, the model should be applied as a part of the QA system to determine the next, most professional, and competent steps, when it becomes apparent that the intelligence data are becoming politicized. The three individuals selected could be from varying specialties within intelligence to generate a broader assessment when determining the politicization while sifting through the evidence. An understanding of the development of the model would provide a clearer pathway to the application of the model and this necessitates more professional training in the assigning of scores according to the percentage requirements to avoid any ambiguities.

In the development of this model, the first two questions raised were,

1. Can the politicization of intelligence be recognized before the release of final intelligence reports?
2. Can the degree of politicization of intelligence be measured quantitatively or qualitatively?

It is clear that the model has answered both the first two questions. The politicization can be recognized and expressed qualitatively by assessing each facet described previously. The quantitative values derived from the model will provide a clearer understanding of the degree of politicization.

It is important to recognize the politicization prior to the release of the intelligence report to the consumer. Therefore, the final intelligence report should include an analysis according to the model. This analysis annexed to the report would explicitly indicate the extent to which the report can be relied upon. Whilst this process exonerates the intelligence officers of any future blame, this process will also lead to establishing good management practices within the intelligence community that is free from any politicization.

The third and the final question raised was,

3. Can the above model be applied to past, confirmed instances of politicization of intelligence to verify the model?

The application of the model to two well-known past incidents displayed that this model is simple and direct to determine the politicization of intelligence in different scenarios. This model was recently applied to recognize the politicization of intelligence in another country through analysis at a distance. The results confirmed extreme politicization. The commission appointed to test the reasons for the failure of intelligence confirmed extreme politicization as the main cause confirming the results of the model. The application of this model may need some streamlined training of officers, who would act as independent personnel applying the model to determine the politicization within projects and reports.

## SOLUTIONS AND RECOMMENDATIONS

The solutions to reducing politicization are to recognize it, quantify it, and present it as the cause for the deviation from true, unadulterated, intelligence data. The management within intelligence must support the officers and insulate them from the influence of politicization. It is suggested that in addition to the training on the application of the STARR model, the intelligence officers, section heads, and managers undergo necessary training and attend regular meetings on the politicization of intelligence. It is important to change the mindset of policymakers and also the management within intelligence to recognize that policy should be developed on good, unbiased intelligence and not the other way.

## FUTURE RESEARCH DIRECTIONS

The model suggested proposed could be further developed to apply under multi-settings and determine the interdependency among two or more projects. The percentage requirement not discussed in this paper can also be improved within the intelligence training unit. A direct improvement of the model could be the addition of a correction factor to the model as a quantitative solution to reduce, reverse, or eliminate the politicization of an intelligence project.

## CONCLUSION

This chapter has discussed the challenge of pollicization within intelligence. The STARR model proposed has confirmed the five facets where politicization happens and how the degree of politicization can be determined. Whilst, a complete absence of politicization may not be possible at any given instance, the recognition will bring about a change and reduction of the influence that reduces the independence of intelligence personnel.

## REFERENCES

Bar-Joseph, U. (2013). The Politicization of Intelligence: A Comparative Study. *International Journal of Intelligence and CounterIntelligence*, *26*(2), 347–369. do i:10.1080/08850607.2013.758000

Betts, R. K. (2003). Politicization of Intelligence: Costs and Benefits. In R. K. Betts, T. G. Mahnken, & F. Cass (Eds.), Paradoxes of Strategic Intelligence: Essays in Honor of Michael I. Handel (pp. 59–79). Academic Press.

Davies, P. H. J. (2019). All in Good Faith? Proximity, Politicization, and Malaysia's External Intelligence Organizations. *International Journal of Intelligence and CounterIntelligence*, *32*(4), 691–716. doi:10.1080/08850607.2019.1621105

De Silva, E. (2003). Intelligence and Policy in Combating Terrorism. In Terrorism in the Asia-Pacific – Threat and Response (pp. 108 – 132). Easter University Press.

De Silva, E. (2017). *Development of a Dynamic Model to Detect and Diminish the Politicization of Intelligence Data* (Unpublished). Virginia Research Institute.

Eisenfeld, B. (2016). The Intelligence Dilemma: Proximity and Politicization–Analysis of External Influences. *Journal of Strategic Security*, *10*(2), 77–96. doi:10.5038/1944-0472.10.2.1583

Gannon, J. C. (2008). Managing Analysis in the Information Age. In *Analyzing intelligence: Origins, Obstacles, and Innovation*. Georgetown University Press.

Gates, R. M. (2006). Guarding Against Politicization: A Message to Analysts. In Ethics of Spying: A Reader for the Intelligence Professional. Scarecrow Press.

Handel, M. (n.d.). The Politics of Intelligence. *Intelligence and National Security*, *2*(4), 6.

Hanni, A. (2016). When Casey's Blood Pressure Rose: A Case Study of Intelligence Politicization in the United States. *Intelligence and National Security*, *31*(7), 963–977. doi:10.1080/02684527.2016.1162401

Hastedt, G. (2013). The Politics of Intelligence and the Politicization of Intelligence: The American Experience. *Intelligence and National Security*, *28*(1), 1, 5–31. doi:10.1080/02684527.2012.749062

Hegemann, H. (2018). Toward 'normal' politics? Security, parliaments and the politicization of intelligence oversight in the German Bundestag. *British Journal of Politics and International Relations*, *20*(1), 175–190. doi:10.1177/1369148117745683

Hulnick, A. S. (2013). Intelligence Theory – Seeking Better Models. In M. Phythian (Ed.), *Understanding the Intelligence Cycle*. Routledge.

Johnson, L. (2003). Bricks and mortar for a theory of intelligence. *Comparative Strategy*, *22*(1), 1–28. Advance online publication. doi:10.1080/01495930390130481

Kent, S. (1949). *Strategic Intelligence for American World Policy*. Princeton University.

Kent, S. (1949) Strategic Intelligence for American World Policy. Princeton University Press.

Marrin, S. (2007). At Arm's Length or At the Elbow? Explaining the Distance between Analysis and Decision Makers. *International Journal of Intelligence and CounterIntelligence*, *20*(3), 401–414. doi:10.1080/08850600701249733

Motley, J. (1987). Coping with the Terrorist Threat: The U.S. Intelligence Dilemma. In S. Cimbala (Ed.), *Intelligence and Intelligence Policy in a Democratic Society* (pp. 169–248). Transnational Publishers, Inc.

Pillar, P. R. (2010). The Perils of Politicization. In L. K. Johnson (Ed.), *The Oxford Handbook of National Security Intelligence* (pp. 472–484). Oxford University Press.

Prados, J. (1986). *Presidents' Secret Wars: CIA and Pentagon Covert Operations Since World War II*. William Morrow.

Ransom, H. H. (1987). The Politicization of Intelligence. In Intelligence and the Intelligence Policy in a Democratic Society. Transnational Publishers, Inc.

Rovner, J. (2011). *Fixing the Facts: National Security and the Politics of Intelligence*. Cornell University Press. doi:10.7591/cornell/9780801448294.001.0001

Seo, H. (2018). Intelligence Politicization in the Republic of Korea: Implications for Reform. *International Journal of Intelligence and Counterintelligence. Taylor Francis.*, *31*(3), 451–478. doi:10.1080/08850607.2018.1466566

Treverton, G. F. (2008). Intelligence Analysis: Between 'Politicization' and Irrelevance. In Analyzing intelligence: Origins, Obstacles, and Innovation. Georgetown University Press.

## KEY TERMS AND DEFINITIONS

**Hard Politicization:** Hard politicization happens when intelligence personnel is directly influenced, coerced, pressurized, threatened to produce the desired report favorable to the policymaker.

**Intelligence Cycle:** In this chapter, the intelligence cycle refers to the process whereby intelligence data are collected and reported. The cycle begins with a policy decision, collection of raw intelligence, processing and analysis, and finally dissemination through the production of the final report.

**Politicization:** In this chapter, politicization refers to the influence by the policymakers or senior, management intelligence officers on the intelligence personnel involved in gathering, processing, and presenting intelligence reports to distort or deviate from the facts.

**Quantitative/Qualitative Model:** This is a model where the user can either generate a piece of descriptive information related to the politicization or obtain a numerical value that indicates the degree of politicization.

**Simple Scale:** This is a numerical range ranging from zero to 2 with positive and negative directions on a two-dimensional scale.

**Soft Politicization:** Soft politicization happens when intelligence personnel is indirectly influenced, coerced, pressurized, threatened to produce the desired report favorable to the policymaker.

## ENDNOTE

1 Viet Cong or Viet Nam Cong San was a Communist Vietnamese guerrilla force together with the North Vietnamese Army fought against South Vietnam from the late 1950s to 1975 and against the USA from early 1960 0 1973.

# Chapter 2
# Law Enforcement Challenges to Gathering Intelligence in the Street:
## The Fourth Amendment

**Joseph R. Budd**
https://orcid.org/0000-0001-5208-630X
*Campbellsville University, USA*

**Michael W. Littrell**
*Campbellsville University, USA*

## ABSTRACT

*Intelligence gathering by law enforcement officers has been used in the conviction of criminals for many years in the United States. Law enforcement officers must ensure that the information gathered and seized does not violate the Fourth Amendment of the United States Constitution. However, officers, even though acting in the spirit of the law, may not be in legal compliance. This chapter identifies and discusses the requirements of a search warrant, the legally accepted exceptions to the search warrant requirements in the United States, and reviews several historical and modern United States Supreme Court cases on the gathering of intelligence by officers.*

## INTRODUCTION

Intelligence gathering in law enforcement has occurred since early times when local law enforcement was the military of the King, Emperor, or ruler of the land.

DOI: 10.4018/978-1-7998-7904-6.ch002

Individuals, sometimes known as *spies*, would infiltrate other lands and gather intelligence to bring back to their superiors. In London, England, in 1748, Sir Henry Fielding employed known thieves to recover stolen goods, returning them to its rightful owner. These individuals, known as the *Bow Street Runners*, would gather intelligence from other known thieves on the whereabouts of stolen property. They would then steal the property back and return it to the owner for a fee. The Bow Street Runners are viewed as one of the first forms of detective work. Later, Sir Robert Peel created the first police force in London and built upon these forms of intelligence gathering to combat crime (Orthmann & Hess, 2013). Across the English Channel in France circa 1811, François Eugene Vidocq, a former criminal, was changing his ways and is credited with being the founder of the first plain-clothed detective division called the Brigade de la Surete, translating to be the *Security Brigade*. In the mid-1800s in the United States, a Scottish immigrant named Allan Pinkerton became the first known detective of the Chicago Police Department in 1849. He is credited with the invention of different methods of intelligence gathering via the use of shadowing and following suspects (Orthmann & Hess, 2013).

The collection of intelligence by officers is a primary way to combat crime. Without this intelligence, officers are unable to gain leads, which can lead to warrants and, hopefully, arrests. However, the method in which officers collect these leads and evidence must follow the protections outlined in the Fourth Amendment of the United States Constitution (Whitebread & Slobogin, 2015). With little guidance from the Courts and Constitution regarding the use of technological advances by the police, they sometimes teeter on the edge of this Amendment for many years when performing criminal investigations. The Fourth Amendment protects individuals against unlawful searches and seizures by government officials. Law enforcement must stay on the cutting-edge use of technology, yet remain within the parameters outlined by our Constitution, which protects our civil liberties. How officers conduct the gathering of intelligence is vital to the integrity of the case being built against a suspect, the integrity of the officer, and the integrity of the department for which they are employed.

The gathering of intelligence or information is essential to police when combating crime. An officer understands the need for robust, reliable intelligence and should know how to obtain the said intelligence legally. Citizens of the United States are protected under the Fourth Amendment of the Constitution, which states:

*The right of the people to be secure in their persons, houses, papers, and effects, against unreasonable searches and seizures, shall not be violated, and no warrants shall issue, but upon probable cause, supported by oath or affirmation, and particularly describing the place to be searched, and the persons or things to be seized. (Para. 1)*

Over the years, law enforcement has tested this Amendment to its fullest. The methods and instruments used to commit crime change almost daily, thus the need for officers to find new ways to combat criminal activity. For the criminal, staying one step ahead of the police in their methods of operation occurs with minimal challenge. However, sometimes officers push the legal boundaries when gathering intelligence; thus, legal challenges arise. A review of these challenges by the Court sometimes happens slowly, delaying guidance for many years. Officers should be educated on the constant challenges of how to perform daily operations—knowing what is legally acceptable when gathering intelligence. This chapter will educate the reader about the Fourth Amendment to the Constitution, to whom it applies, the search warrant process, and exceptions to the search warrant process as applicable to the gathering of intelligence. Furthermore, this chapter will provide an examination of three historic United States Supreme Court cases involving the gathering of intelligence by law enforcement, along with an examination of recent United States Supreme Court cases also involving the gathering of intelligence by law enforcement officers.

## BACKGROUND

### The Fourth Amendment

The fourth amendment to the United States Constitution was enacted on December 15th, 1791, as a part of a ten-amendment package known as the Bill of Rights. These *rights* were put in place to protect the public from the government. Specifically, the fourth amendment protects individuals from illegal search and seizure by the government. The government is defined as any person employed or sub-contracted by a government agency (Whitebread & Sloboggin, 2015). For example, a police officer of a city, state, or federal agency is a governmental official at their level of employment. These protections extend to all who are employed under a governmental agency. Searches that may be conducted by health inspectors, safety inspections, and public-school teachers would fall under the protection of the fourth amendment. The founding fathers wanted to ensure that when evidence is obtained against a citizen for the purposes of a criminal conviction, the evidence should be obtained legally and not violate any of the items outlined in the U.S. Constitution. As stated previously, the fourth amendment (and any of the items in the Bill of Rights) only applies to government officials; constitutionally, therefore, a private citizen cannot violate these rights.

The concept of the violation of only applying to government officials was first tested in *Burdeau v. McDowell* (1921). Here, a group of private individuals who were at one time employees of McDowell entered the business illegally and confiscated items, specifically papers, and then turned them over to Burdeau, who was employed as an Assistant to the Attorney General. These individuals did this solely on their own and without influence or coercion from Burdeau. McDowell argued the items were confiscated illegally and in violation of the fourth amendment. The Court ruled against McDowell in that the amendment was to protect individuals from the government, not from other private individuals. This holding was again confirmed in *Coolidge v. New Hampshire* (1971) when the Court ruled that when a private citizen on their own part turns over items to the government for use in a criminal investigation, the said items may be used as evidence and does not violate the fourth amendment. Later in *Walter v. United States* (1980), the Court stated these actions do not deny the government of the ability to use said evidence (Whitebread & Sloboggin, 2015). However, when a private citizen has been influenced by a government official to obtain items, the seizure of said items would then violate the fourth amendment (Coolidge v. New Hampshire, 1921).

## MAIN FOCUS OF THE CHAPTER

### The Search Warrant

The *search warrant* is a document authorized by a judicial official authorizing law enforcement to search and seize specific items from a person or place. Each search warrant must meet four (4) requirements to be valid. The first requirement is that the search warrant is within good faith of the officer seeking the warrant. Second, the information within the warrant must be based upon probable cause (PC). Probable cause is defined as a set of facts or circumstances which would lead a reasonably intelligent person to believe a crime has, had, or is about to occur. Third, the warrant must be issued by a natural judicial official. Fourth, the warrant must explain in detail the place to person to be searched and the items to be seized. Other items not individually listed on the search warrant may be seized if their discovery falls within the scope of the search. Search warrants are only valid for a specific amount of time and not an indefinite document. The search warrant must be executed within ten days of being authorized. While there are numerous exceptions to the search warrant requirement which we will examine below, let's look at how evidence that is obtained illegally be dismissed.

## Fruit of the Poisonous Tree

The fruit of the poisonous tree doctrine is said to have originated in the case of *Silverthorne Lumber Co. v. United States* (1920). Here, the Government obtained documents illegally, which were used to convict Silverthorne. The United States Supreme Court (USSC) later overturned the conviction due to the illegal way in which the documents were obtained. Justice Frankfurter later coined the term fruit of the poisonous tree in the case of *Nardone v. the United States* (1939), where he stated, "a substantial portion of the case against the accused was a fruit of the poisonous tree" (Whitebread and Sloboggin, 2015 p.34). The fruit of the poisonous tree can be easily described as any evidence which has been collected via illegal means. For example, if the search of a residence is deemed illegal (the poisonous tree), then any evidence (the fruit) collected shall not be permitted to be used in a criminal case against the defendant. However, as with all things, there are exceptions.

Exceptions to policy and procedure are standard, and rules of law have exceptions as well. There will be circumstances that could arise where even when the rule of law is broken (such as an illegal arrest), that fruit from the illegal arrest can be used in a criminal case. An example of this is illustrated in *Rawlings v. Kentucky* (1980). Here, Rawlings was illegally arrested and made incriminating statements. The USSC, however, permitted the use of his statements due to several factors. First, officers did read him his *Miranda* rights after the illegal arrest. Second, Rawlings was in a home, and there were several other individuals present. Third, his statements were made in an unprompted manner and were not uttered in response to direct police questioning. Fourth, it was determined that the Fourth Amendment violation was not deliberate but was a good faith error. Fifth and lastly, the defendant made no dispute that he made the statements involuntarily.

## Exceptions to the Search Warrant

As we learned in the previous paragraphs, there will be exceptions to rules of law. The requirement for a search warrant also has several exceptions in which a warrant would not be needed or practical to obtain. Below, we will briefly discuss the most common exceptions to the search warrant requirement.

### Hot Pursuit

When we hear the term 'hot pursuit,' it takes us back to the childhood days of watching the *Dukes of Hazzard* and hearing Sheriff Rosco P. Coltrane yelling into his microphone that he was in "hot pursuit of them Duke boys." This example is fairly spot on to our exception to the warrant requirement, however hot pursuit does not just mean the car chase we just described. For *hot pursuit* to be valid, several elements need to be met for this exception: (1) the officers must have established probable cause before the start of the pursuit. (2) the starting point of which the pursuit needs to be legal and valid. Officers must be starting the pursuit where they have a legitimate legal right to be. (3) the type of crime that was violated must be of a severe nature. This means that if the officer does not continue their pursuit, serious injury, death, or imminent danger of citizens may occur.

The first case of hot pursuit is found in *Warden v. Hayden* (1967). Police officers were made aware of a robbery that occurred at a taxi company. A driver followed the suspect to a house while he was fleeing the scene. Upon the arrival of the officers, they entered the home, finding the suspect pretending to be asleep in an upstairs bedroom. They further searched the home at the time of his arrest and discovered the clothing and weapon used in the robbery, which were identified by the taxi drivers. The defendant moved to have the evidence suppressed due to an illegal search and seizure of his person and evidence. The Court ruled the officers acted within a reasonable scope as the Fourth Amendment does not expect officers to delay actions when the risk of danger to the public is present. The fact that the defendant brandished a weapon during the robbery even though he did not fire the weapon, we should expect that he would fire the weapon, thus putting the public in danger.

## Search Incident to a Lawful Arrest

The search incident to a lawful arrest is the most common and oldest exception to the warrant requirement for the searching of a person. We have all seen a television show or movie where a person is being arrested. They are told to put their hands against the wall and spread their legs while the officers search the arrestee. This is a full search of a person (excluding body cavities), their clothing, and any property in their immediate possession (purse, backpack, or bag.). The purpose of this exception is that the officer(s) is/are searching for items that could cause harm to the officers, to the arrestee, or contraband in which the arrestee may bring into a secure facility (jail). This exception to the warrant requirement has been a standard in American law and was solidified in *Weeks v. United States* (1914). Just as in the hot pursuit exception, the search incident arrest exception does have elements that need to be met in order to be valid.

The timing of the search is the first element that must be met. The search of the person must be after the individual has been arrested (see the section on stop and frisk for when a pat-down may precede arrest). This element is in place to prevent officers from *looking* for evidence that could lead to an arrest but having probable cause to make the arrest, thus making the warrantless search legal. Furthermore, the search must come within a reasonable amount of time after the individual has been arrested. There is no definite timetable of what is reasonable, but a reasonable time is what an average person would believe to be reasonable. If officers do not search items in possession of the arrestee in a reasonable amount of time, officers should seek a warrant.

The last element to discuss when searching incident to arrest is the scope of the search. Until *the United States v. Rabinowitz* (1950) developed the *Armspan Rule*. Upon a legal arrest of the defendant, officers then conducted a warrantless search of his small one-room office, which included all the contents of the office, such as desk drawers, file cabinets, and other items. The Court ruled that even though officers would have had time to obtain a search warrant, the search was deemed legal as to the semi-public area of the office and the fact that the size of the office being small that the defendant had almost immediate access to anything in that space.

## The Automobile Exception

As with the previous exceptions to the warrant requirement we have discussed, the automobile exception is the second most common practiced exception besides the search incident to arrest exception as described previously. In *Carrol v. the United States* (1925), officers observed a vehicle that appeared to be overloaded and, by a visual look, could see the vehicle was sitting much lower than it should. This observation, along with the fact that the vehicle was traveling in an area heavily known for bootlegging of alcohol, officers stopped this vehicle and searched it. During the search, officers discovered 68 bottles of illegal alcohol. The defendants moved to request the search and seizure be deemed illegal due to the officers not having a proper search warrant. The Court did not agree and upheld the warrantless search and seizure based on two elements; (1) The officers were able to articulate probable cause to the justification to the stop and search and (2) officers would not have had time to reasonably detain the defendants in order to obtain a search warrant. The automobile exception is based on the fact that obtaining a proper search warrant would take too long, and evidence could then be lost due to the mobility of the area being searched. Over the years, officers, lawyers, and judges have involuntarily extended the automobile exception to other movable vehicles such as airplanes, boats, and trains.

Elements of the automobile exception focus on the vehicle itself and how the vehicle is being used. In *California v. Carney* (1985), officers were challenged with a hybrid situation, a Recreational Vehicle (RV) stationary in a public parking lot. The Court aggreged that while the RV did present many of the same characteristics as a home, thus afforded the expanded privacy protections. They also agreed that the manner in which the RV was being used should determine if the automobile exception applied. Since the RV was parked in a public lot, not connected to utilities, thus made the RV appear more like a vehicle than a home; as a result, the automobile exception applied in this situation.

The next element for the automobile exception is an element found in every exception, probable cause. For any exception to the warrant requirement to be met, officers must have probable cause before the search being conducted. As in *Carroll*, officers established probable cause before the stop itself. However, there are a few circumstances in which probable cause is not necessary. An example of this is found in *New York v. Class* (1986), where officers entered a vehicle to verify the Vehicle Identification Number (VIN). The Court ruled that due to the fact that motor vehicles pose a lesser expectation of privacy and are regulated by State and Federal regulations and licensing requirements when the VIN cannot be viewed via the windshield, the minimal intrusiveness of the VIN verification is valid as long as the officers are there legitimately.

## Plain View

The *plain view* exception to the warrant requirement permits officers to *seize* evidence that is in *plain view* of the officer(s). Simply put, if the officer(s) have the right to be in a place (legitimately), they have the right to see any items which are visible to any person in the same position. The *plain view* exception was first tested in *Coolidge v. New Hampshire* (1971). In *Coolidge*, the dilemma the Court faced was if officers were able to seize evidence without a warrant. Consequently, the warrant they did possess was not valid due to it not being authorized by a neutral and detached judge but was authorized by the State Attorney General, who acted as a justice of the peace signed the warrant. Although the warrant was deemed to be invalid, the lawfulness of the officer's presence fell under a good faith exception. The Court ruled that officers are permitted to seize items without a warrant if: (1) the officer(s) have a legitimate right to be in a location, (2) the items sized are in plain view, and quickly evident to any individual, and (3) the items seized must be discovered inadvertently.

However, *the plain view* is just not as simple as being able to see an item and seizing it as evidence. *Arizona v. Hicks* (1987) changed the understanding of the *plain view*. In *Hicks*, officers were legitimately at a residence conducting an investigation of another separate crime noticed stereo components within the residence in *plain view*, which he believed matched the description of the make and model of items that had been reported stolen. To verify this, the officer moved the components to view and compared the serial numbers to the one reported stolen, which matched. Hicks was charged with the possession of stolen items along with other non-related charges from the officer's previous investigation. The Court upheld Hicks' challenge that the items were seized without a warrant. The Court stated that although the officer was in the apartment legitimately and was able to view the stereo equipment in *plain view*, to verify the serial numbers, the officer had to move the items, which then constituted as a search as the serial numbers were not in *plain view*.

## Stop and Frisk

As discussed in each exception to the warrant requirement above, officers need *probable cause* to fall within the requirements of an exception to the warrant requirement under the Fourth Amendment. However, the *stop and frisk* is an exception within an exception to the warrant requirement. The Court first acknowledged this exception in *Terry v. Ohio* (1968). The Court loosened the *probable cause* requirement and described the new requirement as *reasonable suspicion*. Under *reasonable suspicion*, officers may have more than just a 'hunch' of criminal activity, but less than *probable cause*. In other words, the officer can articulate why they believe criminal activity has, is, or will occur, and the search of the person is strictly limited to a pat-down of the outer clothing of the citizen for officer safety.

In *Terry* (1968), officers were conducting a stakeout of a department store area in which there had been several previous burglaries. Detectives with more than 30-years of combined experience were observing Terry and another suspect loitering at a street corner by the department store. During this surveillance, the detectives noticed the suspects taking the same path to and from the department store, each stopping at the same window (more than 20 times), then meeting up again and talking. The detectives approached the suspects and identified themselves as police officers and requested each of their names. The suspects were not clear in their responses and mumbled an inaudible name. The detectives fearing that the suspects were armed, turned them around, and patted down the outer clothing of each individual. Terry was found to have a revolver on his person in the coat pocket. Other items that were discovered were tools to commit burglaries such as bolt cutters and a crowbar. The suspects were charged and contested because they were not under arrest when they were searched.

The Court disagreed with Terry and stated:

*.....When a police officer observes unusual conduct which leads him to conclude in light of his experience that criminal activity is afoot and the person whom he is dealing with may be armed and dangerous.... He is entitled to the protection of himself and others in the area to carefully conduct a limited search of the outer clothing.*

Stop and frisk then became what we know today as a *Terry Stop*. For a *Terry Stop* to be legal, officers must have a reasonable suspicion of criminal activity. As stated earlier, this suspicion must be more than just a hunch, but be facts in which the officer(s) can articulate to. *Minnesota v. Dickerson* (1993) added a new term to a *Terry Stop* with the term, *plain feel*. This term is used to describe that when an officer is patting down a suspect's outer clothing and *feels* what they believe to be an item that could be used as a weapon or contraband, the officer may enter the pocket or clothing to retrieve said item. The *plain feel* doctrine expanded the scope of the search for officers during a *Stop and Frisk* event.

## Consent Searches

The last exception to discuss is the consent of an individual to waive their right to officers being required a warrant to search. As early as 1921 in *Amos v. the United States*, the Court agreed that the valid consent of an individual is sufficient to waive the prerequisites of probable cause and the search warrant requirement under the Fourth Amendment. As with previous exceptions to the search warrant requirement, certain elements must be met for consent to be considered valid. The Court has stated that for consent to be valid, it must be made voluntarily and willingly. *Schneckloth v. Bustamonte* (1973) led the way for defining that consent must be made voluntarily. Here, Bustamonte was in a vehicle that was stopped by officers for defective equipment (a burned-out heading and a burned-out license plate light). The officers discovered six men in the vehicle, only one who had a valid driver's license who was the passenger. During routine questioning, the passenger stated the vehicle belonged to his brother and was not his. When officers asked for permission to search the vehicle, he permitted them. During the search, stolen checks were discovered, and Bustamonte was charged with possession of the checks with intent to defraud. To determine the validity of the consent, the Court used the totality of the circumstances to establish that consent of the individual is valid when he gives consent voluntarily, and no coercion exists. Officers need to only ask for consent to search and need not inform the individual of their right to refuse consent. We see here that the consent was also made willingly, and no coercion from the officers was made.

Along with the voluntariness of the consent, the consent to a search must also be made willingly. As stated in *Schneckloth*, the consent was provided without any coercion or threats from the officers, thus made willingly. The coercion or threat of force of the officers may differ in each situation, primarily depending on how the individual may perceive the threat or coercion. In *Johnson v. the United States* (1948), the Court stated that officers exhibited coercion when they stated they would conduct the search even without the proper warrant in hand. Furthermore, in *Bumper v. North Carolina* (1968), the Court held that the mere presence of six officers claiming to have a valid warrant to an elderly woman was considered a "show of authority" and was considered coerced (as the officers did not have a valid warrant). In the *United States v. Mendenhall* (1980), we see that even with similarities to *Johnson* and *Bumper*, we have a different outcome. In *Mendenhall*, the Court applied the totality of the circumstances to this case.

Here, Mendenhall was approached by members of the Drug Enforcement Administration (DEA) at an airport as she was suspected of traveling with narcotics. When officers met with Mendenhall, they identified themselves and asked for her identification. The identification she provided did not match the name on her airplane ticket. When asked about this oddness, she stated she just felt like it. She was then asked to accompany the officers to another location, and she did voluntarily. It was then discovered that she had a second plane ticket in another name and that she had been traveling for several days but had no luggage. This promoted further suspicion, and a female officer was brought in. The officer then asked if she could search her person, Mendenhall agreed. After a partial disrobing, the officer was handed over packages of heroin by Mendenhall. The Court viewed this differently than *Johnson* and *Bumper* as there was no coercion or threats to Mendenhall, and she was just asked if she would go with the officers, and the initial questioning by officers was very brief. The officers, in this case, also instructed Mendenhall two times that she could refuse the consent, which the Court decided was an essential and relative factor in the willingness of this case.

## HISTORICAL COURT CASES INVOLVING THE POLICE AND SEIZURE INVOLVING INTELLIGENCE GATHERING

The United States Supreme Court is the highest Court in the United States. Therefore, decisions made by the Court affect the entire nation. No other Court, agency, or individual is able to overturn a ruling by the Supreme Court, not even the President. Therefore, these rulings made by the Court stand until changed by the Court. Usually, when the Court changes direction on a previous ruling, it is due to the change in social acceptance. For example, what we see today in malls and clothing stores with women's lingerie would have been considered obscene many years ago, but today is acceptable. Thus, the Court applies modern standards to each case they hear. The Court selects approximately 100 cases per year that have been presented to them for review. These cases are selected based on which have the most severe constitutional issues. Below is a summary of three historic United States Supreme Court cases involving the police and the Fourth Amendment as it pertains to the gathering of intelligence of criminal activity.

## Katz *v.* the United States 389 US 347 (1967)

This case was argued on October 17, 1967, in front of the United States Supreme Court and was decided on December 18, 1967. The constitutional issues the Justices were reviewing was if the police were required to obtain a search warrant for the wiretapping of a public payphone. This case reviewed several issues such as a person's expectation of privacy in a public area, the requirement of law enforcement to obtain a search warrant for a wiretap, and if the seizure of recorded statements fell under the Fourth Amendment protections.

Katz was under suspicion of 'running numbers' and conducting illegal betting and gambling covering several States, including Los Angeles CA, Miami FL, and Boston MA, via the use of a public telephone booth. Since the illegal activity crossed the state line, the Federal Bureau of Investigation (FBI) was the lead law enforcement agency. Understanding that obtaining a wiretap is difficult, agents took another approach to gather intelligence. The phone booth Katz was using for his illegal activity was located in a public area. Agents put a listening device on the outside of the phone booth. This, so they thought would not be an intrusion into the inside of the phone booth where anyone using it upon closing the door would have an expectation of privacy. Katz was initially convicted of eight counts of illegally transmitting wagering information. Katz appealed, citing that the collection of evidence, this being his recorded conversations were obtained illegally via illegal eavesdropping by agents was, in fact, a search and seizure under the Fourth Amendment. The seizure of his words is considered a physical item, thus protected under the Fourth Amendment, and due to the fact that the Fourth Amendment protects people and not places, he was thus protected in the phone booth when he closed the door as he had an expectation of privacy form others hearing his conversations. The United States Supreme Court overturned the lower Court's decision and agreed with Katz that he was protected under the Fourth Amendment as per Justice he had a reasonable exception of privacy when using the phone booth and closing the door. The Court stated in the majority opinion:

*The Government's activities in electronically listening to and recording the petitioner's words violated the privacy upon which he justifiably relied while using the telephone booth and thus constituted a "search and seizure" within the meaning of the Fourth Amendment. The fact that the electronic device employed to achieve that end did not happen to penetrate the wall of the booth can have no constitutional significance.*

## Importance to Police Intelligence Gathering

The use of a wiretap for investigations was used to gather intelligence on a suspect for many years and continues today. Historically, the wiretap was an actual electronic connection to an individual's home or business phone, where offices would listen and record conversations. These wiretaps, as expected, would require a search warrant signed by a judge as wiretapping was and still is considered a 'dirty business' as stated by Justice Holmes in *Olmstead v. United States* (1928). Officers in Katz did think outside the box as they understood they could not enter the phonebooth to place the listening device, but still did not fully understand the intrusion into the privacy expectation of the phone booth. This case clarified the 'people not places' language of the Fourth Amendment to illustrate that even in a public area, individuals do have some expectations of privacy. When in doubt, officers should always attempt to gather intelligence and obtain a search warrant before recording any conversations in which the other party is not aware of being recorded by a person with whom they are directly speaking.

## Spinelli v. the United States 393 US 410 (1969)

This case was argued on October 15th and 16th, 1968, in front of the United States Supreme Court and was decided on January 27, 1969. The constitutional issues the Justices reviewing were if there was enough probable cause in the application for the search warrant, which was issued. This case reviewed the elements of probable cause and if there was sufficient information provided to agents by a confidential informant to illustrate probable cause under *Aguilar v. Texas* (1964).

A search warrant was issued to agents with the FBI in an attempt to identify and collect evidence of an illegal gambling operation of the defendant, William Spinelli. In the search warrant affidavit, agents listed that Spinelli was known by the local police as a gambler and an associate of other know gamblers. They also stated that they had visually tracked Spinelli for five days and received information from a confidential informant that Spinelli was conducting his business by using specific telephone numbers. The search warrant was executed, and items seized indicted the illegal gaming operation. Spinelli challenged the validity of the search warrant as they argued it did not meet the particularity requirements outlined in *Aguilar*.

The Supreme Court had the task of deciding if agents met the probable cause requirement to obtain the search warrant. Here, the Court agreed with Spinelli that agents did not follow the particularity requirement outlined in Aguilar several years earlier. The Court stating in the majority opinion said:

*The tip describes the accused criminal activity in sufficient detail that the magistrate knows that he is relying on something more substantial than a casual rumor or an accusation based merely on an individuals' general reputation.*

### Importance to Police Intelligence Gathering

Ensuring intelligence gathered meets the basic requirements for a search warrant is crucial to the integrity of the investigation. After *Spinelli*, the court created the *Aguilar-Spinelli* test to determine the legitimacy of information received from confidential informants or the general public. However, twenty-four years later, in *Illinois v. Gates* (1983), this test was overturned, and the court said that when issuing a search warrant based on the information from the general public or confidential informants, it should be based upon the "totality of the circumstances." Officers need to review all information when gathering intelligence, not just the word of informants or citizens, even if the information is more than an average respectable citizen would be able to observe. Being able to articulate the facts and circumstances in a clear and concise manner ensures the search warrant will meet the requirements to be issued

## MODERN COURT CASES INVOLVING POLICE INTELLIGENCE GATHERING

In modern times, the Supreme Court attempts to keep pace with questions arising out of the use of technological advances, but because of the length of time required for a case to wind its way through the justice system, rulings on these issues often occur many years after the constitutionality question arises. These next three cases take a look at how the Court has dealt with the police's use of technology related to the Fourth Amendment. The first case looks at the use of GPS tracking devices by the police, the second case examines if the police can search a cell phone immediately after the arrest of a person, and the third case looks at how the police use Cell-site location information collected by cell phone carriers and if a warrant is required.

### The United States *v.* Jones 565 US _ (2012)

This case, which was argued in front of the United States Supreme Court in November 2011 and Decided in 2012, arose from a Court of Appeals decision out of the District of Columbia Circuit. The Justices in this case, within the meaning of the Fourth Amendment, were asked to evaluate the constitutionality of attaching a GPS (Global Positioning System) device to a person's vehicle, and its subsequent use to monitor the location and movements of that vehicle on public streets. Justice Scalia delivered the majority opinion of the Court.

In 2004, Antoine Jones, a nightclub owner in Washington, D.C., was suspected of trafficking narcotics by the joint FBI and Metropolitan Police Department task force. The police utilized various investigative strategies to surveil Mr. Jones, including installing cameras focused on his business and pen registers and wiretaps of his mobile phone. As a result of the information gathered from these strategies, the police in 2005 requested a search warrant to use an electronic tracking device on the Jeep registered to Mr. Jones's wife, but Mr. Jones was the exclusive operator of the vehicle. A warrant was granted authorizing the police to install the tracking device on the Jeep within the District of Columbia within ten days.

However, on the 11th day, not in D.C., but in Maryland, the police installed the GPS tracking device on the undercarriage of Jones's Jeep while parked in a public parking lot. During the next 28 days, the police tracked the vehicle's whereabouts, and on occasion, had to replace the battery of the GPS device while the Jeep was parked in another public parking lot in Maryland. More than 2,000 pages of data were generated from the location history of the vehicle, which was broadcast via cellular phone to the police.

Mr. Jones and several alleged co-conspirators were indicted on multiple counts, including conspiracy to distribute and possess with intent to distribute five kilograms or more of cocaine and 50 grams or more of cocaine base in violation of Federal law. Before trial, Jones filed a motion to suppress the evidence from the GPS device from being admitted as evidence at his trial. The District Court granted that motion, but only in part. The Court ruled, at the time, that only the data collected while the vehicle was parked in the garage adjoining his residence would be excluded; the remaining data would be admissible because "'[a] person traveling in an automobile on public thoroughfares has no reasonable expectation of privacy in his movements from one place to another.'" (quoting the *United States v. Knotts*, 460 U.S. 276, 281 (1983)). Jones's October 2006 trial resulted in a hung jury on the conspiracy accusation.

In the spring of 2007, a grand jury returned a new indictment against Mr. Jones and the others with the same alleged conspiracy. At trial, the Government presented the same GPS evidence from the first trial, which placed Mr. Jones at the alleged conspirators' stash house that contained $850,000 cash and 97 kilograms of cocaine, and 1 kilogram of cocaine base. This time, the jury found Mr. Jones guilty, and the Court sentenced him to life in prison.

The U.S. Court of Appeals for the District of Columbia reversed Mr. Jones's conviction because of the admission of the data derived from the warrantless use of the GPS device on Jones's vehicle. The Court of Appeals ruled that the use of this data violated the Fourth Amendment, and the case was eventually granted certiorari to the U.S. Supreme Court. The Court stated: "We hold the Government's installation of a GPS device on a target's vehicle, and its use of that device to monitor the vehicle's movements constitutes a "search."

The Court wanted to be clear that in this case, the police physically occupied private property in order to facilitate the acquisition of the location data of Jones's Jeep. That by placing the GPS device on the Jeep, the Government "trespassory inserted the information-gathering device," and this action by the police demonstrates the importance of property to the Fourth Amendment. The Court, in its majority opinion, said:

*The text of the Fourth Amendment reflects its close connection to the property since otherwise it would have referred simply to "the right of the people to be secure against unreasonable searches and seizures"; the phrase "in their person, houses, papers, and effects" would have been superfluous.*

## Importance to Police Intelligence Gathering

In a variety of police investigations, the locations of the persons of interest in the investigation can be vitally important evidence. The ability of the police to gather this information like that which is available from a GPS device, in the traditional sense, is tedious and time-consuming. Gone are the days, where the police need to sit for hours in a car surveilling targets of importance. Because of advances in GPS technology, most of us carry a GPS tracking device on us every day in the form of a smartphone. While this case does not address smartphones, the spirit of the case establishes a procedure through which the police, in an attempt to gather specific data, must traverse in order to be successful in its admittance at trial.

Moving forward, the police must request and be granted a search warrant in order to gather information about a target's whereabouts when gathered through electronic means. This does not likely preclude officers from manually surveilling targets and tracking them through traditional eyes-on techniques.

## Riley *v.* California 573 US 373 (2014)

This case, in combination with another case, the *United States v. Wurie* (2014) generated another Fourth Amendment question for the Court. Can the police, without a search warrant, search digital information on a cell phone seized pursuant to a person's arrest? Chief Justice Roberts delivered the majority opinion in this 2014 decision.

In the first case, David Riley was stopped while driving for an expired license plate. During the traffic stop, the officer discovered that Riley had a suspended driver's license. The officer impounded Riley's vehicle, and another officer conducted an inventory search. This search uncovered two handguns hidden under the car's hood leading to the arrest of Riley for possession of a concealed and loaded firearm.

The officer searched Riley incident to his arrest. During this search, the officer located items associated with the "Bloods" street gang. After this discovery, the officer seized the smartphone he found in Riley's pants pocket. After this seizure, the officer looked through the phone and located contacts that had the letters "CK" preceding the name of the contact. The officer, based on his experience and training, believed this stood for "Crip Killers" slang for members of the Bloods gang.

A couple of hours later, while back at the police station, another officer who had experience in investigating gangs again examined Riley's phone looking for evidence related to gang activity. The detective testified that he went through Riley's phone, looking for videos and photos of guns or other related information. The detective focused on videos he located on the device of young men sparring while someone in the background yelled in encouragement the word "Blood." The officers also located a photo of Riley standing in front of a vehicle that had allegedly been involved in a shooting a few weeks prior.

Riley was charged with firing at an occupied vehicle, assault with a semiautomatic firearm, and attempted murder in connection with the prior week's shooting. The state alleged that Riley did so for the benefit of the street gang, which is an aggravating enhancement to the final sentence. Before trial Riley filed a motion to suppress all the evidence recovered from his smartphone because it violated the Fourth Amendment in that, the police had conducted a search of his phone absent a search warrant under circumstances that were not justified as exigent. The trial Court rejected this argument. During the trial, the police testified about the contents of the phone, and Riley was convicted on all three counts and was sentenced to an enhanced indeterminate sentence of 15 years to life in prison. The California Court of Appeals affirmed his case based on California Supreme Court case law, and the California Supreme Court denied Riley's petition for review of his case. The Supreme Court of the United States, on the other hand, agreed to hear the case.

In the second case, a police officer who was conducting routine surveillance observed Brima Wurie make an apparent drug sale from a car. Wurie was arrested and taken to the police station where the police seized two cell phones from his person. One of the phones was a flip phone, and this phone became an issue in this case. Within the first five to ten minutes after arriving at the police station, the officers noticed the phone was receiving multiple calls from "my house," which was observed from the phone's external screen. Eventually, the officers opened the phone where they saw his wallpaper of a woman holding a baby, and they then accessed the call log to see what number was associated with "my house," they used an online phone directory to trace that phone number to an apartment.

Officers went to the apartment, and they saw Wurie's name on the mailbox and looked in the window and saw a woman who resembled the woman in the photograph on the phone's wallpaper. They petitioned for and were granted a search warrant for the residence and found 215 grams of crack cocaine, marijuana, drug paraphernalia, a firearm and ammunition, and cash. Wurie was charged with distributing crack cocaine, possessing crack cocaine with intent to distribute, and being a felon in possession of a handgun. Wurie, before trial, attempted to suppress the evidence from the search of the apartment, arguing that the search of his residence was the result of the unconstitutional search of his cell phone. This motion was denied, and Wurie was found guilty at trial and sentenced to 262 months in prison.

A divided panel of the First Circuit Court of appeals reversed the denial of Wurie's appeal to suppress the evidence and vacated his conviction. This Court ruled, at the time, that cell phones are distinct from other possessions and that they may be searched incident to arrest without a warrant because the amount of personal data they hold poses a minor threat to the interests of the police.

The Court, in these cases, decided that officers must get a warrant before conducting a search of a cell phone, in most cases. They opined,

*Modern cell phones are not just another technological convenience. With all they contain and all they may reveal, they hold for many Americans "the privacies of life," Boyd supra, at 630. The fact that technology now allows an individual to carry such information in his hand does not make the information any less worthy of the protection for which the Founders fought. Our answer to the question of what police must do before searching a cell phone seized incident to arrest is accordingly simple – get a warrant.*

## Importance to Police Intelligence Gathering

The Court recognized in their ruling the potential for evidence to be destroyed by being remotely wiped from a device. They also recognized that a device could be encrypted automatically after a period of time. The Court opined that in some instances, there might be an exigent circumstance upon which officers may search a phone immediately. The Court also recognized that some steps are necessary to disable a phone from automatically locking to prevent data destruction or encryption and compared those steps to similar procedures used to secure a scene to preserve evidence while awaiting a warrant. These steps are outlined in *McArthur*, 531 U.S. 326.

In the years since this case was heard and decided, many advancements in cell phone encryption technology have occurred. Guidance from this case on dealing with these advances may help determine what to do with specific devices. The ability to bypass the encryption on certain devices is dependent on what happens to those devices upon seizure. Having procedures in place in accordance with this ruling to ensure the protection of the data on the devices is critical to the successful extraction of the data after a search warrant is issued.

## Carpenter *v.* United States 585 US _ (2018)

This case came to the Supreme Court by way of the US Court of Appeals from the Sixth Circuit. The question, in this case, has similarities to the *Jones* case mentioned previously in this chapter but deals with historical location data. The question before the Court was whether the government searches the Fourth Amendment when it accesses historical cell phone records that give a detailed history of the user's movements. This case was argued in November of 2017 and decided in June of 2018.

In 2011, the police arrested four men suspected of the robberies of several Radio Shack and T-Mobile stores in Detroit. One of those arrested confessed to the police that during the past four months, he and a group of others had robbed nine stores in Michigan and Ohio. This person was able to identify 15 accomplices who aided in these various robberies and was able to provide many of their cell phone numbers to the FBI. The FBI then reviewed his phone records to identify other numbers with which he had communicated around the time of the robberies.

Based on this information gathered from the suspect and his phone records, the prosecutors on the case requested Court orders to obtain cell phone records for Timothy Carpenter and many of the other suspects in the case. Under the Stored Communications Act, a 1994 amendment allows for the government to compel the disclosure of come telecommunications records based on reasonable grounds that the records are pertinent to a criminal investigation. In this case, Federal Magistrate Judges issued orders to MetroPCS and Sprint to disclose "cell/site sector for [Carpenter's telephone] at call origination and call termination for incoming and outgoing calls" during the four months under investigation by the FBI. The result of these orders was 127 days from MetroPCS and two days of records from Sprint at a time when Carpenter's phone was "roaming" in Ohio. Combined, the government had nearly 13,000 location points on Carpenter's location.

Carpenter was charged with six counts of robbery and six counts of carrying a firearm during a federal crime of violence. Carpenter filed a motion before trial to suppress the cell-site data because, he argued, that the government obtained this data in violation of the Fourth Amendment. His argument was based on the fact that the government obtained the records without a search warrant supported by probable cause; the Court denied his motion. At trial, seven witnesses indicated Carpenter was the leader of the operation. The FBI agent in the case testified that he produced maps that placed Carpenter's phone near four of the robberies. Carpenter was convicted on all but one of the firearms counts and sentenced to more than 100 years in prison.

The Court of Appeals for the sixth circuit upheld his conviction by ruling that Carpenter lacked a reasonable expectation of privacy in his location data because he had shared it with his cell phone company – and that these records were a business record and not protected by the Fourth Amendment.

The Court ruled that the process used to obtain the records obtained in this case by the FBI was a search under the Fourth Amendment. The Court opined that the Fourth Amendment not only protects property interests, but also interests when "an individual "seeks to preserve something as private." The Court recognized that the location data kept by a third party, in this case, the cell phone companies, do not fit neatly within previous rulings by the Court, but that it meets at the intersection of an expectation of privacy in one's physical location and an expectation of privacy in the information given to a third party.

This case is reminiscent of the *Jones* case as it relates to the tracking of an individual, in this instance; however, the data was not collected by the police directly, but by a third-party company – in which the Court ruled a person has an expectation of privacy.

## Importance to Police Intelligence Gathering

In *Jones*, the Court ruled that live tracking of a person would, in most cases, require a warrant. In this case, the Court similarly found that historical tracking of a person, through their records, should also require a warrant, in most cases. As technology advances, the ability to track a person too changes. Now, a person can be tracked via their Wi-Fi signal, Bluetooth signal, and advertiser identifiers, these technologies are similar to those mentioned in this case, but different in many ways. While the connection to a cell tower is required for your cell phone company to provide you service and records, they collect and maintain from you. Other trackable signals from your devices are freely broadcast as a convivence to the device user, and the Court has not addressed in this case how the police should handle the interception of those signals.

In each of these modern cases, the Court examined how the police use technology as a way to develop and collect intelligence on a person's whereabouts. In each case, the Court cautioned the police by expanding the reach of the Fourth Amendment to GPS devices, cell phone searches, and historical cell-site records. These actions by the Court may place constraints on the government to take an extra step but ensure the rights and process of the individuals the police investigate. In the future, the Court will, undoubtedly, deal with similar cases as technology grows to incorporate new forms of communication and tracking.

## FUTURE RESEARCH DIRECTIONS AND CONCLUSION

The gathering of intelligence by officers of the law has been occurring since we first saw modern police forces. As first seen in the Bow Street Runners in London under Sir Henry Fielding to the modern police forces of today. Officers gathering this intelligence to be used in a criminal prosecution need to ensure the methods they employ are within Constitutional and Case Law guidelines outlined in the Fourth Amendment to the United States Constitution and by opinions of the United States Supreme Court. Ensuring these are followed does not necessarily ensure a conviction in a court of law, but ensures the officers are abiding by the rules of law. However, with the ever-changing use of technology, there may not be a precedent on the area of intelligence gathering and how officers are gathering intelligence. Officers should always maintain current legal updates to changes to search and seizure rules from opinions from Court cases. Understanding when a search warrant is required and when an exception to the warrant requirement can be applied is essential in the construction and integrity of the case. Currently, there is no future research relevant to search and seizure as the Courts are reactive to cases that are brought before them.

## REFERENCES

Adams v. Williams (1971) 407 U.S. 143

Aguilar v. Texas (1964) 378 U.S. 108

Alderman v. United States (1967) 394 U.S. 165

Arizona v. Hicks (1987) 480 U.S. 321

Bumper v. North Carolina (1968) 391 U.S. 543

Burdeau v. McDowell (1921). 256 U.S. 465

California v. Carney (1985) 471 U.S. 386

Carpenter v. United States (2018) 585 U.S.

Carrol v. United States (1925) 267 U.S. 132

Coolidge v. New Hampshire (1971) 403 U.S. 443

Illinois v. Gates (1983) 462 U.S. 213

Johnson v. United States (1948) 333 U.S. 10

Katz v. United States (1967) 389 U.S. 347

Miller, L. S., Hess, K. M., & Orthmann, C. H. (2017). *Community Policing: Partnerships for Problem Solving* (8th ed.). Cengage.

Minnesota v. Dickerson (1993) 508 U.S. 366

Nardone v. United States (1939) 308 U.S. 338

New York v. Class (1986) 475 U.S. 106

Olmstead v. United States (1928) 277 U.S. 438

Orthmann, C. H., & Hess, K. M. (2013). *Criminal Investigations*. Cengage.

Rawlings v. Kentucky (1980) 448 U.S. 98

Riley v. California (2013) 573 U.S. 373

Schneckloth v. Bustamonte (1973) 412 U.S. 218

Silverthorne Lumber Company v. United States (1920) 251 U.S. 385

Spinelli v United States (1969) 393 U.S. 410

Terry v. Ohio (1968) 392 U.S.1

United States Constitution, Amendment IV United States v. Jones (2012) 565 U.S. 400

United States v. Mendenhall (1980) 446 U.S. 544

United States v. Wurie (2014) 728 F.3d 1

Walter v. United States (1980) 477 U.S. 649

Weeks v. United States (1914) 232 U.S. 383

Whitebread, C. H., & Sloboggin, C. (2015). *Criminal Procedure: An Analysis of Cases and Concepts* (6th ed.). Foundation Press.

## KEY TERMS AND DEFINITIONS

**Armspan Rule:** A rule developed in the case of *United States v. Rabinowitz* (1950) where officers conducting a legal search incident to arrest may search the immediate areas of the arrestee.

**Automobile Exception:** An exception to the *search warrant* requirement brought forth in *Carrol v. United States* (1925) where officers upon establishment of probable cause may search a vehicle without a warrant due to the mobility of said vehicle where evidence could easily be moved.

**Consent:** Where an individual provides officers consent to search without a warrant. The consent must be made voluntarily and willingly.

**Fruit of the Poisonous Tree:** A term used to describe evidence (the fruit) that has been illegally obtained (the poisonous tree) by officers and is being used against a defendant in a court of law.

**Good Faith:** Where officers conduct an illegal search or arrest of an individual but at the time of the search or arrest did not know they were doing it illegally.

**Hot Pursuit:** An exception to the warrant requirement where officers actively engaged in the pursuit of a suspect may enter areas normally protected under the Fourth Amendment such as a home, building, or structure where there is an expectation of privacy.

**Plain View:** A term used when officers are in a location legally and have the right to see said items. The officer has the right to be able to collect the item(s) as evidence.

**Probable Cause:** A set of facts or circumstances which would lead an intelligent person to believe a crime is, has, or about to occur.

**Search Incident to Arrest:** An exception to the search warrant requirement where officers may search an individual or an area (see armspan rule) upon a legal arrest.

**Search Warrant:** A document-based upon probable cause and signed by a neutral and detached judge authorizing law enforcement the ability to search and seize persons and items.

**Stop and Frisk:** A rule-based upon *Terry v. Ohio* (1968) which allows officers to conduct pat-down of a person's outer clothing for the purpose of officer safety.

# Chapter 3
# The United States Intelligence Community:
## Improving Interagency Interoperability

**Eugenie de Silva**
*National American University, USA*

## ABSTRACT

*The purpose of this work is to examine interagency cooperation within the United States (US) Intelligence Community (IC). To elucidate the importance of interagency interoperability, two cases wherein IC agencies failed to appropriately collaborate are presented: 1) the September 11th attacks of 2001 and 2) the failed bombing by Umar Farouk Abdulmutallab, also referred to as the underwear bomber. This work begins with a brief review of how interagency issues have quite deep roots in the IC. Then, readers are presented with a review of the two cases that is followed by an in-depth analysis of the factors that were common to both failures. Ultimately, the variations in modus operandi (MO), a lack of clear guidelines, and bureaucracy were identified as the three primary factors of failure in both of the cases. Therefore, the work concludes by recommending improved training and educational opportunities for those in the IC in addition to the establishment of an independent entity that would be responsible for overseeing and guiding interagency activities.*

## INTRODUCTION

Within the United States (US) intelligence field, it has proved to be paramount that information sharing and interagency cooperation be held in the highest regard. Throughout history, there have been major instances of interagency failures within

DOI: 10.4018/978-1-7998-7904-6.ch003

the Intelligence Community (IC). Each of these debacles has presented ample opportunities for security officials to learn vital lessons about the most beneficial strategies to maintain national security. Accordingly, this work provides readers with an opportunity to review two cases of failures that have resulted from failed interagency interoperability: 1) the September 11$^{th}$ attacks of 2001 (herein referred to as the 9/11 attacks); and 2) the failed Christmas bombing by Umar Farouk Abdulmutallab, also known as the underwear bomber. Through an analysis of the factors leading to the inefficient cooperation amongst agencies, this work also offers recommendations for the improvement of existing structures within the IC.

As is known, the US IC is comprised of eighteen agencies and organizations that are allocated unique responsibilities with regard to the maintenance of national security. Over the course of history, the IC has essentially undergone an evolutionary process to arrive at the structure it currently possesses. Yet, contemporary organizational and intelligence mechanisms within the IC remain insufficient to handle the wide-ranging and ever-changing threats posed to the US. Albeit advances in security certainly manage the risks, there are structural issues in the IC that may undermine true progress within the field.

The IC has a clear pattern of updating policies, establishing or restructuring agencies/organizations, and even developing new strategies to address novel threats or failures (where applicable). Additionally, members of the IC seek to "collect, analyze, and deliver foreign intelligence and counterintelligence information to America's leaders so they can make sound decisions to protect our country" ("Mission," n.d.). Therefore, the community not only works internally to identify methods of enhancing security, but also endeavors to offer logical, sound analyses for intelligence consumers to take further steps to protect the nation. Notwithstanding the constant efforts of intelligence practitioners to ameliorate the standards of the discipline, there have been many failures that have shed light on those issues that have been deeply ingrained in the IC as a collective institution. These issues and ways to address them constitute the focus of the recommendations section of this work.

## BACKGROUND

There is clear evidence that security practitioners have continuously sought to identify best practices and strategies through the formation of various internal commissions and committees. For example, consequent to the "fall of the Soviet Union [but prior to] the September 11 attacks, six bipartisan blue-ribbon commissions, three major unclassified government initiatives, and three think tank task forces" were established to investigate security practices (Zegart, 2005, p.86). Such initiatives highlight the importance placed on perpetual growth and improvement within the field. It is also imperative to recognize that intelligence professionals diligently work to rectify mistakes and overcome failures as and when they arise. The most notable example is the production of the Final Report of the National Commission on Terrorist Attacks Upon the United States, otherwise known as the 9/11 commission report.

In response to the devastating 9/11 attacks of 2001, the US witnessed the "IC's largest reorganization in more than 30 years" (Rosenbach & Peritz, 2009, p.14). The attacks made the shortcomings of intelligence practices glaringly apparent to intelligence professionals and the nation. Accordingly, based on the recommendations of the 9/11 commission report, the Intelligence Reform and Terrorism Prevention Act (IRTPA) was created with the aim of enhancing the IC's capabilities (Tamanaha, 2010, p.419). The IRTPA promoted information sharing, established greater oversight mechanisms, and implemented "new rules for intelligence and law enforcement" (Tamanaha, 2010, p.425).

Despite the inherent value of the 9/11 commission findings and the IRTPA, the conclusions of the 9/11 commission report were not unique or new. To the members of the general public, it may seem that the establishment of the IRTPA was indicative of the IC's pattern of immediately responding to new issues. However, for those with knowledge of the history of intelligence, it is readily apparent that the primary, structural issues identified within the report were identical to discussions that had been prevalent for years prior to the 9/11 attacks.

In a 1996 House Intelligence Committee staff report, it was posited that the IC "suffered from a lack of [...] integration between individual agencies" (Zegart, 2005, p.86). For many years, the IC established interagency committees as a means of rectifying these issues that were so easily discernible amongst agencies. Although the issues had not become a major point of discussion amongst members of the public, it is clear that government officials were aware of the severity of the interagency problems that faced the IC. Therefore, the inception of the IRTPA could be viewed as offering resolutions to long-standing issues of interagency, and not simply to those that had newly arisen.

The intelligence field prides itself on forethought and strategic planning. Ergo, the IC would have benefited from enacting changes to its intelligence sharing and interagency practices when these notions were first considered, rather than remaining complacent until the issue was immensely exacerbated. Thus, it would seem only rational to posit that the very act of remaining complacent until physical violence occurred was an intelligence failure. If the IC was aware of such shortcomings prior to the attacks, then one must question whether there was a purposeful decision not to amend the intelligence processes or whether there existed underlying conditions within the field that made improvements unfeasible.

And so, to understand the most beneficial strategies to rely upon when moving forward, one must review historical instances of interagency cooperation. By reviewing past failures, one may acquire practical knowledge of how best to ensure that history does not repeat itself; thus, enabling the community to effect genuine, positive change.

## MAIN FOCUS OF THE CHAPTER

### Interagency Interoperability – Failures

This work has sought to only explore examples of intelligence failures related to a lack of interagency cooperation. Therefore, it is hoped that readers understand that a conscious decision was made to not focus on the myriad of factors that could lead to various intelligence failures. The decision to maintain focus on interagency cooperation, however, should not be mistaken for the disregard or dismissal of the disastrous effects of other factors.

There are many forms of intelligence failures that range from errors in the analytical process to the reliance on inexact data. In fact, in many instances within the intelligence field, one mistake could result in a snowball effect that results in more serious dilemmas. Of course, one could certainly devote an entire research study to the various elements of intelligence failures. Yet, the focus of this paper has been purposefully made narrow to ensure the primary topic is not obfuscated by an abundance of data. Notwithstanding, it is also herein argued that politicization should, at the minimum, be one factor that is included in any discussion of intelligence failures as it is one of the most pervasive issues observed within the field. To fail to acknowledge this issue would be to neglect a major, pertinent aspect that is unfortunately deeply entangled in the workings of the IC.

Due to the very nature of the discipline, there are many unfortunate instances wherein politicization of intelligence occurs and thus undermines the mission statement of the IC. Unfortunately, the role of intelligence professionals can become extremely dependent on their political counterparts or consumers (Lowenthal, 2017, p.280). For example, it has been observed that once policymakers have been in office for several years and have become more familiar with the intricacies of the IC, they "tend to have higher expectations and to become more demanding" (Lowenthal, 2017, p.282). Consequently, an unfavorable relationship is formed wherein a policymaker may expect the IC to provide reports that advance his/her/their agenda, whilst the intelligence officials may consciously or subconsciously offer analyses that are "meant to please a policymaker," (Lowenthal, 2017, p.286).

A discussion of the element of politicization is especially pertinent when considering the failures regarding the 9/11 attacks as it can prove the aforementioned argument of the snowball effect of intelligence errors. The emotional responses invoked by the attacks seemingly made it possible for political motivations to lead the nation into an unwarranted war based on erroneous and fallacious intelligence. The lack of interagency cooperation leading up to the 9/11 attacks essentially laid the foundation for such improper actions to be consequently taken by the government.

External political motivations of the various branches of government are visible throughout the IC, and many interagency rivalries and bureaucratic mechanisms (as discussed later in this work) are also worsened as a result. Thus, as one may recognize, there is an inherent relationship between the factors discussed within this work and the politicization of the field. Therefore, readers must understand that a lack of interagency cooperation is simply one of many factors that contribute to failures within the IC. These factors do not occur within a vacuum. Hence, gaining a more holistic view of actions that could lead to failure can result in a more informed and rational discussion of plans for improvement. With this information taken into consideration, one may shift attention to failures that have resulted from issues in interagency cooperation.

## Case One: Lack of Interagency Cooperation

The 9/11 attacks of 2001 have been classified as "the most brazen and shocking terrorist attacks conducted by a sub-state group in history" (Ilardo, 2009, p.171). However, the physical devastation of the attacks was worsened by the realization that the US IC had ample information to predict and possibly prevent the attacks from taking place. When considering the events leading to these tragic attacks, the lack of interagency cooperation between the CIA and FBI is typically highlighted as a major example of a failure of agency integration in the IC.

The inability of these two intelligence organizations to set aside bureaucratic friction and maintain collaborative practices became the center of attention during inquiries into the attacks. The issues between the CIA and FBI are deeply rooted and have been acknowledged by those in the IC for many years. For example, in the 1990s, the IC sought to improve its practices to more adequately handle the threats posed by post-Cold War adversaries. Amidst these efforts, intelligence personnel had to "fight a deep-rooted competitiveness between the FBI and the CIA, dating back to J. Edgar Hoover's days, when the two agencies competed for each other's turf" (Gilmore, 2002). Therefore, it is unsurprising that the CIA and FBI have "harbor[ed] [long-standing] mutual distrust" that has been furthered by their "different internal cultures" for years (Tamanaha, 2010, p.428).

According to the 9/11 commission report, one of the several instances of failed interagency interoperability between the two agencies came about in January of 2001. The agencies were working together with regard to the investigation of the USS Cole bombing. The agencies were made aware of an individual known as "Khallad," who was a senior security officer for Osama Bin Laden (9/11 Commission, 2004, p.266). However, the agencies were also under the impression that "Khallad and Khalid al Mihdhar might be one and the same" (9/11 Commission, 2004, p.266). Thus, without the knowledge of the FBI, the CIA requested that a surveillance photograph of al Mihdhar be shown to a CIA source to help clarify his identity (9/11 Commission, 2004, p.266).

Whilst the source had previously identified images of Khallad with high levels of confidence, the source did not recognize the photograph of al Midhar; accordingly, the notion that Khallad and al Midhar was the same person was immediately disproved (9/11 Commission, 2004, p.266). Regrettably, the CIA did not share this information with the FBI. Without this knowledge, the FBI was unaware of the possible close ties between Khallad and al Midhar, and was also unable to begin investigations into his whereabouts (9/11 Commission, 2004, p.267).

Under ordinary circumstances, one may typically assume that the failure to inform the FBI was a careless mistake. Yet, further insight into the culture of the agencies may reveal that the CIA and FBI had underlying motivations that could have consciously or subconsciously guided officials away from genuine synergy. For example, reports show that both agencies instructed their personnel to share the least information with one another (Riebling, 2010, p.446).

In the months leading up to September of 2001, interagency cooperation continued to fail in online communications and even in-person meetings. For instance, in May, a CIA officer based at the FBI's International Terrorism Operations Section made the decision to continue to focus his efforts on assessments of Malaysia without providing support to the domestic investigations of the FBI (9/11 Commission, 2004, p.267). The agent was aware that Mihdar had obtained a US visa, and Nawaf al-Hazmi had arrived in Los Angeles in January of 2000, yet he did not share this data outside of the CIA (9/11 Commission, 2004, p.267). The reasoning behind the CIA official's decision not to inform the FBI was underpinned by the CIA's typical procedures in handling cases. Once the officer's inquiries had resulted in a lack of useful information for CIA purposes, he swiftly "moved on to different things" (9/11 Commission, 2004, p.268).

Similarly, in June of 2001, FBI personnel and the aforementioned CIA officer held a meeting wherein the USS Cole bombing was discussed. During the discussions of the activities in Malaysia, the CIA officer withheld information about Mihdhar obtaining a US visa, in addition to the fact "that his visa application indicated that he intended to travel to New York, that Hazmi had traveled to Los Angeles, and that a source had put Mihdhar in the company of Khallad" (9/11 Commission, 2004, p.269). Additionally, one FBI agent decided not to share reports that tied Mihdhar to a terrorist facility in the Middle East, since she believed that it would be inappropriate without the approval of the Justice Department's Office of Intelligence Policy and Review (OIPR) (9/11 Commission, 2004, p.269).

Had the FBI agent shared all information, those at the meeting would have been able to identify how Mihdhar was linked to the suspected facility, based on their "work on the embassy bombings case" (9/11 Commission, 2004, p.269). Along those lines, since the CIA officer did not share any information, Mihdhar was able to obtain a new US visa just two days after the meeting was held, and he flew to New York on the 4$^{th}$ of July (9/11 Commission, 2004, p.269).

Throughout the months leading to the 9/11 attacks, the CIA and FBI proved that they were not only restricted by improper guidelines about information sharing, but also by bureaucracy and cultural differences amongst the agencies. Whereas these issues were supposedly addressed by the IRTPA, one may turn focus to the 2009 case of Umar Farouk Abdulmutallab wherein such issues were again identified.

## Case Two: Lack of Interagency Cooperation

On Christmas day of 2009, Abdulmutallab boarded Northwest Flight 253 with the intent of detonating a bomb when approaching the destination of Detroit (Hawley, n.d., p.2). Abdulmutallab was a member of al-Qaida who managed to successfully pass through the US airport security measures, despite having "80 grams of pentaerythritol tetranitrate (PETN) [...] sewn into his underwear" (Spade, 2011, p.1). Fortunately, Abdulmutallab failed to ignite the substance according to his plans, and passengers immediately "noticed that both Abdulmutallab's pants and the wall of the aircraft had caught fire" (Spade, 2011, p.1). At this point, a passenger managed to tackle Abdulmutallab, whilst a flight crewmember extinguished the fire (Spade, 2011, p.1).

Although Abdulmutallab was unable to successfully detonate the bomb, he should never have had the opportunity to board the plane with the dangerous materials. The case may seem to be a straightforward instance of the Transportation Security Administration (TSA) failing to adequately scan and conduct security checks of Abdulmutallab prior to boarding the flight. Nonetheless, this case was that which actually had ties to failed information sharing amongst intelligence agencies. According to reports, Abdulmutallab's father had contacted the CIA to provide information about the extremist views that his son held ("Source: CIA Failed," 2009). The CIA did not further investigate this information and it was not shared with other agencies that may have more carefully considered the repercussions of dismissing the information.

Additionally, according to the Senate Select Committee on Intelligence (SSCI) (2010), the CIA "did not disseminate key reporting until after the 12/25 attempted attack" (p.5). The SSCI also posited that had the CIA disseminated the information throughout the IC, "other intelligence officers outside of the CIA and NCTC who tracked intelligence on Yemen and [...] Arabian Peninsula[] may have made the connection between the information provided" (2010, p.5). The failure to share information prevented in-depth analyses, and the variations in the operational foci of the IC members left vital data unnoticed.

Per the SSCI (2010), analysts' "competing priorities contributed to the failure" in this case (p.9). The CIA, National Security Agency (NSA), and the National Counterterrorism Center (NCTC) were focused on possible terrorist threats within Yemen (Senate Select Committee, 2010, p.9). Thus, they disregarded clear indicators of possible attacks within the US. Although each of the agencies was seemingly focused on the same objectives, they failed to take into consideration all elements of the threats at the domestic and international levels.

## Factors of Failure

Through a systematic review of the above cases, one may identify three specific factors that were common to both failures: 1) Differences in Modus Operandi (MO); 2) Lack of clear guidelines for intelligence sharing; and 3) Widespread interagency competitiveness and bureaucracies.

### Modus Operandi

All members of the IC maintain the common objective of protecting the nation and providing evidence-based analyses to policymakers. Notwithstanding, it is unequivocally clear that each agency and organization has distinct approaches to contribute to the IC's overall mission. The variations in procedures make difficult uniformity in interagency operations and can result in major intelligence failures.

Within the first case, it was clear that the two involved agencies were unable to recognize the urgency and innate necessity of upholding collaborative processes to predict and prevent an attack on US soil. The two agencies held, and seemingly continue to hold, very different opinions about intelligence and its role. For the FBI, "intelligence is the fodder of prosecutions, while the CIA's focus is on intelligence as a stepping stone to more knowledge" (Gilmore, 2002). In the case of the failures prior to 9/11, one of the CIA officials responsible for failing to share information with FBI personnel argued that the organizational functions were one of the reasons why certain information was not shared. In particular, the agent posited that the CIA "tended to play a 'zone defense,'" whereas the FBI had a tendency to "play 'man-to-man'" (9/11 Commission, 2004, p.268). According to the officer, it seemed that the objectives and focus of the organizations resulted in divisions that were not his responsibility to bridge.

With regard to the second case, the MO of several agencies failed to adequately consider the possibility of domestic attacks in comparison to attacks carried out abroad. The CIA, NSA, and NCTC strongly focused their efforts on Yemen. Thus, the agencies remained unwavering in their initial foci even when confronted with data that would have typically been readily indicative of a possible national security threat.

## Inadequate and Inflexible Guidelines

A lack of a solid foundation for intelligence professionals to base their investigations can result in immense failures. Despite the strong educational backgrounds and professional training of intelligence personnel, they cannot be expected to adequately carry out their responsibilities if the IC does not offer clear guidelines for their success. Therefore, when evaluating historical instances of failures, one is able to realize the dire impact of existing intelligence systems.

Due to the need for confidentiality in the IC, a strong "legal wall" has been "built to protect intelligence sources and defendants" (Gilmore, 2002). Unfortunately, these legal walls have resulted in lessened interagency cooperation and greater confusion amongst personnel. The guidelines for intelligence officers have not remained consistent throughout the IC. Therefore, whilst practitioners may understand how to carry out their duties within their agency, they may find it difficult to collaborate with fellow intelligence officials from other agencies wherein guidelines may greatly vary.

In fact, it has been reported that within the IC there have been instances of "conflicting directives assign[ing] overlapping [...] responsibilities to three different DOD entities, creating confusion as to which DOD office is actually responsible for coordinating with law enforcement agencies" (Pendleton, 2010, p.10). These types of issues were the most significantly prevalent in the case of 9/11. The FBI agents involved in the case made the decision not to share intelligence with certain other officers, due to a fear that it was against their regulations. If the agents were offered more straightforward guidelines, then they would have realized that the unique circumstances made it acceptable for the data to be shared.

## Bureaucracy

The intelligence field is fraught with bureaucratic structures that divide agencies and organizations and result in "overlapping agency responsibilities, redundant assignments, [and] conflicting authorities" (Olson, 2008, p.224). It is also regrettable that "'turf' conflicts" and "agency 'tunnel vision'" have resulted in the continuation of an intelligence culture "characterized by a professional but narrow focus on individual agency missions" (McConnell, 2007, p.52; Segall, 2010, p.69). Agency divisions have also resulted in increased internal secrecy, which not only makes information sharing difficult, but also lessens the sense of community within the field.

Currently, researchers assert that there are three categories of secrecy identified in the government. The first category is genuine national security secrecy, which relates to the "body of information which, if disclosed, could actually damage national security in some identifiable way" (Aftergood, 1996). The second category is political secrecy, which pertains to "deliberate and conscious abuse of classification authority for political advantage" (Aftergood, 1996). The third and final category is bureaucratic secrecy, which refers to "the tendency of all organizations to limit the information that they release to outsiders so as to control perceptions of the organization" (Aftergood, 1996).

In the aforementioned cases, it seems that bureaucratic secrecy may have inadvertently resulted in intelligence failures. The desire to limit the sharing of information may now be instinctive within the agencies; therefore, it is possible that officers subconsciously do not share because that is simply how they have been trained. These officers may not be aware of the underlying bureaucracy that initially led to such limited information sharing practices. However, ignorance should not be considered as bliss and complacency should not be tolerated. Therefore, it is herein argued that all intelligence professionals have the responsibility to understand the history of intelligence so that they can be equipped with the knowledge to prevent the repetition of historical intelligence failures.

The desire to control perceptions of an agency may have also backfired as the failures resulted in widespread negative views of the involved agencies. Nevertheless, these issues, as aforementioned are not new to the IC. Interagency rivalries may be traced back, in part, to the formation of the National Security Council (NSC) consequent to the National Security Act of 1947 (Maher, 2006, p.7). The objective of the NSC has been to "unify interagency approaches to national security issues" and also take responsibility for "the general direction and coordination of intelligence operations" (Maher, 2006, p.7). Yet, it has been argued that the NSC is "at the mercy of particular presidents--to be used, reshaped, or ignored as they prefer" (Maher, 2006, pp.7-8).

Those in the executive branch believe that the strong influence may be beneficial in centralizing affairs to more successfully handle foreign policy (Maher, 2006, p.10). However, the negative effects have also become extremely evident to those outside the branch. In particular, the inadvertent gravitation toward the NSC being viewed as "an entity of federal power in its own right" may have led to the "intimidat[ion] or overrid[ing] of other interagency players" (Maher, 2006, p.10). The management of foreign policy by the President through the NSC inherently causes a "rise[] in prominence" within the field (Maher, 2006, p.10). This not only leads agencies to withhold constructive opinions and deferring to the NSC, but also to the NSC not even consulting other agencies due to its perceived importance and status (Maher, 2006, p.10). Ultimately, information sharing and interagency coordination are compromised due to the "inter-departmental and agency rivalries [that] develop in reaction to the rise of certain personalities in both the NSC and NSC staff" (Maher, 2006, p.10).

## SOLUTIONS AND RECOMMENDATIONS

The rectification of the aforementioned common failures of interagency cooperation in the US necessitates systemic reconstruction. It has been reported that "[o]nly when a bureaucracy is really pushed to change will any major action actually take place" (Halperin & Klapp, 2006, p.99). The IC has consistently undertaken actions to improve interagency efforts, including calls for improved oversight, and the establishment of interagency management systems (Dahl, 2007, p.13). Therefore, the implementation of new guidelines for information sharing practices would not resolve the current underlying issues within the intelligence arena.

Any recommendations for improved interagency efforts must holistically consider all factors preventing coordination. Not only is every agency structured quite differently, but they also have different agency-level missions. They each contribute to national security differently; hence, one cannot strive for integration without also realizing that each agency has different legal constraints, "habits[,] and practices" (Olson, 2008, p.229). Furthermore, without completely restructuring the entire government to alter commonplace practices, there can never be complete interagency coordination. For instance, take into consideration how Congress appropriates funds. It has been reported that the "timing for approving money works on a schedule that is only partly amenable to interagency coordination" (Olson, 2008, p.230). Therefore, an individual offering any recommendations must be cognizant of the pitfalls of the current structure of the government. To effect change, one must identify a solution that mitigates the issues and provides a reasonable, attainable solution for all involved.

### Steps Forward

The actions proposed within this paper relate to altering the atmosphere of the IC through systematic changes to cultural norms within agencies. There must be a combination of steps aimed at eradicating the internal turf wars of the IC by focusing on the mindsets of individual intelligence personnel. The critical thinking skills of intelligence officers must be honed to promote greater rationality. Once these steps have been successfully taken and the IC can provide empirical evidence that the competitive nature of agencies has been eliminated or minimized, then new policies or guidelines could be more effectively introduced.

Thus, the first step would involve consistent, mandatory training throughout the IC. This training should be devoted to raising awareness of the sense of community amongst IC agencies. Further, this training should be uniform for every agency. This would enable all agency employees to recognize that they are equal members of the community. There may be misconceptions that one agency is superior to another; hence, the training should strongly elucidate that each member is valuable, unique, and one element of a larger community. Along those lines, it should be taught that competing with another agency is undermining one's own mission. It is herein asserted that the training should highlight how enforcing bureaucratic secrecy in an effort to maintain a more idealistic view of an agency is equivalent to purposefully sabotaging the efforts of the IC. Yearning to maintain control over perceptions of an agency should be realized through honest, law-abiding, ethical intelligence work, not by shielding important information from other agencies.

The second step involves altering how agencies view current interagency guidelines. The policies that have been established should not solely be viewed as recommendations or suggestions. The IC should recognize them as clear rules that have stringent penalties for failing to comply. However, as previously mentioned, it is also understood that an agency may deliberately classify information to avoid sharing it with other agencies. Such an agency could possibly argue that they are within their rights not to share, due to the need for confidentiality. To handle such cases, there should be an external review team, which leads to the third step.

The third step involves appeals to Congress for the establishment of an independent entity devoted to oversight and guidance of interagency activities. In fact, some researchers advocate for the enactment of an updated and expanded "version of the Contingency Operations Oversight and Interagency Enhancement Act of 2011" (Mauser, 2013, p.21). This would allow an independent office to "direct coordination and collaboration" amongst government organizations (Mauser, 2013, p.21). An office that has no other involvement in intelligence activities can provide objective support to the community, which would also support the aforementioned steps.

## CONCLUSION

In its entirety, interagency collaboration has proved to be a significant issue throughout the history of the IC. The atrocious 9/11 attacks of 2001 placed a major spotlight on the inner workings of intelligence agencies. Subsequently, the 9/11 commission report provided the necessary reform of the field, especially with regard to enhanced integration and information sharing practices. Alas, eight years later, the failed Christmas bombing by the notorious, "Underwear Bomber" again highlighted the same failures by agencies to adequately work with one another. Through the assessment of both cases, it has been herein determined that the failed interagency cooperation was the result of three main factors: 1) Widely varying MOs; 2) Lack of clear guidelines, and 3) Bureaucracy and interagency rivalry.

The differences in objectives and practices within the agencies made difficult the task of coordination amongst one another. In addition, agency officials refrained to share data even when they understood the benefit it would have for ongoing investigations. This was primarily due to confusion about the guidelines on information sharing and in what instances sharing was acceptable and appropriate. These issues were further exacerbated by the inherent interagency competitiveness. The desire to maintain positive perceptions of the agency and or simply the innate rivalry amongst agencies led agents to feel as though they had no responsibility in sharing information with one another.

The identified issues make clear that there are deeply rooted issues that cannot be resolved by surface-level Courses of Actions (COAs). Accordingly, this work has sought to present a strategy that first handles the issues through rigorous, consistent training across the IC. The training would help to change the incorrect assumptions that certain agencies are more important or more useful to the intelligence arena. Furthermore, this could help lay the foundation for the next step, which involves changing how intelligence professionals perceive interagency collaboration guidelines. These guidelines should be recognized as not only important, but mandatory in the applicable instances. Personnel should not simply view the guidelines as suggestions to be followed at one's own discretion. The first two steps would be supported by the last step that concerns the establishment of an independent entity to conduct oversight of interagency activities, and provide unbiased assessments of how agencies are carrying out their interagency responsibilities.

Unless the overall structure of government is altered, it is unquestionable that the coordination problem will remain an issue. Nonetheless, taking steps to improve true synergy in the IC must precede policy changes that simply force agencies to interact with one another. When an agency feels controlled to do something, other issues arise, such as bureaucratic secrecy. Therefore, the development of acceptance and understanding of the roles each agency plays and how they should and could support one another will be the first true step forward.

## REFERENCES

Aftergood, S. (1996, October 9). *Secrecy and accountability in U.S. intelligence.* Federation of American Scientists. https://fas.org/sgp/cipsecr.html

Commission. (2004, July 22). *The 9/11 commission report.* https://www.9-11commission.gov/report/911Report.pdf

Dahl, K. R. (2007, July). *New security for new threats: The case for reforming the interagency process.* The Brookings Institution. https://www.brookings.edu/wp-content/uploads/2016/06/dahl20070731.pdf

Gilmore, J. (2002, December 22). *CIA-FBI cooperation - Some recent history.* PBS. https://www.pbs.org/wgbh/frontline/article/cia-fbi-cooperation-some-recent-history/

Halperin, M., & Clapp, P. (2006). *Bureaucratic politics and foreign policy.* Brookings Institution Press.

Ilardo, G. J. (2009). The 9/11 attacks—A study of Al Qaeda's use of intelligence and counterintelligence. *Studies in Conflict and Terrorism, 32*(3), 171–187. doi:10.1080/10576100802670803

Maher, J. E. (2006). *Interagency unity of effort. The strategic interagency coordination center (STRIACC).* Air War College. Retrieved October 25, 2020 from https://pdfs.semanticscholar.org/c471/7c533d8e9bd469847450f1d8b08d90040d84.pdf

Mauser, D. P. (2013). *U.S. government interagency reform needed in support of national security.* United States Army War College. Retrieved October 31, 2020 from https://apps.dtic.mil/dtic/tr/fulltext/u2/a589428.pdf

McConnell, M. (2007). Overhauling intelligence. *Foreign Affairs, 86*(4), 49–58. https://www.jstor.org/stable/20032414 9/11

Office of the Director of National Intelligence. (n.d.). *Mission.* https://www.intelligence.gov/mission

Olson, W. J. (2008). Interagency coordination: The normal accident or the essence of indecision. In G. Marcella (Ed.), *Affairs Of State: The Interagency And National Security* (pp. 215–254)., https://www.jstor.org/stable/resrep11925.8

Pendleton, J. H. (2010, June 9). *Key challenges and solutions to strengthen interagency collaboration*. Government Accountability Office. https://www.gao.gov/new.items/d10822t.pdf

Riebling, M. (2010). *Wedge: From Pearl Harbor to 9/11: How the secret war between the FBI and CIA has endangered national security*. Simon and Schuster.

Rosenbach, E., & Peritz, A. J. (2009). *Confrontation or collaboration? Congress and the Intelligence community*. Belfer Center for Science and International Affairs. https://www.belfercenter.org/sites/default/files/files/publication/IC-book-finalasof12JUNE.pdf

Segall, R. (2010). The Intelligence Community: Resolving conflicts between agencies for national security. *American Intelligence Journal, 28*(1), 67-77. https://www.jstor.org/stable/44327131

Senate Select Committee on Intelligence. (2010). *Attempted terrorist attack on Northwest Airlines flight 253*. https://www.congress.gov/111/crpt/srpt199/CRPT-111srpt199.pdf

Source: CIA failed to circulate report about bombing suspect. (2009, December 29). *CNN*. Retrieved October 28, 2020 from http://www.cnn.com/2009/CRIME/12/29/airline.terror.cia/index.html

Spade, M. (2011, December 27). *Case 33: The underwear bomber*. Ohio State University. https://politicalscience.osu.edu/faculty/jmueller/33UDWR7.pdf

Tamanaha, B. Z. (2010). Are we safer from terrorism? No, but we can be. *Yale Law & Policy Review, 28*(2). https://digitalcommons.law.yale.edu/ylpr/vol28/iss2/7

Zegart, A. B. (2005). September 11 and the adaptation failure of U.S. intelligence agencies. *International Security, 29*(4), 78–111. doi:10.1162/isec.2005.29.4.78

## KEY TERMS AND DEFINITIONS

**Bureaucracy:** A form of organization characterized by a strict hierarchical structure and chain of command system and stringent division of labor that preserves uniformity.

**Intelligence:** Information that has been collected, processed, and analyzed in support of the maintenance of national security.

**Intelligence Community:** The collection of eighteen intelligence agencies and organizations within the United States that work separately to uphold national security.

**Interagency:** Involving two or more agencies or organizations.

**Interagency Interoperability:** The ability of intelligence agencies to fairly share information, communicate effectively, and provide support across organizational borders.

**Modus Operandi:** A specific approach to handling certain matters or patterns of working.

**Politicization (in Intelligence):** The act of skewing intelligence to fit a specific political narrative or perspective.

# Chapter 4
# Countering Radicalization in the 21st Century

**Eugenie de Silva**
*National American University, USA*

## ABSTRACT

*The aim of this work is to provide a discussion of radicalization, especially as it has been presented in existing literature. This chapter begins with a focus on how radicalization is defined and how debates surrounding the definition of the term could have pragmatic and theoretical consequences. Further, this work highlights current discourse on the radicalization process. The work also includes a review of the risk factors that may typically lead one to radicalization. To do this, the three main overarching themes, including push, pull, and personal factors, are spotlighted. Finally, the work concludes with a three-pronged course of action (COA) to prevent the radicalization process, mitigate the violence carried by those who have already been radicalized, and also rehabilitate those who have undergone the radicalization process.*

## INTRODUCTION

To truly consider the topic of radicalization, one must adopt a holistic approach that is underpinned by an understanding that there is little consensus on the topic. Thus, if what is sought is a strategy to prevent radicalization, then one must first embark on a literary journey to examine the multitude of perspectives regarding what is radicalization, what factors make one more or less vulnerable, and how does the radicalization process unfold. Accordingly, the adoption of an objective standpoint is necessary to comprehend the breadth of studies on radicalization.

DOI: 10.4018/978-1-7998-7904-6.ch004

In any field, researchers are bound to hold varying beliefs, convictions, and standpoints on issues. Although this diversity can be problematic in a pragmatic sense, it can be highly beneficial for academics. In fact, as is posited later in this work, the work of an academic who takes the contrasting views of a field and develops a theory that bridges any gaps could possibly arrive at a practical, real-world solution to a pressing issue. This logically leads to the question, "Is it possible to close the divide that currently stands between researchers who focus on radicalization?"

With this information and this question at the forefront of the analyses, this work was produced. Through a review of the primary opinions within the field, the strategy for preventing and mitigating radicalization and rehabilitating those radicalized is presented with an emphasis on integrating the seemingly disparate viewpoints to achieve a form of harmony in the field.

## BACKGROUND

### Radicalization – Defined

Within the fields of intelligence and security, there is an unfortunate pattern with regard to a lack of uniform definitions of concepts and terms. One of the most well-known examples of this is the failure to adopt one universally accepted definition of terrorism. This lack of consistent definitions also spans to the notion of radicalization. Currently, the existing body of literature includes many wide-ranging definitions from researchers who interpret the concept from their unique perspectives. Therefore, prior to any analyses, it is imperative to offer an explanation of how radicalization is herein construed and defined.

According to many researchers, radicalization refers to "the process of developing extremist ideologies and beliefs" (Borum, 2011, p.9). Researchers who adopt this definition clearly posit that individuals who are radicalized may embrace or be sympathetic to extremist beliefs. Yet, they also assert that the act of embracing extremist ideas is not entirely suggestive that an individual will engage in extremist actions (Borum, 2011, p.9). On the other hand, researchers, such as Donatella Della Porta and Gary LaFree (2012) view radicalization as the "escalation process leading to violence" (p.6). This is inherently contradictory to the former views of the concept, which assert that violence is not guaranteed with radicalization. To further elucidate the contradictions within the literature, one may consider academic discussions that contend radicalism should never even be considered as synonymous with extremism, due to relative differences in the reliance on reason and rationalism by radicals (Schmid, 2013).

Along these lines, one could further argue that many of the current definitions have greater issues, since they have also failed to accurately define "violence" in the contexts of their work. It is undoubted that violence certainly extends beyond direct, physical harm. Therefore, could the adoption of a negative, radical, cultural viewpoint that intrinsically disparages a specific population be a form of cultural violence? If so, in such instances, it would seem only logical that radicalization be considered a form of violence, rather than a process leading to violence.

These academic or theoretical debates in defining radicalization can lead to pragmatic issues in counter-radicalization and even counter-terrorism operations. The variations in how radicalization is understood can lead to major differences in the ways in which intelligence or security efforts are directed. A successful Course of Action (COA) for countering radicalization requires a true understanding of what is radicalization. Therefore, until consensus is achieved amongst academics and practitioners about the definition of radicalization, researchers should always offer straightforward explanations of the definitions they rely upon in their investigations into the topic.

Accordingly, for the purposes of this work, radicalization is viewed as the "process of developing extremist beliefs, emotions, and behaviors" (Trip et al., 2019, p.2). For further clarity, extremist beliefs are herein defined as "profound convictions that oppose the fundamental values of society, the laws of democracy, and universal human rights by advocating the supremacy of a particular group (racial, religious, political, economic, social, etc.)" (Trip et al., 2019, p.2). These workplaces a priority on the examination of radicalization leading to extremism and terrorism, but does not necessitate that physical violence be present to signify radicalization. However, it is accepted that individuals may become fundamentally involved in the triangle of violence (physical, structural, and cultural) (Galtung, 1969).

## Radicalization Process

According to researchers, radicalization tends to be a "gradual process" (Schmid, 2013, p.20). Furthermore, it has been made abundantly clear that the process of radicalization leading to violent extremism or terrorism can "vary by individual, group, type of belief system, and context" (Lynch, Mason, & Rodriguez, 2015, p.iv). The motivations that result in one engaging with the radicalization process can also influence how the process progresses.

There are many who hold the opinion that radicalization can be presented as a linear process. As a result, models have been developed to highlight the step-by-step process of radicalization of terrorism. For example, in 2005, Fathali Moghaddam developed a "staircase to terrorism" model that "used the metaphor of a narrowing staircase leading to the terrorist act at the top of a building" (p.161). This model included six steps in the process to terrorism: 1) "Psychological Interpretations of Material Conditions;" 2) "Perceived Options to Fight Unfair Treatment;" 3) "Displacement of Aggression;" 4) "Moral Engagement;" 5) "Solidification of Categorical Thinking and the Perceived Legitimacy of the Terrorist Organization;" and 6) "The Terrorist Act and Sidestepping Inhibitory Mechanisms" (Moghaddam, 2005, pp.162-166).

Moghaddam (2005) argued that the higher an individual metaphorically climbs the "staircase," the less viable options they will be able to identify, "until the only possible outcome is the destruction of others, or oneself, or both" (p.161). Upon closer investigation, it seems that progression within the process was primarily based on individual motivations, such as perceived "options to fight unfair treatment" that they may be facing (Moghaddam, 2005, p.163). These factors are further explored later in this paper. Nonetheless, Moghaddam (2005) recognized that such models were intended to provide general frameworks, rather than to be utilized as "formal model[s] to be tested" (p.162).

On the contrary, there are many studies and researchers who disagree and disapprove of the idea that radicalization can be regarded as a "linear 'conveyor belt' moving from grievance, through radicalization, to violence" (Patel, 2011, p.8). This perspective was reinforced by a 2008 study conducted by the United Kingdom's (UK) Military Intelligence, Section 5 (MI5) that concluded that the process of embracing violence was extremely complex and therefore radicalization could logically not be linear (Security Service MI5, 2008). This was further corroborated by a Department of Homeland Security (DHS) supported report that declared "unlikely that any single theory can integrate all the influences that bring individuals to radical political action, although a conceptual framework in which to view these influences may be possible" (McCauley & Moskalenko, 2008, p.429).

The commonality amongst each of the aforementioned articles is the presentation of similar or even the same risk factors leading to radicalization. The sole difference is the outlook on the structural characteristics of radicalization being linear versus nonlinear. Therefore, due to the subjectivity within the literature, the articles upon which one decides to rely will determine what stance one adopts. If one chooses to holistically assess the discourse on radicalization, as is the case for this paper, then one can objectively identify the pros and cons of both viewpoints.

The prescription of a linear process is particularly beneficial for law enforcement and intelligence personnel who must observe and predict those individuals who may be more likely to be radicalized or are already undergoing the process. Such linear assessments are pragmatically beneficial as they allow practitioners to generally understand radicalization and actively apply the knowledge. However, from an academic standpoint, a nonlinear explanation of the radicalization process is the most reasonable. The distinctive case studies of those who have been radicalized that fail to fall within the bounds of any specific process are evidence of the nonlinear characteristic of radicalization. Thus, one should be aware that the true nature of radicalization may be nonlinear, but there is a pragmatic necessity to assess it in the context of linear processes to support investigations and operations. With this information taken into consideration, one can progress to the discussion of the common risk factors amongst those who have undergone the radicalization process.

# MAIN FOCUS OF THE CHAPTER

## Risk Factors Leading to Radicalization

Over the years, researchers and practitioners have identified many baseline factors of individuals who have been radicalized. Accordingly, it has become possible to use this information to recognize those who may be susceptible to radicalization, and then develop prevention strategies. Whilst literature on this topic is vast, there are many risk factors that seem to be commonly illuminated. Hence, to systematize discourse on radicalization risk factors, authors and practitioners commonly refer to specific types of factors under the categories of "push," "pull," and "personal." Therefore, to understand the variety of risk factors leading to radicalization, one must be cognizant of the meanings behind these categories.

### Push Factors

The concept of a "push factor" is utilized as a means of describing a key factor that is quite structural in nature. For instance, push factors include, but are not limited to "loss of legitimacy, geopolitical factors, state repression, relative deprivation, [and] inequality" (Vergani, et al., 2018, p.861). These structural issues can create unfavorable conditions for individuals wherein they feel as though violent extremism is a rational and beneficial way forward. In fact, the structural and thus contextual factors can also inherently become the "root cause[s]" of pull and personal factors.

Notwithstanding the fact that there are many different push factors, the most commonly cited factor in literature is the "relative deprivation of a social group" (Vergani, et al., 2018, p.866). When an individual believes that their social group has been threatened, or perceives that there are prevalent social injustices, they may be radicalized to resort to extremism as a solution. This push factor makes it more likely that the pull factors will lead to radicalization, which is discussed in more detail in the following section of this work.

Another push factor leading to radicalization is unemployment and thus poverty. The desire to provide for one's self and one's family can lead an individual to join an extremist group even if they may not initially hold such radical views. Whereas authors posit that poverty itself is not the sole reason for radicalization, it is the effects of poverty, such as "idleness and low self-esteem" that are problematic (Hassan, 2012, p.18).

Another push risk factor is a lack of education amongst a population. Individuals may have access to religious education, yet the inadequate general education opportunities can make it difficult for persons to "pursue different avenues in life" (Hassan, 2012, p.19). Without appropriate knowledge and problem-solving skills to join the workforce, seek further education, or simply work toward societal betterment, these individuals may turn to radicalism as their only viable and easy option (Hassan, 2012, p.19).

## Pull Factors

The aforementioned definition of push factors makes clear how factors, such as societal or structural inequalities, could unintentionally leave a population more vulnerable to radicalization. However, pull factors are those that are intentionally enticing to certain individuals, based on their backgrounds. These factors spotlight the "aspects that make extremist groups and lifestyles appealing to some people" (Vergani, et al., 2018, p.858). These factors generally include ideologies, the sense of belonging to a group, and other similar engaging incentives (Vergani, et al., 2018, p.858).

To elaborate, persons may become radicalized as the result of a yearning to protect, strengthen, or further their ideological beliefs within society. The ideological underpinning of radicalization can make it possible for individuals to rationalize and justify their violence. Therefore, extremist groups may capitalize on an individual's desire to do what they believe is ideologically just.

Consequently, to influence individuals to become involved in violent extremism, the pull factor of reputation or heroism is a common tactic. This also ties to the push factor of societal restrictions or inequalities; for instance, in societies wherein youths are viewed as powerless and worthy of less respect, extremist groups may use the promise of "immediate respect and access to power" to inveigle this particular population (Hassan, 2012, p.19). By understanding the structural inequities within a certain society, extremist groups are able to target populations and take advantage of their personal factors. This is indicative of the interconnected nature of push, pull, and personal factors.

## Personal Factors

Moving forward, personal factors are closely related to pull factors; however, they extend into the "individual characteristics that make certain individuals more vulnerable than their circumstantially comparable peers" (Vergani, et al., 2018, p.858). Personal factors leading to radicalization include "psychological disorders, personality traits, and traumatic life experiences" (Vergani, et al., 2018, p.858). According to researchers, psychological issues are wide-ranging, but typically include depression, loneliness, and low self-esteem (Vergani, et al., 2018, p.871). These factors are quite straightforward and simpler to identify, especially if individuals have been officially diagnosed with a disorder.

Au contraire, personality traits may require more in-depth observations. An individual's personality offers the foundational knowledge needed to determine how he/she/they could be influenced to be involved or to sympathize with extremist beliefs. Take for instance "ideological activists," who have charismatic personality types "motivated by idealism and a strong sense of justice" (Alonso et al., 2008, p.12). It is reported that these individuals may be more susceptible to the radicalization process, due to their possible rationalizations of the necessity of political violence in support or defense of their ideological standpoints (Alonso et al., 2008, p.12).

Along those lines, the discussion of political violence leads to those individuals who may certainly be intelligent and socially adapted, yet also are "impressionable and easily manipulated" (Alonso et al., 2008, p.12). These types of persons have a tendency to be exploited to "embrace violent forms of militancy through a combination of loyalty to the leader and political activism" (Alonso et al., 2008, p.12). Whilst these individuals may be educated and well-accepted within society, their overall naivety makes them malleable and thus quite vulnerable to external influences.

In addition, individuals with criminal backgrounds, a history of family problems, and/or "negative social backgrounds and careers" may seek "violent activism" as a coping mechanism for their personal issues (Alonso et al., 2008, p.13). Their traumas commonly lead them to be "action-oriented, aggressive" individuals with a "high readiness for violence" (Alonso et al., 2008, p.13). This is particularly beneficial to extremist groups, since they are able to hone the indignation of these individuals to promote intense violence and radical actions.

## SOLUTIONS AND RECOMMENDATIONS

To counter-radicalization, a three-pronged COA should be adopted to address the issue at various stages of the cycle: 1) Prevention; 2) Management; and 3) Rehabilitation. One should first consider preventative measures to possibly predict and then deter individuals from falling victim to the radicalization process. However, if individuals have already been radicalized, it is important to focus on management capabilities to thwart violent or extremist activities, whilst also mitigating the effects of radicalization. Finally, in cases wherein radicalized individuals have either sought help or been imprisoned for radical, illegal behavior, rehabilitation to promote progressive, positive mindsets and productive reintegration into society should be prioritized.

## Prevention

It is herein posited that the most propitious way forward to prevent radicalization is through the adoption of a long-term, positive peace strategy. According to Johan Galtung (1964), commonly referred to as the father of peace studies, positive peace is the "integration of human society" (p.2). For a "prevention" stage of a COA, positive peace would play a major role since it is an "optimistic" approach that promotes "peace by peaceful means" (Grewal, 2013, p.4).

Therefore, education would seemingly be the first long-term strategy to counter radicalization. Education would support counter-radicalization efforts in three main ways. Firstly, by preventing structural issues through curriculum reform that could possibly lead to societal changes. Secondly, by undermining the allure of extremism as a means to cope with difficulties by providing individuals with greater knowledge and means of reconciling issues. Thirdly, by supporting individuals to personally progress, engage in self-improvement, and understand healthy coping mechanisms for personal trauma. At this stage, it would be beneficial to view radicalization as a nonlinear process. This would enable one to view all possible risk factors and consider them when reforming educational systems.

Educational curricula (including the ways in which information is presented and how individuals are treated) should be tailored to prevent isolation of individuals in academic settings (and thereby also social settings). This includes focusing on the elimination of the "us" versus "them" dichotomies that may be present in the educational materials. This would help to prevent the aforementioned risk factors relating to isolation or the desire to feel a sense of belonging within a group. It could also help to prevent the development of any resentment by a certain group. The instructional materials within the academic arena should be reviewed and modified where necessary to ascertain that diversity is embraced. Further, educators should be made aware of the domestic and international risks of allowing their students to feel like outcasts.

Along these lines, another prevention mechanism would be the establishment of integrative, collaborative centers for security professionals to consult with educators. This would be conducive to an open, straightforward discussion of what information or support educational professionals may need and what data security personnel may require from the educators. A respectful, balanced center could help to fill the lacuna in societies around the globe with regard to academic-practitioner engagement and relationships.

## Management

Although prevention strategies may be preferred, it is not guaranteed that individuals will not fall victim to the radicalization process. Thus, the management of the actions of those who have already undergone the process will always be a necessity. Unlike the prevention stage, the management stage may benefit from the adoption of a linear outlook on radicalization. Analyzing radicalization as a linear process can help officials to understand, based on where an individual falls within the steps of the process, how best to mitigate or counter the issues.

Furthermore, if a nation aims to counter radicalization, then all terms, concepts, and policy objectives must be effectively explained. As it stands, reports show that "policies swing almost erratically," due to the "lack of a clearly defined path to radicalization" (Vidino, 2010, p.9). Government personnel must make it a priority to clarify their ultimate goals, immediate objectives, and strategic pathways to success. Counter-radicalization efforts cannot be handled in a haphazard manner; rather, officials must devote considerable time to the determination of a rational, methodical solution.

It was Galtung (1964) who explicated that negative peace refers to the "absence of violence [or] absence of war;" this is particularly applicable to this second stage of management (p.2). In order for management measures to be successful, security officials must first ensure the cessation of any major physical violence that is active within the city, state, or nation in question. Whereas prevention may align with positive peace measures, management must focus on negative peace processes to ascertain that officials can deter direct violence stemming from radicalization.

The management process, however, must be tailored to the context or culture in which it is applied. Although this paper was written from the perspective of an academic in a Western culture, it is herein maintained that there should be no westernization of management strategies in other cultures. Westernization should not be confused with globalization or modernization; hence, avoiding the pitfalls associated with forcing the adoption of a disparate culture will allow for more functional and rewarding management approaches.

Management would include the day-to-day activities of security and intelligence professionals. By monitoring common avenues used for radicalization (i.e. via the Internet), professionals can ensure that any imminent threats to society (particularly direct, physical violence) may be thwarted. The maintenance of societal peace against physical violence would allow the positive peace measures time to flourish.

## Rehabilitation

Although the illegal, immoral, and, at times, inhumane actions of radicalized individuals may seem to simply necessitate imprisonment, there must be opportunities for rehabilitation. Radicalization is known to take place within prison environments; therefore, even in cases of individuals with life sentences, rehabilitation can allow individuals to understand the irrationality of their actions whilst ensuring that they no longer seek to spread their harmful ideology. In these situations, the experts would most likely be psychologists and psychiatrists who could offer support in the rehabilitation processes.

Although there may be many strategies to promote rehabilitation amongst the population of those who have undergone radicalization, restorative justice is an approach that would be especially advantageous. Restorative justice focuses on bringing both victims and perpetrators together, voluntarily, "to identify, understand and possibly transform a conflict and repair the harm that originated by such crime or conflict" (Radicalisation Awareness Network [RAN], 2020, p.2). These practices are aimed at reinstating justice by "focusing the sense of responsibility towards another human being (previously considered as a target, an enemy or as a monster), not towards the law or the state" (RAN, 2020, p.4). Typical restorative justice methods include "victim-offender mediation, discussion circles, and conferencing" (RAN, 2020, p.2). These practices place a strong emphasis on ensuring voluntary opportunities for those radicalized and the victims of their extremism to have an open dialogue.

Research has also shown that restorative justice can prevent criminals from reoffending (RAN, 2020, p.4). Therefore, the adoption of such an approach would also be considered as a positive peace approach to counter radicalization. The incarceration of those who have been radicalized and been involved in violent extremism is only one aspect of the solution to the problem of radicalization. The rehabilitation of individuals would be more substantive in helping to improve the overall wellbeing of society. In fact, restorative justice approaches could help to realize a society wherein individuals can believe that their government and criminal justice system will support them to accept responsibility for crimes, make amends for past actions, peacefully reintegrate into society, and recognize the unwarranted nature of extremism.

## Multidisciplinary Cooperation

To enhance the COA, multidisciplinary approaches must be interwoven throughout the prevention, management, and rehabilitation stages. Multidisciplinary cooperation would offer invaluable insight into the most advantageous practices and overall strategies for counter-radicalization. The integration of professionals from many fields can ascertain that efforts are based on rational, systematically analyzed assessments. To tackle the issue of radicalization, there must be input from experts outside the intelligence or security arenas, such as social scientists, natural scientists, humanities, etc.

Even in instances wherein the topic may not be typically relevant in one's own discipline, the problem-solving skills and methodologies of different subjects could possibly be applied effectively. For example, the inclusion of experts in linguistics could enable the development of strong academic materials to promote positive peace throughout educational institutions; thereby, reducing the risk of future radicalization. Similarly, experts in theological studies could provide vital data about certain ideological extremism, whilst sociologists would undoubtedly contribute considerable knowledge on intricate societal patterns and social behaviors. Therefore, the multidisciplinary interconnectedness would allow for the adoption of a holistic view of radicalization. This could possibly lead to innovative and unique methods of predicting, preventing, mitigating, and rehabilitating those involved in radicalization.

## CONCLUSION

In its entirety, the topic of radicalization is that which is inundated with varying perspectives and strategies. Discourse on radicalization is divided into those who view the process as linear and those who hold the belief that it is nonlinear. Although literature seems to posit the notion that the two views are always contradictory, it has been herein suggested that they can be complementary when applied to various stages of a three-step counter-radicalization COA that is underpinned by multidisciplinary cooperation.

According to the existing literature on this topic, there are many push, pull, and personal risk factors that most commonly lead to radicalization. Push factors are typically structural in nature and relate to issues of social inequalities, poverty, state repression, and other similar problems. These factors are notably common in cases of those who have been radicalized, since their environments essentially "push" or lead them on a pathway wherein extremism is viewed as a logical or rational choice. On the other hand, pull factors relate to those that may entice or lure individuals toward extremism. The factors, such as ideology and the desire to be a part of a larger community or group of people, can be exacerbated by the aforementioned push factors. Similarly, personal factors, which include psychological disorders, personality traits, and life trauma, can be noted as playing a major role in which individuals may be more susceptible to radicalization especially in relation to push and pull factors.

The negative structural factors or push factors leading to radicalization may be minimized through a COA consisting of prevention, management, and rehabilitation strategies. Preventative measures based on a nonlinear view of radicalization would include educational reform and the establishment of integrated security centers to engage academics and practitioners about best practices. Although there are certainly more possible prevention mechanisms, these two would provide a solid foundation for the progressive development of such practices throughout society.

Moving forward, management strategies would include the daily activities of security and intelligence officials to remove direct, physical violence. These activities would ensure that there is a non-violent (physically) environment wherein the positive peace measures can prosper. A quality management strategy requires well-defined terms and objectives. Hence, individual governments or even all members of the international community, collectively, should clearly elucidate long-term goals, definitions of radicalization and other important terms, and short-term objectives.

Although there should be a general consensus about the meanings of concepts, there need not be one manner in which counter-radicalization efforts are carried out. For instance, management plans must be culturally appropriate and suited to the needs of a city, state, or even nation's population. Thus, the strategies need not be westernized to be appropriate. Rather, the development of any strategy should be focused on upholding the law, moral, and ethical standards, and improving national security.

Lastly, the rehabilitation stage of the COA would include promoting restorative justice. This would allow those radicalized to openly discuss their opinions and beliefs and also speak with their victims in safe environments for all parties. A restorative justice approach would be a positive peace process that could help individuals to understand that there are mechanisms in place to aid in the recovery process from radicalization. This would also aid in the prevention of those radicalized further indoctrinating others to their extremist ideology consequent to being incarcerated.

Finally, multidisciplinary integration and cooperation should be woven throughout the entire COA. By embracing professional perspectives from a range of fields, one would be able to assess the topic of radicalization without being confined to the limits of one's own discipline. Overall, this could aid in the development of a holistic pathway to preventing and managing radicalization within society.

## REFERENCES

Alonso, R., Bjorgo, T., Porta, D. D., Coolsaet, R., Khosrokhavar, F., Lohlker, R., Ranstorp, M., Reinares, F., Schmid, A. P., Silke, A., Taarnby, M., & De Vries, G. (2008, May 15). *Radicalisation processes leading to acts of terrorism.* European Commission Expert Group on Radicalisation. https://www.clingendael.org/sites/default/files/pdfs/20080500_cscp_report_vries.pdf

Borum, R. (2011). Radicalization into violent extremism I: A review of social science theories. *Journal of Strategic Security, 4*(4), 7–36. doi:10.5038/1944-0472.4.4.1

Galtung, J. (1964). An editorial. *Journal of Peace Research, 1*(1), 1–4. https://www.jstor.org/stable/422802. doi:10.1177/002234336400100101

Galtung, J. (1969). Violence, peace, and peace research. *Journal of Peace Research, 6*(3), 167–191. https://www.jstor.org/stable/422690. doi:10.1177/002234336900600301

Grewal, B. S. (2003, August 30). *Johan Galtung: Positive and negative peace.* Auckland University of Technology. http://www.activeforpeace.org/no/fred/Positive_Negative_Peace.pdf

Hassan, M. (2012). Understanding drivers of violent extremism: The case of al-Shabab and Somali youth. *CTC Sentinel, 5*(8), 1-24. https://ctc.usma.edu/wp-content/uploads/2012/08/CTCSentinel-Vol5Iss84.pdf

Lynch, L. E., Mason, K. V., & Rodriguez, N. (2015). Radicalization and violent extremism: Lessons learned from Canada, the U.K. and the U.S. *National Institute of Justice.* Retrieved October 21, 2020, from https://www.ncjrs.gov/pdffiles1/nij/249947.pdf

McCauley, C., & Moskalenko, S. (2008). Mechanisms of political radicalization: Pathways toward terrorism. *Terrorism and Political Violence, 20*(3), 415–433. doi:10.1080/09546550802073367

Moghaddam, F. M. (2005). The staircase to terrorism. A psychological exploration. *The American Psychologist, 60*(2), 161–169. doi:10.1037/0003-066X.60.2.161 PMID:15740448

Porta, D. D., & LaFree, G. (2011). Guest editorial: Processes of radicalization and de-radicalization. *International Journal of Conflict and Violence, 6*(1), 4–10. doi:10.4119/ijcv-2926

Radicalisation Awareness Network. (2020, January 14). *The role of restorative justice in preventing and responding to violent extremism.* https://ec.europa.eu/home-affairs/sites/homeaffairs/files/what-we-do/networks/radicalisation_awareness_network/ran-papers/docs/ran_rvt-exit_role_of_restorative_justice_dublin_3-4_122019_en.pdf

Schmid, A. P. (2013). Radicalisation, de-radicalisation, counter-radicalisation: A conceptual discussion and literature review. *International Centre for Counter-Terrorism – The Hague.* Retrieved October 19, 2020, from https://www.icct.nl/download/file/ICCT-Schmid-Radicalisation-De-Radicalisation-Counter-Radicalisation-March-2013.pdf

Security Service MI5. (2008). *Behavioural science unit operational briefing note: Understanding radicalisation and violent extremism in the UK.* http://image.guardian.co.uk/sys-files/Guardian/documents/2008/08/20/mi5.pdf

Trip, S., Bora, C. H., Marian, M., Halmajan, A., & Drugas, M. L. (2019). Psychological mechanisms involved in radicalization and extremism. A Rational Emotive Behavioral Conceptualization. *Frontiers in Psychology, 10*, 1–8. doi:10.3389/fpsyg.2019.00437 PMID:30894828

Vergani, M., Iqbal, M., & Barton, G. (2018). The 3 Ps of radicalisation: Push, pull and personal. A systematic scoping review of the scientific evidence about radicalisation into violent extremism. *Studies in Conflict and Terrorism, 43*(10), 854–893. doi:10.1080/1057610X.2018.1505686

Vidino, L. (2010). Countering radicalization in America. Lessons from Europe. *United States Institute of Peace Special Report, 262,* 1-16. https://www.usip.org/sites/default/files/resources/SR262%20-%20Countering_Radicalization_in_America.pdf

## KEY TERMS AND DEFINITIONS

**Linear Process (in Radicalization):** The notion that there is a straightforward, step-by-step path to radicalization.

**Multidisciplinary:** The combination or involvement of multiple academic or professional disciplines in an effort to resolve or tackle one issue.

**Nonlinear Process (in Radicalization):** The notion that the path to radicalization is not always sequential or straightforward, but rather rests upon a multitude of complex factors.

**Personal Factor (in Radicalization):** The risk factors that stem from within an individual that make them more likely to be radicalized (i.e. psychological disorders, life trauma, and personality traits) in comparison to their peers.

**Pull Factor (in Radicalization):** A factor that is purposefully enticing to individuals and highlights aspects of extremist groups that may lead individuals to become involved in violent extremism.

**Push Factor (in Radicalization):** A risk factor that is structural in nature (i.e., unfair geopolitics and societal inequality) that causes unfavorable conditions for individuals, which then leads them to believe that violent extremism is a viable solution.

**Risk Factor (in Radicalization):** That which increases the likelihood of one being radicalized.

# Section 2

# Chapter 5
# Regionalism in South Asia From Pre to Post Pandemic

**Asanga Abeyagoonasekera**
*Parliament of Sri Lanka, Sri Lanka*

## ABSTRACT

*Overly complex interdependencies develop systemic risks and flow into our international system. A lesson from the pandemic is the importance of managing systemic risks due to globalization. The entire world is facing a trust recession due to the rise of populist politics and protectionist sentiments. We should regain trust and strengthen economic globalization and promote multilateral agenda. There are four factors identified for the widening trust deficit. If the trust is restored, there will be definite positive outcomes such as strong intra-regional trade, developed economy, and cross-border security. The pandemic exacerbated domestic nationalist viewpoints in many nations; taking this opportunity, pandemic nations like Sri Lanka had parliamentary elections and amended the constitution, shifting power to the president. The present ultra-nationalism and populist policies would further fuel and instill domestic malign mercantilism.*

## INTRODUCTION

The paper will examine Globalization and its Systemic Risks ignored due to political factors of ultra-nationalism and populism where leaders confined their interest to their national borders. Political trust with the polity was built on this toxic environment by many national leaders in South Asia with national security at the helm. The global risk of the Pandemic has pushed many global leaders in a dual policy prescription to focus inwards to manage the pandemic in their national boundaries and at the same

DOI: 10.4018/978-1-7998-7904-6.ch005

time, pushed towards a global agenda on strengthening multilateralism. Reactivation of SAARC which was dormant since 2014 and establishing a SAARC fund during the COVID19 pandemic in South Asia is seen as a positive sign towards reactivation of regionalism in the present challenging environment.

The core question of the paper is how will the political leadership evolve from a nationalist standpoint in pre-pandemic to a multilateral/regional focus during and post-pandemic? And how would they build political trust in this transition time from pre to post-pandemic? To stay on the trajectory of improving regionalism in one of the least integrated regions of the world, there are four factors discussed to strengthen regionalism in South Asia.

## GLOBALIZATION: COMPLEX INTERDEPENDENCIES & SYSTEMIC RISKS

Globalization has brought us many benefits, integrating communities, rapid transportation networks to urbanization to megacities. Robert Keohane and Joseph Nye call this the 'complex interdependencies' (Nye 2011) is what the world has experienced. Further, the scholarship published back in 1977 suggest conventional thinking have overemphasized states and has over aggregated power, this was the predominant failure to understand before the largest terror attack on the US soil 9/11, that the most powerful nation could be vulnerable to small bands of terrorists attributed to patterns of asymmetrical interdependence. While globalization was seen by many as a benefit to uplift human conditions from poverty and bring people closer to the technological advancements of the 4$^{th}$ industrial revolution (Schwab 2016), the patterns of asymmetries in globalization were developing along with the progress. The patterns of asymmetries triggered multiple threats from terrorism, financial crisis to the present-day pandemic. It is as if there was not much investment done by policymakers to understand these asymmetries and risk factors of globalization.

These overly complex interdependencies would develop systemic risks within the system.

With great benefit, there are risk factors that flow into our international system. While many national leaders confine their focus on national issues, they tend to ignore systemic risks generated from rapid globalization between countries. What triggered in the dawn of 2020 was a global systemic risk which most nations couldn't cope with due to the rapid spread of the Pandemic. Most leaders have been pushed to a multilateral platform by the Pandemic. Pandemics and the health risk from Globalization are areas not discussed broadly across nations and are somewhat absent or limited in the international relations agenda. What happens in Wuhan (WHO 2020) China ended up in so many countries so fast due to the '*Butterfly defect*' in globalization. The butterfly defect concept was introduced by Prof. Ian Goldin, referring to the work of American mathematician Edward Lorenz (Lorenz 1963) work in Chaos theory which found the 'Butterfly Effect'. Explaining how a hurricane formation is influenced by minor perturbations such as the flapping of the wings of a distant butterfly several weeks earlier. A small change in one place can lead to major differences in a remote area. In the same manner, negative unintended ripple effects of Coronavirus that triggered in Wuhan ended up affecting many nations including Iran, Italy, Spain, and the USA currently holding the highest infected cases.

Globalization creates systemic risks from micro distresses from the closely-knit systems and connections we have built. While immense health benefits we have felt from Globalization the responsible health officials did not identify the systemic risk from a Pandemic such as Coronavirus that could trigger one day. According to Goldin and Mariathasan (Goldin and Mariathasan, Butterfly Defect 2014) 'Globalization, population growth, and urbanization have facilitated the transmission of infectious diseases. The complexity of Global travel and global integration any patient zero is now but a few degrees of separation from formerly isolated communities', was clear from the present Pandemic we all are facing. According to Goldin, Systemic risks cannot be removed because it is endemic to globalization. It is a process to be managed, not a problem to be solved. Systemic risks from complex trade, finance, cyber, travel, and other networks grow in scale and interact as they pass through major hubs, they become more complex and unstable. Over complacency and trust in the existing national health care and multilateral health system World Health Organization(WHO) was a clear failure as explained by Prof. Ian Goldin "WHO has been starved of much-needed resources and authority, not least by the US and other rich countries" (Goldin, Contagion: Systemic Risks of Globalisation 2020). Systemic risks could only be managed from a multilateral platform where nations and institutions work together for a common cause. What world politics faced in the last several years was opposite to this phenomenon, a more nationalist agenda confining to national boundaries with a growing political trust deficit among nations.

## PUBLIC TRUST IN GOVERNMENT

The prevalence of low-level political trust among nations will narrow the space for multilateralism to flourish. Trust among nations to enter and invest into a multilateral platform is an essential prerequisite. National leaders working on their nationalist agenda's confined to the boundaries, looking inward will not facilitate the process of cross border integration.

During a crisis such as a pandemic, how will trust play a role? How will domestic political trust among government and public translate to support regionalism during the Pandemic? While trust in political establishments has eroded during pre-pandemic, a crisis usually questions public trust with the government. When assessing crisis and trust, during the 9/11 terrorist bombing trust between the public and government establishment was strong. Even after the 2004 Asian Tsunami which killed almost 35,000 in Sri Lanka, the humanitarian operations carried out by the government were trusted by the civil society. In a different crisis in 2008, the financial crisis US government was at the lowest when it came to public trust. In fighting the pandemic public tend to reach out to the government for information and security and usually trust with the Government should be high. This situation differs from nation to nation like the USA under President Trump and Brazilian leaders lost popularity and trust, leaders in nations such as Sri Lanka managed to win public trust due to successfully managing the crisis in the initial wave of the Pandemic but lost trust in the present environment. According to Goldin and Muggah 'Countries with functional democracies such as New Zealand did not bend the curve, they crushed it. Meanwhile, nations with populist leaders experienced soaring rates of infection and death' (Goldin and Muggah, Terra Incognita 2020).

However, most leaders tend to look inward and not reach out for regional-level solutions in the pandemic environment. This impacts the post-pandemic globalization agenda and strengthening regionalism especially in regions such as South Asia. Deglobalization sentiments afloat have widened the public trust deficit, further exacerbates when multilateral agencies such as WHO are questioned for its conduct, and funds withdrawn by the USA by President Trump administration. This geopolitical tense atmosphere will have a direct impact on globalization. Public trust in political establishments around the world perhaps is at its lowest due to several phenomena. According to a Pew Research finding, trust in the US government has plunged from 75 percent of the population in the 1960s to a historic low of 17 percent today (PEW Research Center 2019). While democracies in Europe have faced declining trust since the 2008 financial crisis (Archer, Kristjan, and Ron-Levey 2020).

## POLITICAL TRUST AND MULTILATERALISM IN SOUTH ASIA

South Asia is one of the least integrated regions with fragile democracies with traits of semi authoritarianism lagging civil political space and violent terrorism and border disputes are common in the region. The deep polarization in political partisan lines in almost every South Asian country has a direct effect on public trust. Apart from this, you would see a dangerous fault line in partisan politics in South Asia which is ethnoreligious politics and ultra-nationalism. The global phenomenon of populist politics has probably been manifested in South Asia.

In Sri Lanka, the ultra-nationalist political landscape, protecting sovereignty and ensuring national security has won the majority voter base in the last Presidential election. The 'Hindutva' agenda of Prime Minister Modi in India is another example from the region of growing populist ultra-nationalist sentiments in the region. These leaders build political trust with the public by securing their national values ensuring national security as the primary objectivity. This trend is evident not only in South Asia but also in the global arena in many corners of the world.

The ultra-nationalist political forces will be a new challenge for economic globalization in South Asia which is least integrated as a region with less intra-regional trade. Growing ultra-nationalist and populist policies in South Asian countries will create a bottleneck for intra-regional trade and further could worsen during the post-pandemic with the global financial recession. According to Professor Razeen Sally, the present unstable environment of the Pandemic with contested geopolitics revolving around the competition will squeeze global trade and globalization. 'Domestic malign mercantilism' with more state intervention and restricted markets will see a different kind of capitalism coming out of this pandemic (Sally 2020). If South Asian leaders propel domestic malign mercantilism, this would further reduce the space for regional integration and economic globalization. The protectionist space would grow in each nation. Thus, the present ultra-nationalism and populist policies would further fuel and instill Domestic malign Mercantilism in South Asian nations reducing space for regionalism and promoting intra-regional trade.

## Regionalism and Intra-Regional Trade in South Asia

On 23rd May 2020 a phone conversation between President Gotabaya Rajapaksa of Sri Lanka and Indian Prime Minister Narendra Modi took place where Sri Lankan President sought from Government of India for a USD 1.1 billion special SWAP facility to top up USD 400 million under the South Asian Association of Regional Cooperation(SAARC) Facility to deal with foreign exchange issue of the country. Indian Premier assured, "We are ready to help under terms that are favorable to Sri Lanka.". (Srinivasan 2020) A month ago, SAARC the dormant regional institution from 2014 was recommenced to fight the ongoing Pandemic. India pledged US$10 million and Sri Lanka the second-highest US$5million for regional health hazard, the largest humanitarian health crisis the region has faced in decades. Total contributions towards the fund amount to US$21.6m. Apart from SAARC, 'India participated in a virtual G20 leaders summit, a foreign ministerial meeting of the BRICS(Brazil, Russia, India, China, and South Africa) grouping and with seven Indo-Pacific partners including Japan, United States, and Australia. Financial assistance was provided to South Asian countries by various multilateral institutions and bilateral donors, including the World Bank, the US, China, Japan, and the United Kingdom.

India provided crisis assistance to regional countries, including supplies of medical equipment to Bangladesh, food to Afghanistan, and sent a team of 15 doctors to Kuwait, a team of 14 medical experts to the Maldives. India is the largest provider of generic drugs globally and drawing on its prominent growing pharmaceutical industry to provide supplies including the anti-malarial drug hydroxychloroquine and paracetamol, to 85 countries' (Solanki 2020). However, the Indian vaccine diplomacy at the global level changed with the domestic constraints from the second wave of the Pandemic infecting millions of Indians. India's absence in vaccine diplomacy is filled by China in countries like Sri Lanka.

Pandemic has got leaders to interact more and speak to each other discovering bilateral and regional collaborative approaches to overcome the prevailing hazard which is usually not the case during the pre-pandemic era as regionalism was not the most favorable topic due to cross border security tension. It was the security dynamics in 2019 which changed the course of the Indian and Sri Lankan elections. In India, it was the Balakot attack and in Sri Lanka, the Easter Sunday Bombing that made national security the determinant factor for election. Regionalism was swept under the carpet and the nationalistic drive was seen in the election year 2019 in both India and Sri Lanka.

The regional dynamics have been altered with the Pandemic just like in Europe. According to Judy Dempsey, Senior fellow at Carnegie Europe 'Whenever there is a crisis, European Union leaders have the habit of saying that the bloc will emerge stronger. They have been repeatedly disproved of this slogan, which has lost all meaning (Dempsey 2020).' The importance of Multilateralism is discussed from Europe to South Asia where leaders have dismantled multilateral organizations such as SAARC in the past is now finding ways of discussing activating health funds and strengthening regional cooperation. The ultra-nationalist narrative is in a way weakened by the Pandemic showing a direction and an opportunity towards regional cooperation and promoting multilateral efforts as a much mutually beneficial way forward especially in times of a humanitarian crisis.

The post-pandemic environment could be turned into an opportunity for an increase in intra-regional trade and the region could work towards building trust among the nations for trade. In South Asia, the virtuous circle between trust and trade has been broken by a history of mutual distrust rooted in historical conflict and size asymmetries across economies which prevent South Asian countries from reaping the full economic benefits of geographical proximity and complementary resources endowments. Trust deficit and negative stereotypes are perpetuated by a lack of people-to-people interaction (Sanjay and Mathur 2018). The leader-to-leader frequent interaction such as between India-Sri Lanka is in a positive trajectory with the present regime of President Gotabaya Rajapaksa. This gives the opportunity to explore many avenues in economic and security cooperation and especially work towards a regional agenda.

According to a recent Brookings report 'Despite geographical proximity and the existence of bilateral and multilateral free trade agreements (FTAs), South Asia is one of the least economically integrated regions in the world. Owing to protectionist policies, high logistics cost, lack of political will, and a broader trust deficit, intra-regional trade in South Asia remain well below its potential at 5% of the region's global trade.' (Riya and Sareen, India's limited trade connectivity in South Asia 2020). The present trade environment makes this region one of the least integrated regions in the world. When compared to other regions such as East Asia, South Asian intraregional trade is less than 6% (World Bank 2019). The region lacks connectivity in goods, people, services, knowledge, and foreign investment(FDI) to ensure economic growth. The trust deficit among the regional nations is high due to protectionist policies driven by nationalist political sentiments. Trade liberalization initiatives have been long delayed. Bay of Bengal Initiative for Multi-Sectoral Technical and Economic Cooperation (BIMSTEC) has been under negotiation for more than 15 years, SAFTA and South Asian Economic Union no longer feature in New Delhi's regional focus.

Indo-Lanka FTA dates back two decades with negotiations on the Comprehensive Economic Partnership Agreement (CEPA) is delayed due to ultra-nationalist political forces who have voiced against in Sri Lanka and protectionist measures in place. The nationalist forces usually tend to be part of the power politics supporting and forming the government coalition to gain a majority for the Government in power. The ultra-nationalist forces are a key obstacle that has stalled multilateral trade liberalization in the region and broken trust in intraregional trade. To pursue higher intraregional trade and trust among nations there should be clear political leadership to keep away domestic protectionist measures and promote trade interdependence.

India's trade with the regional countries takes a larger percentage in South Asia with an increasing trade deficit in favor of India. 'India's largest export market in the region is Bangladesh, followed by Sri Lanka and Nepal, whereas the largest imports by value come from Myanmar, Sri Lanka, and Bangladesh. All countries in the neighborhood have a trade deficit with India, the highest being Bangladesh with a deficit of US$7.6 billion, followed by Nepal at US$6.8 billion (2018). The trade deficit has been increasing (Figure 1). (Riya and Sareen, Brookings 2020)[1]

The increasing trade deficit in favor of India with a larger percentage of Indian exports to the regional countries tends to be a discussion point among political groups critical of trade liberalization in Sri Lanka. The CEPA between India and Sri Lanka is seen by the ultra-nationalist as an agreement in favor of India to further widen the trade deficit facilitating more Indian imports to flood the Sri Lankan market. This growing trust deficit is a key feature among India and its neighbors due to the political trust deficit. This deficit of trust in Sri Lanka with India tends to take a political dimension due to India's involvement in the countries domestic politics in the late 1980's to resolve the Tamilian grievances. Indo-Lanka political trust has eroded between New- Delhi and Colombo after the Sri Lankan government's recent strong China tilt in its foreign policy. The East Container Terminal which was agreed a few years ago to India was revisited by the government and politicized as a concern for protecting the sovereignty of the country while Chinese projects such as the Port City Project were awarded to China without any concern on sovereignty.

*Figure 1.*

*India's trade surplus with N8 has been increasing*

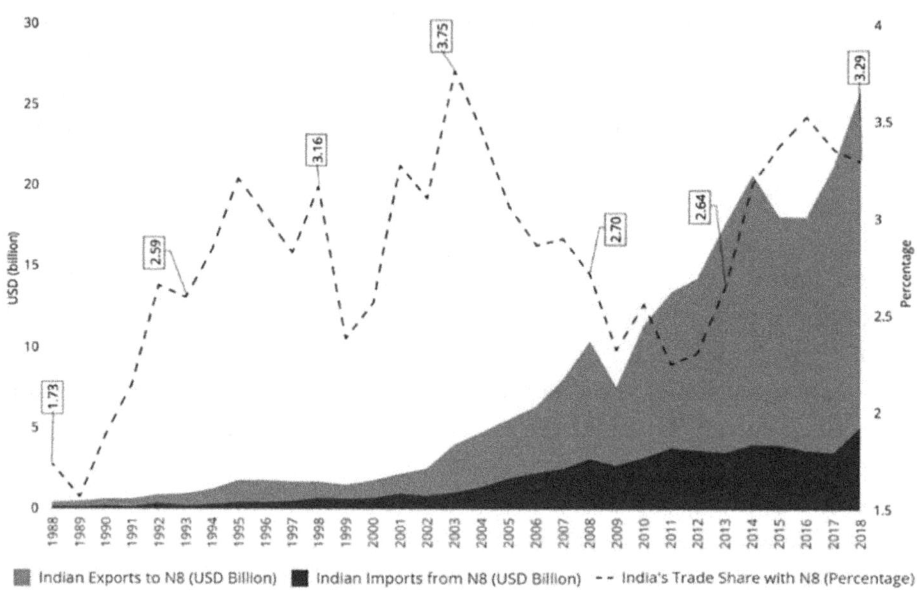


N8: Afghanistan, Bangladesh, Bhutan, Maldives, Myanmar, Nepal, Pakistan, and Sri Lanka
Source: WITS, World Bank

## Four Factors for the Trust Deficit in the Region

Why has trust eroded among South Asian nations? There are four important factors.

First, is the reaction to globalization from the South Asia nations. The global financial crisis in 2009 and its slow recovery has exacerbated this trend with governments blamed for failing to prevent the crisis and then compounding the difficulties in failing to engineer a swift recovery. More specifically the dislocations that have occurred in our interconnected global economy. Many people believe that it has not delivered fair outcomes and that there is a lack of accountability for leaders and those who have gained the most (Lipton 2018). Further adding to this, global leaders such as the US President Trump speaking of closing its borders to ultra nationalist-populist sentiments, questioning the multilateral global organizations has aggravated the trend. However, there is hope from President Biden's policies to reactivate the multilateral agenda. In the present context of the post-pandemic environment with multilateral institutions such as WHO struggling with limited resources and contested geopolitical environment between the USA and China, deglobalization will take precedence over globalization and multilateralism. The reaction from South Asian nations to globalization itself will be a significant factor in the post-pandemic.

Second, weak domestic state institutions in South Asia are a long-standing political and economic challenge. The weak institutions with the weak regulatory mechanism in place will be vulnerable to strengthen regionalism and intra-regional trade. With inconsistent government policies, time to time has affected to build strong institutions that support regionalism. Weak institutions are products of high-level corruption, loss-making, less transparency, and political interferences which have serious procedural fairness stemming to trust deficiency among the public. The government institutional level contribution for large infrastructure projects such as China's Port City Project was minimum due to interference and crippling of the bureaucratic level negations by the higher leadership. The weak institutions have a severe effect on the national economy and towards strengthening regional trade.

Third, the rise of populism and semi-autocratic models in South Asia is another obstacle to build trust among the neighboring countries. A scholar from the University of Amsterdam Roodjuin Matthis argues that populism is incompatible with the liberal pillar of contemporary democracies and tends to breed "the tyranny of the majority" (Chowdhury and Ziaus 2019). Majoritarian government with the ethnoreligious feature is visible in many south Asian nations. The rise of 'Hindutva' in India, Sinhalese Buddhist sentiments in Sri Lanka will only pull nations inwards, a more insular protectionist mode with ultra-nationalism at the helm in local politics. This trend will not promote regionalism nor promote intra-regional trade. The protectionist measures have created a space for extra-regional nations to strengthen bilateral trade. The populist sentiments have only eroded and slowed the growth potential of South Asia. In many South Asian nations, populist and ultra-nationalist sentiments are supported by alliances and coalitions supporting governments to create and establish political power in the legislature by the ethnoreligious majoritarian sentiments. This becomes a hindrance to building trust outside the borders with the neighboring nations to promote economic trade. It appears that there is a relationship between the rise of the aforesaid sentiments and a reduction of building trust outside the borders with neighboring nations to promote economic trade.

Fourth, corruption and transparency are factors hindering regionalism in South Asia. Widespread corruption undermines efficiency and effectiveness in the overall government, and it implies an absence of moral principles. With weak institutions, 'it thrives on an institutionalized lack of accountability and corruption invokes uncertainty and inequality both at the macro-level (policies that are agreed upon by government) and at the micro-level (the implementation of these policies in daily life). As such, corruption is the epitome of bad-quality government (Meer 2017). Further identifying corruption is the major explanation of cross-national differences in the political trust where trust rates are substantially lower in countries where corruption is high. Most South Asia nations including Sri Lanka (93rd place) fall behind at a weak place in the Global Corruption Perception Index (Corruption Perception Index 2019) year on year. Trust between government and civil society is widened due to high-level corruption. In Sri Lanka, the previous Sirisena-Wickramasinghe Government had a substantial impact after the central bank bond scam (Reuters 2019), where the trust between Government and civil society eroded to the lowest ebb. The present government has also failed to address the concern on high-level corruption adequately and punish the corrupt such as the former governor of the central bank residing in Singapore. The public has lost trust in the government due to inefficiency in fighting high-level corruption. This widespread corruption has a direct impact on economic growth and on developing regional trade agenda. Political distrust among the public would spill over to regional level trade. The fairness of the process affects the local level and regional level, as transparency of the processes in place is vital for intra-regional trade. The more transparent and less corrupt a regime is more it protects democratic values in the society, this value which will enhance the trust among government and civil society, and regional nations.

## CONCLUSION: FUTURE RESEARCH DIRECTIONS

South Asia will face a daunting challenge in the post-pandemic period. First with its already toxic ultra-nationalist and populist political environment in many countries 'deglobalization' will be further embraced. Political leadership evolving from a nationalist standpoint in pre-pandemic to a global/multilateral focus during and post-pandemic is an essential focus area to be invested. While pandemics are a threat to the entire human race, there is an opportunity we could discover by working towards a common global agenda, strengthening global and regional integration. India as a regional power and its ability in the absence of strong regional cooperation to undertake a meaningful regional leadership role is essential. To increase and strengthen its collaboration with South Asian neighbors and extend to key Indo-Pacific partners will have an important impact in overcoming the humanitarian crisis, improving its trade and economic challenges caused by COVID-19 across South Asia. It was an unblemished factor in South Asia and many regions the growing nationalist sentiments in politics in the pre-pandemic era. In the present transition time from Pandemic to post Pandemic, it's time to discover where the least investments and focus was made specially in managing systemic risks due to Globalization. If well managed, we could evade or minimize the next global catastrophe.

We are in a trust recession due to the rise of populist politics and protectionist sentiments. Trust can be rebuilt, and we should invest to regain trust and strengthen economic globalization and promote multilateral agenda amidst 'malign mercantilism' and growing ultra-nationalism in the post-pandemic world. Four factors in South Asia widen the trust deficit. Respective governments in South Asia must invest in these factors to build trust in the domestic arena and the regional arena. With a level of trust among the closely knit south Asian geography, there will be definite positive outcomes to strengthen intra-regional trade, develop economic activity and cross border security.

## REFERENCES

Archer, K., & Ron-Levey, I. (2020). *Trust in Government Lacking on COVID-19's Frontlines.* Accessed 01 2021. https://news.gallup.com/opinion/gallup/296594/trust-government-lacking-frontlines-covid.aspx

Chowdhury & Ziaus. (2019). *Populism and how it impacts democracy.* Accessed 01 2021. https://www.thedailystar.net/opinion/perspective/news/populism-and-how-it-impacts-democracy-1714120

Dempsey, J. (2020). *Carnegie Europe.* Accessed 01 2021. https://carnegieeurope.eu/strategiceurope/81352

Goldin & Mariathasan. (2014). *Butterfly Defect.* Princeton Press.

Goldin, I. (2020). *Contagion: Systemic Risks of Globalisation.* Accessed 01 2021. https://www.oxfordmartin.ox.ac.uk/blog/contagion-the-systemic-risks-of-globalisation/

Goldin, I., & Muggah, R. (2020). *Terra Incognita.* Penguin.

Index, C. P. (2019). Accessed 01 2021. https://www.transparency.org/en/cpi#

Lipton, D. (2018). *IMF.* Accessed 01 2021. https://www.imf.org/en/News/Articles/2018/04/30/sp042618-trust-and-the-future-of-multilateralism

Lorenz, E. (1963). Deterministic Nonperiodic Flow. *Journal of the Atmospheric Sciences, 20*(2), 130–141. doi:10.1175/1520-0469(1963)020<0130:DNF>2.0.CO;2

Meer, T. W. G. van der. (2017). *Political Trust and the "Crisis of Democracy".* Accessed 01 2021. https://oxfordre.com/politics/view/10.1093/acrefore/9780190228637.001.0001/acrefore-9780190228637-e-77

Nye, J., & Keohane, R. (2011). *Power & Interdependence.* Pearson.

Pew Research Center. (2019). *Public Trust in Government: 1958-2019.* Accessed 01 2021. https://www.people-press.org/2019/04/11/public-trust-in-government-1958-2019/

Reuters. (2019). *Sri Lankan Central Bank Bond Scam.* Accessed 01 2021. https://www.reuters.com/article/us-sri-lanka-bond-arrests/sri-lanka-arrests-ex-central-bank-deputy-governor-four-other-over-alleged-bond-scam-idUSKCN1R62D8

Riya, S., & Sareen, N. (2020). *Brookings.* Accessed 01 2021. https://www.brookings.edu/research/indias-limited-trade-connectivity-with-south-asia/

Riya, S., & Sareen, N. (2020). *India's limited trade connectivity in South Asia.* Accessed 01 2021. https://www.brookings.edu/research/indias-limited-trade-connectivity-with-south-asia/

Sally, R. (2020). *LKYSPP.* Accessed 01 2021. https://lkyspp.nus.edu.sg/news-events/events/details/the-future-of-asian-trade-and-globalisation-after-covid-19

Sanjay, K., & Mathur, P. (2018). *A glass half full: The promise of regional trade in South Asia.* World Bank Publication.

Schwab, K. (2016). *WEF.* Accessed 2021 01. https://www.weforum.org/about/the-fourth-industrial-revolution-by-klaus-schwab

Solanki, V. (2020). *IISS.* Accessed 01 2021. https://www.iiss.org/blogs/analysis/2020/04/sasia-why-indias-response-to-covid-19-matters-to-us-all

Srinivasan, M. (2020). Accessed 01 2021. https://www.thehindu.com/news/international/gotabaya-seeks-additional-11-billion-swap-facility-from-modi/article31662546.ece

WHO. (2020). *Pneumonia of unknown cause – China.* 01 05. Accessed 03 15, 2021. https://www.who.int/csr/don/05-january-2020-pneumonia-of-unkown-cause-china/en/

World Bank. (2019). *World Bank's World Integrated Trade Solution (WITS)*. World Bank.

## ENDNOTE

1 Sinha, Riya, and Niara Sareen. 2020. *India's limited trade connectivity in South Asia*. (26 May. Accessed 05 2020.) https://www.brookings.edu/research/indias-limited-trade-connectivity-with-south-asia/.

# Chapter 6
# COVID-19 Vaccine Nationalism and Politicization:
## Global Competition for Vaccine Amidst Pandemic Break-Out and Risk to Health Security

**Savithri Sellapperumage**
*University of Colombo, Sri Lanka*

## ABSTRACT

*The COVID-19 pandemic has swept the world uprooting people from their livelihoods and toppling the economy of the world. Thus, to everyone's interest, producing a vaccine became the priority to gain at least half the normalcy in day-to-day activities of the world. With over a year passing, several states have come to the front in producing vaccines, having completed tedious processes of research and clinical trials. The next mammoth task at hand is distribution and administration in countries. However, with only a few countries gaining the advantage of production, they are seen to exercise power politics in purchasing and distribution of the vaccine. Developing countries have succumbed to a difficult predicament amidst balancing the great powers and the financial inability to obtain the vaccination. Therefore, the chapter explores the political dimension to vaccine distribution and the plight of developing nations in obtaining the vaccine. Further, the chapter observes the global initiatives taken to address the issue and the impact of distribution on health security.*

DOI: 10.4018/978-1-7998-7904-6.ch006

## INTRODUCTION

The COVID-19 pandemic, since its first known case back in 2019, has given birth to a global humanitarian crisis, affecting global health, economy, politics, and social wellbeing. Amongst the sectors impacted, world health experienced the heaviest blow in 2020. As of 29th of January 2021, the global cases have increased beyond 100 million and it has caused over 2 million deaths. Irrespective of size and power, nation-states around the world were anticipating the introduction of a vaccine to return to normalcy and save countries' economies.

Since several vaccines have been released since the end of 2020, wealthy countries such as the USA, Canada, UK, and China have become pioneers of production as well as the biggest buyers of the vaccine. Many of these countries are blamed for hoarding the vaccines and follow protectionism at the same time leaving a vacuum for world leadership (Sytas, 2021). Thus a regional approach to fulfilling vaccine needs must be observed.

It is proven now more than ever that health security must be achieved by collective action across countries, hierarchies of societies as well as individual action within countries as the virus at hand do not distinguish between state boundaries, rich or the poor.

Even though vaccines have been developed, access to vaccines for 8 billion people around the world would take months or even years. Amidst distribution efforts, the administration of the vaccine will have to overcome financial challenges, health policies of countries, refusal of people to obtain the vaccine. As much as local preparedness is addressed by each country, the success rate of national-level action will be futile as only a handful of countries are capable of producing, purchasing as well as effective dissemination. Therefore, global level action must be taken in vaccine administration.

Therefore, the chapter expects to understand the issue of vaccine nationalism, regional context to the provision of vaccines, the plight of developing and least developing countries, and the risks to the health security of developing countries such as Sri Lanka.

## BACKGROUND

Availability of Vaccines can be identified as the end result of the culminating process of R&D, distribution, governing tools with regards to acquiring the vaccine, financial capacity in purchasing the vaccine, etc. To understand how a vaccine works; upon injection, "it activates the immune system and induces both innate and adaptive immune responses thus leading to the production of antibodies, in the case of humoral response, or to the generation of memory cells that will recognize the same antigen, if there is a later exposure. Periodic repeat injections can improve the efficacy and effectiveness of inoculations" (Hussein, Chams, Chams, Sayegh, Badran, Raad, Gerges-geagea, Leone & Jurjus (2015). Vaccines programs have been in execution as early as 1960 led by World Health Organization. For instance, "Small Pox Eradication Program commenced in 1960 and it was wiped out from the world by 1967… and the Polio Eradication Initiative in Africa from 1993 to 2002, the number of endemic countries fell from 34 to just two" (The immunization program that saved millions of lives, 2014). Therefore, it is evident that for a current pandemic situation, eradication or controlling of the disease might take up years.

## What Are the Vaccinations Available?

After a year of testing and trial, two vaccinations were made ready early in 2020 namely; the Pfizer-BioNTech COVID-19 vaccine and Moderna's COVID-19 vaccine (Centre for Disease Control and Prevention, 2021). As of December 2020, another large-scale (Phase 3) clinical trials were in progress or being planned for three COVID-19 vaccines in the United States; AstraZeneca's COVID-19 vaccine, Janssen's COVID-19 vaccine, and Novavax's COVID-19 vaccine (Centre for Disease Control and Prevention, 2021). However, AstraZeneca's COVID-19 vaccine is also being utilized as of January 2021 (Gallagher, 2021). Several other vaccines have also come onto the stage and their effectiveness is as follows.

*Table 1.*

| | |
|---|---|
| Pfizer-BioNTech vaccine | 95% effective |
| Moderna's vaccine | 94.5% effective |
| Oxford University AstraZeneca's vaccine | 90% effective |
| Janssen's vaccine | 66% effective (Still in a trial) |
| Russian Sputnik V vaccine | 92% effective |
| Novavax's vaccine | 89% effective (Still in phase 3 clinical trial) |

Source: Author Derived from; Gallagher, 2021 and Bland & Davis, 2021.

However, as researchers delve into the evolution of the virus, "scientists have identified at least eight strains of coronavirus doing the rounds globally" (Economic Times, 2020). Therefore, the ability of the vaccines to answer to the many strains of the virus is worrisome and questionable.

## Global Health Security

The Human Development Report of 1994, presents "New Dimensions of Human Security" with seven components pertaining to Human Security; Economic Security, Food Security, Health Security, Environmental Security, Personal Security, Community Security, and Political Security. Thus global health security is identified as a requirement to ensure human security across the globe.

*Global Health Security can be defined as the activities required, both proactive and reactive, to minimize the danger and impact of acute public health events that endanger people's health across geographical regions and international boundaries. (World Health Organization, n.d)*

The current threat to health security is posed through the pandemic break-out of Covid-19 and the international community, governments are faced with the challenge of protecting people and citizens. Covid-19 tools production and distribution including test kits and vaccine production are executed at a rapid pace that the accessibility and availability of the vaccine must be analyzed to measure the impact on health security across the world.

## Theories and Concepts

### Nationalism

Nationalism can be defined in several ways and it rarely that two definitions outline the same meaning. However, at a gist, it can be defined

Hayes explains that "in simplest terms, nationalism may be defined as a fusion of patriotism with the consciousness of nationality." (Kecmanovic, 1996) Nationalism is defined in a similar way by Snyder in his book The Dynamics of Nationalism. Readings in Its Meaning and Development of 1964 mentions that "Nationalism is a condition of mind, feeling, or sentiment of a group of people living in a well-defined geographical area, speaking a common language, professing a literature in which the aspirations of the nation have been expressed, being attached to the common traditions, and, in some cases, having a common origin." Thus Nationalism transcending beyond sentiments of belonging to a nation or a community develops into a desire of inculcating and reserving strength in comparison to other nations/communities and becoming one of the strongest.

Hertz further develops the concept through presenting four elements of national aspirations: 1) the striving for national unity, 2) the striving for national freedom, 3) the striving for separateness, distinctiveness, individuality, originality, or peculiarity, and 4) the striving for distinction among nations (Hertz, 1944). Striving for distinction among nations shall lead to striving for a sense of domination.

In vaccine administration, the nations are showing a tendency in striving for domination through exercising nationalism. Accordingly, Vaccine Nationalism is where "countries prioritize their own vaccine needs and is forecast to handicap, not just the global health recovery but the economic one, too" Understanding in terms of Hertz's four elements of nationalism, it perhaps satisfies all four where ultimately it jewels a sense of domination. In the current context, states are competing with each other to overcome the impact of the pandemic to bring back balance, freedom for people, and a sense of unity gaining the advantage specially developed countries have at hand in terms of economic and political power to rise above other countries and use the opportunity to gain an advantage over other less capable countries by securing vaccines for themselves and themselves only.

## Regional Security Complex

Security Complex Theory was first introduced by Buzan through his book "People States and Fear" in 1983 and he introduced a security architecture with a region as its locus point (Buzan, 1983). He further delves into the theory and expressed that it was the post-cold-war world that catalyzed the prominence of regional level security (Buzan & Weaver, 2003). A regionalist perspective is emphasized by Buzan and Weaver juxtaposed with neorealist and globalist perspectives of politics (Buzan & Weaver, 2003). In the post-cold war era, space for cooperation, and even conflict is often grounded within the regions. Buzan and Weaver opine that the regional level has risen due to; diminishing of superpower rivalry, the ability of global power to intervene has also decreased. And most of the great powers in the post-cold war international system are now 'lite powers' (Buzan and Segal 1996), where domestic dynamics keep them from political relationships, engaging with trouble spots with the world (Buzan & Weaver, 2003).

Therefore, analysis of international political, social, economic relations can be executed at a regional level and perhaps is a comparatively effective means of addressing security issues as well. In the current crisis of global pandemic, regional addressing of crisis and search solutions also have come to the surface. In understanding the regional response, the following figure provides insight.

Therefore, it is significant to implore the regional security complex (RSC) response in relation to the pandemic.

*Figure 1. Post-Cold War regional security complex of Asia*
*Source: (Buzan & Weaver, 2003)*

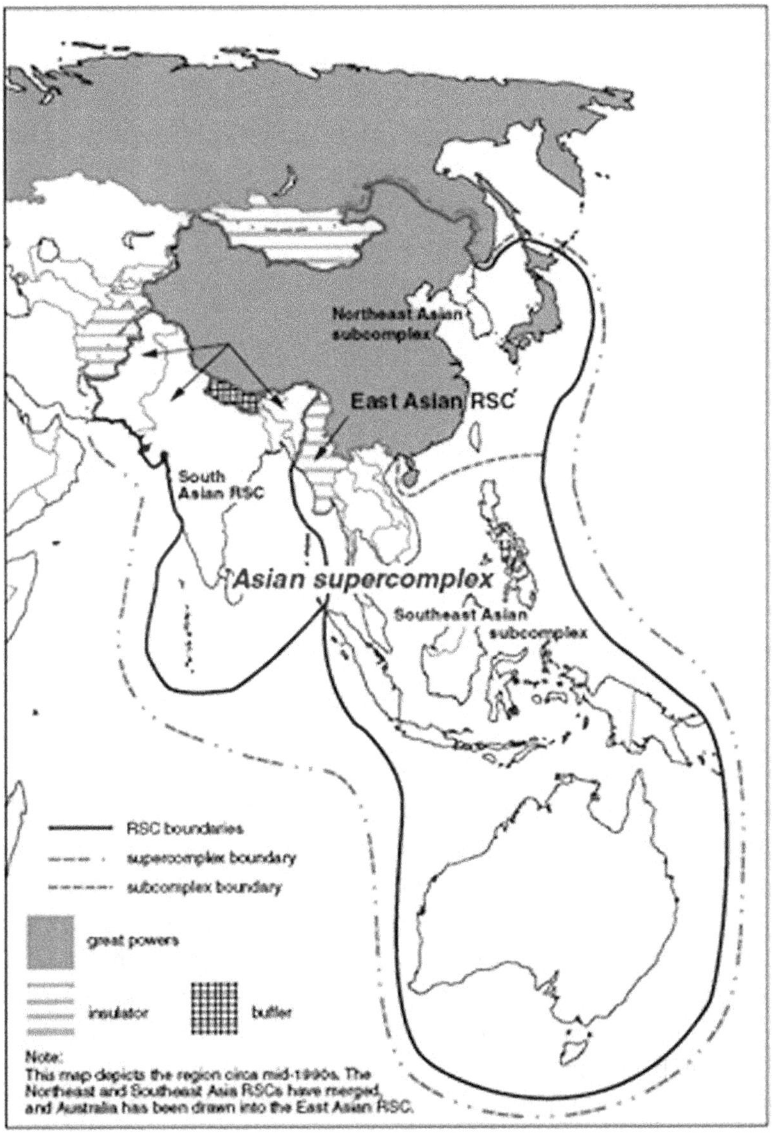


## Public Good Provision

The concept of "global public goods" (GPGs) suggests a possible framework. In this expression, "Goods" encompass a range of physical commodities (such as bread, books, and shoes) but includes services (such as security, information, and

*Figure 2. Covid-19 vaccination administered per 100 people from Dec. 20th to Jan 28th. Source: Our World in Data, 2021*

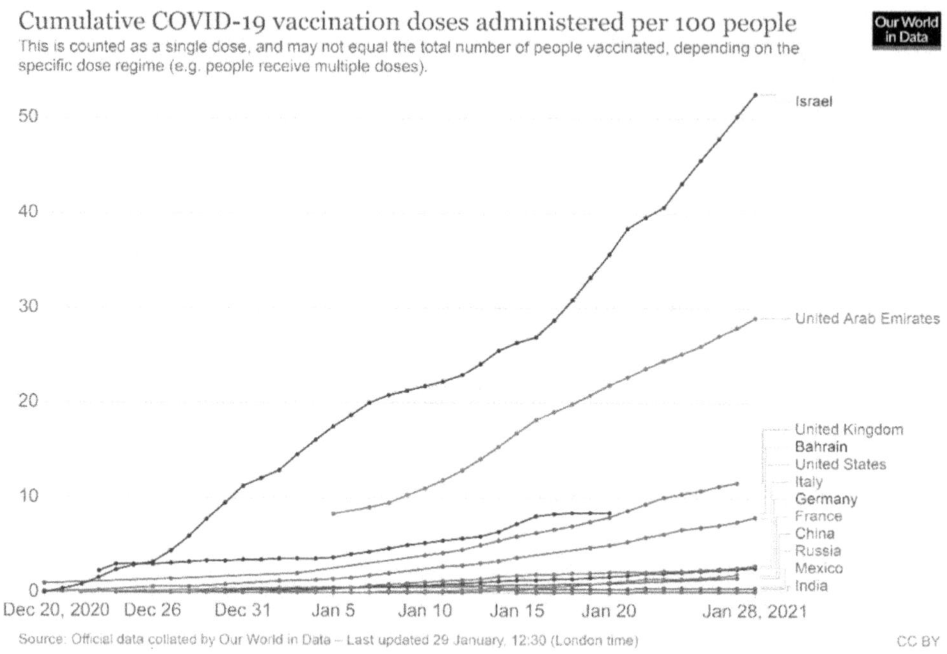


travel), distinguishing between private and public goods. Most goods are ''private''; their consumption can be withheld until payment is made in exchange for them, and once consumed they cannot be consumed again. In contrast, ''public'' goods are provided no one can be excluded from consuming them (they are non-excludable), and one person's consumption of them does not prevent anyone else's (they are non-rival in consumption). For example, no one in a population can be excluded from benefiting from a reduction in risk of infectious disease when its incidence is reduced, and one person benefiting from this reduction in risk does not prevent anyone else from benefiting from it as well (Smith, 2003).

Therefore, Global Public Goods are from those which benefits are reaped across borders; for instance, reduction in emission of CO2 from one location would help avoid global warming.

As such during the period of a pandemic, it is imperative that health care such as vaccines, test kits are considered a global public good in order to mitigate the pandemic. Hoarding vaccines and leaving countries with no access to vaccines will ultimately help keep the virus alive.

*Figure 3. Covid-19 vaccines administered on Jan. 28th, 2021*
*Source: Our World in Data, 2021*

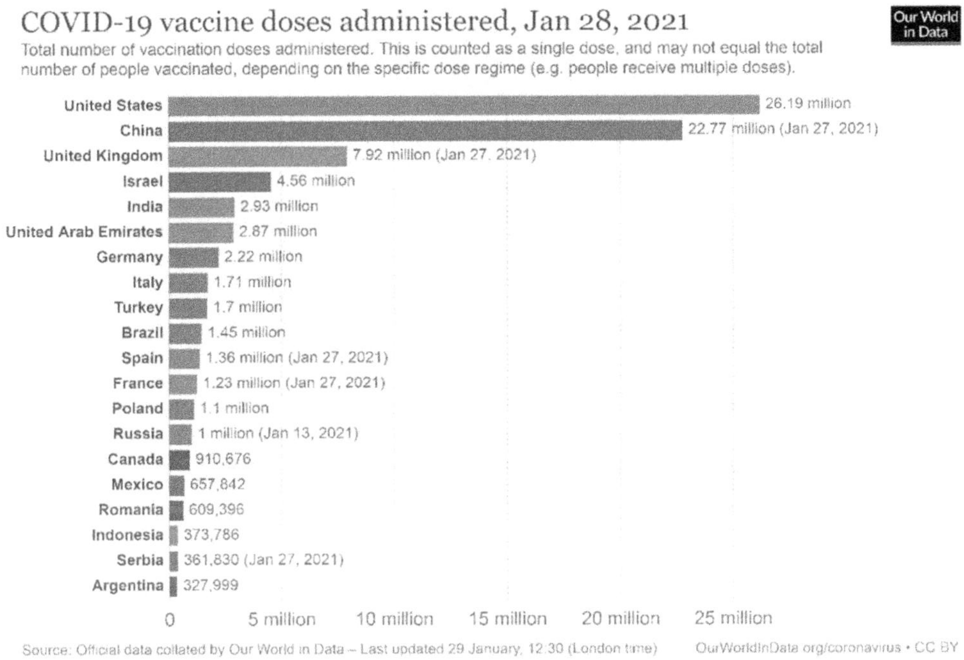


## Vaccine Nationalism

The Power struggle became evident among the states around the world over grabbing the vaccine and the developing and the least developing countries yet again are painfully understanding their "place" in the international system.

From Figure 2 and 3 world powers such as the USA, UK, Israel, China have reserved top positions in vaccine administration monthly as well as in daily vaccine rollout. Developing regions such as Africa, and Asia, although few countries have depicted numbers, are yet to provide vaccines to their citizens.

When the above two maps are juxtaposed, a stark observation can be made that countries with developed economies are in forefront of providing vaccination to their people. According to Duke Global Health Innovation Centre,

*High-income countries currently hold a confirmed 4.2 billion doses, upper-middle-income countries hold 1.1 billion doses, and lower-middle-income countries hold 444 million doses, and low-middle income countries hold 270 million. Many high-income countries have hedged their bets by advance purchasing enough doses to vaccinate their population several times over.*

*Figure 4. Covid-19 vaccination administered in Jan 2021 across the world*
*Source: Our World in Data, 2021*

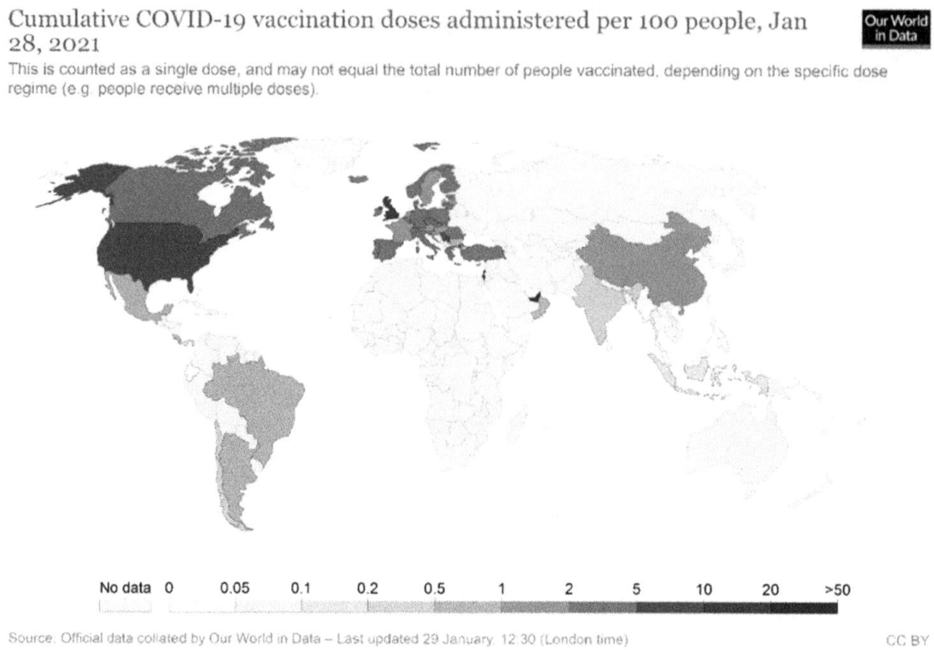


*Figure 5. Country groups by stage of industrialization*
*Source: Upadhyaya, 2013*

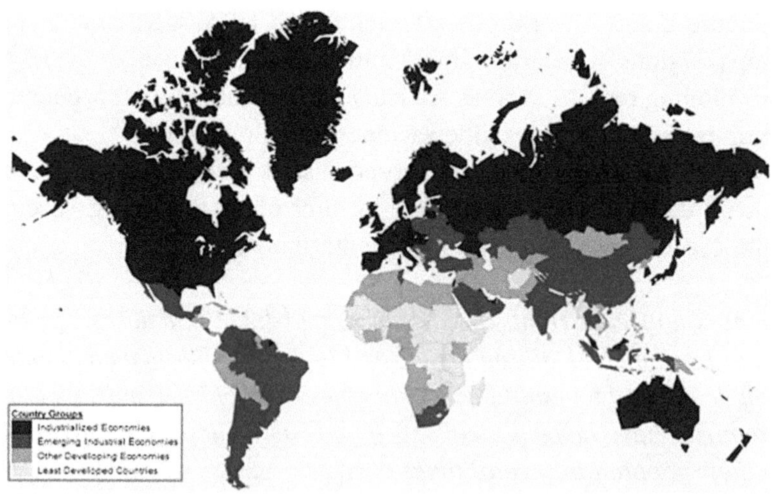

The race to develop a vaccine started back in 2020 in the wake of the pandemic itself. Now that a year has passed and several vaccines are out, the race is on to purchase vaccines enough for each country. Naturally, countries of higher fiscal power have become the front runners of the race which has left the lower-income countries in the waiting. The figure below depicts the unequal distribution and availability of vaccines around the world based on fiscal power.

*Figure 6. World access to Coronavirus vaccine*
*Source: The Economist, 2021*

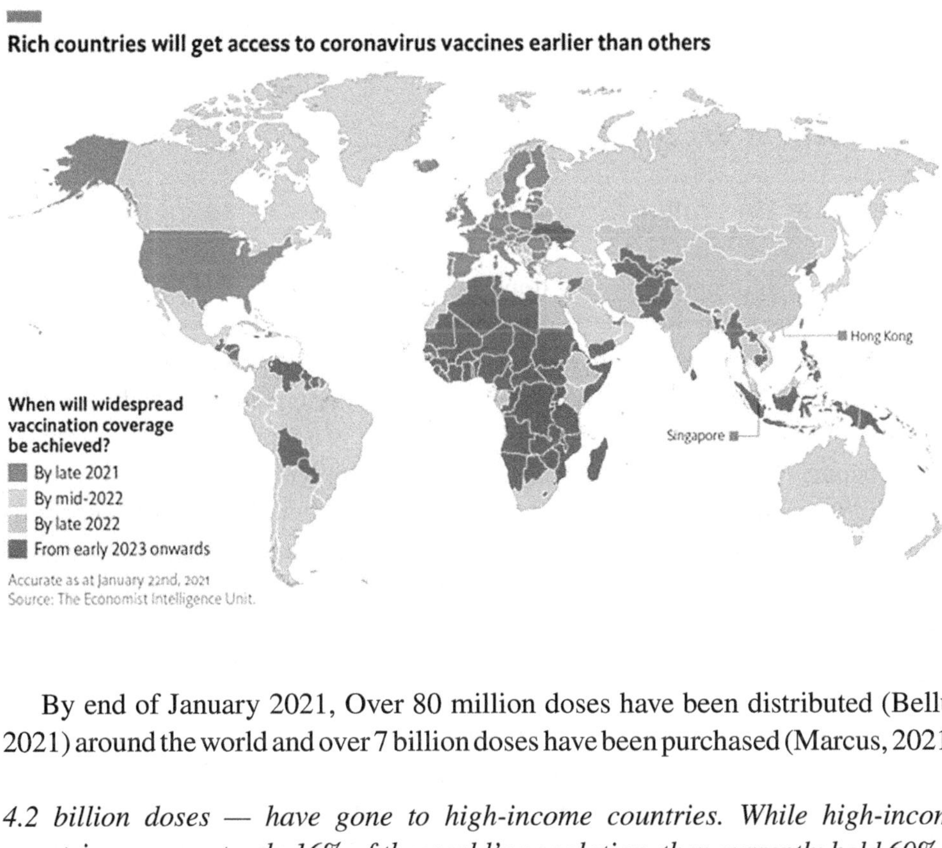


By end of January 2021, Over 80 million doses have been distributed (Belluz 2021) around the world and over 7 billion doses have been purchased (Marcus, 2021).

*4.2 billion doses — have gone to high-income countries. While high-income countries represent only 16% of the world's population, they currently hold 60% of the vaccines for COVID-19 that have been purchased so far. Canada tops the list having purchased enough vaccines to cover more than five times their population. Most other high-income countries have more than 100% coverage, and some can cover their populations several times over (Marcus, 2021).*

Due to higher purchases by richer countries they have secured deals of priority manufacturing slots for 2021, "meaning that even if other countries make purchases now, they may have to wait months or even a year for delivery." Remarked Taylor from Duke University. Therefore, it explains the above figure 05 where lower-income countries will have to wait till at least 2023 to roll out doses.

Therefore, the world economy is set to experience positive development by mid-2021 (The Economist, 2021). However, with the economic interdependence, the global gross domestic product (GDP) will face an inevitable loss even though rich countries achieve successful administration of vaccines. Therefore, there is a definite need for collective action on a global vaccination process. This need has been identified by the World Health Organization in spearheading the COVAX initiative to achieve equitable access to eligible countries.

## Regionalism in Vaccine Roll Out

### In Relation to Sri Lanka

In the current crisis of pandemic, it is important to observe the global politics at hand. The USA was experiencing political turmoil at home and in the wake of vaccine rollout, the UK was experiencing new strains of the Virus and the COVAX facility steered to enhance equitable access to the vaccine is experiencing low funding. Great powers are blamed even more for hoarding and exercising protectionism measures on the vaccine (Sytas, 2021). In such a context, in applying Buzan and Weaver's assumptions where domestic dynamics are keeping greater powers from engaging with trouble spots of the world, we can understand the significance of focusing on regional level integration; how the Regional Security Complex has come into play in addressing the vaccine administration.

When it comes to Asian Super Complex, as shown in the figure, the powers in the region are India and China. It is reported that China is already set to roll out vaccines based on its own national interests (Cook, 2021). Even India is extending her arm especially in Sri Lanka Therefore, access to vaccines will also depend highly on vaccine diplomacy and will perhaps spill over with political, economic relations with countries. Thus 'vaccine diplomacy' has come to play a role in deepening cooperation within the region.

Discussion of Indian assistance to obtain Covid-19 Vaccine came into the spotlight with the arrival of the Indian External Affairs Minister's high-level visit to Sri Lanka from 5$^{th}$ to 7$^{th}$ January in 2021. With the Sri Lankan government express of interest in obtaining the vaccine, the External Affairs Minister of India agreed to address the request (Jaishankar, 2021).

*Figure 7. Vaccine diplomacy*
*Source: Avantha Artigala, 2021*

*Reflecting on our Neighbourhood First policy, India has supported Sri Lanka's efforts to tackle Covid through timely medical assistance. I should place on record our appreciation to the Sri Lankan Government for its assistance and facilitation in the evacuation of Indian nationals who were stuck here. We are now looking at post-Covid cooperation and I carry back with me Sri Lanka's interest in accessing vaccines from India and I shared with the Hon'ble Foreign Minister, as Prime Minister Modi has said, India sees International cooperation in this area as its duty.*

Minister S. Jaishankar referring to India's 'Neighbourhood First' policy emphasized it is India's duty in engaging in cooperation in the area. Moreover, the cultural and geographical proximity between the two countries further enables partnership as mentioned by the minister himself at the beginning of remarks made in Colombo. Therefore, the application of RSC is highlighted where it proves the effectiveness of regional level address of issues.

Accordingly, India sent half a million free doses of the COVID-19 vaccine to Sri Lanka on the 28$^{th}$ of January which will be administered to front-line health care workers Miglani & Karunatilake, 2021). The high-level ministerial visit and act of cooperation carried out by Delhi in hopes of deepening ties with its neighbors comes at a time where discussions on the 2019 agreement on East Container Terminal (ECT) of Colombo Port are at a pressure point facing opposition across the country and trade unions.

Figure 7 depicts the effects of vaccine diplomacy interpreted by a cartoonist and how India is applying leverage on the ECT project through it.

As one of the world's biggest drug producers, India is set to produce Oxford-AstraZeneca vaccine at home and has sent consignments of coronavirus vaccines under grant assistance to Bhutan, Maldives, Nepal, Bangladesh, and Myanmar as well. The role of India in the RSC, therefore, is reiterated and the manner in which India is utilizing the leverage to inculcate relations with the regional partners further enables her to establish her position as a leader in Asia.

Moreover, further talks have been in play in obtaining 300,000 vaccines from China along with monetary assistance to Sri Lanka (The Hindu Business Line, 2021). Sri Lanka's relations with China have been on and off and observing the power politics of the region Sri Lanka must balance the two key players of the region. In application of the RSC theory of Buzan, here we can identify how North-East Asian Sub-complex is intervening in the South Asian Security Complex in relation to figure 01.

## Positive Regional Approach in Vaccine Roll Out

With the power politics at play and engaging in vaccine diplomacy as an extension of national interest, the question arises whether there is a nudge in solidarity among states to overcome the global issue at hand. However, signs of altruism are showing as New Zealand has agreed to provide vaccines to the pacific as well.

*We now have agreements in place with four providers, covering three different types of vaccine technology and we have secured more than enough doses to cover our entire population plus the Pacific (Arden et al, 2020).*

Accordingly, neighboring nations such as Tokelau, Cook Islands, Niue, Samoa, Tonga, and Tuvalu will have access to the vaccine based on each of their need (Diaz, 2020). It will ultimately help New Zealand to achieve pre-Covid normalcy with neighboring countries achieving immunity at the same time as it reduces the possibility of re-spreading the virus at the same time enables economic activities to recuperate. It is yet another instance where regionalism has come to the rescue and how an RSC helps in demarcating the issue through which solutions can be addressed within the region.

The unifying approach of the African region on equitable distribution is admirable. Dr. Ahmed Ogwell, Deputy Director at the Africa Centres for Disease Control and Prevention (Africa CDC), stated,

*...for us at Africa CDC and African Union there is really no option but the equitable distribution of vaccines. If we don't do that, then the virus will never go away because the virus does not respect borders. Neither does it respect position in society and which part of the world someone comes from. So equitable distribution of vaccines is an absolute must if we are going to get a good grip on this pandemic. For us, it makes absolutely no sense for a very healthy, relatively young individual in one part of the world to be getting vaccinated while a health worker on the front lines in another part of the world is not getting vaccinated. This sort of skewed arrangement will not be good for public health and will certainly open us up to even more spread of this virus in the future (Marcus, 2021).*

Ogwell further clarified the distribution of the vaccine to be carried out considering the whole of Africa as a block and will be protecting the most vulnerable first. The approach that has been built on a sense of regionalism has brought hopes of normalcy catalyzed through observing rationale measures of vaccine administration.

## The Plight of Least Developed Countries in a Global Approach to Vaccine Roll Out

While several developing nations have found relief through a regional approach, a global approach has also been in discussions in the rescue of developing and small power nations.

### COVAX Facility

The ACT (Access to Covid-19 Tools) Accelerator is an initiation executed by WHO as a collaboration to accelerate development, production, and equitable access to Covid-19 tests, treatments, and vaccines. It was launched in 2020, April and was prompted by the Director-General of the WHO, the President of France, the President of the European Commission, and the Bill & Melinda Gates Foundation. The ACT Accelerator hopes to bring together governments, scientists, businesses, civil society, and philanthropists, and global health organizations such as Bill & Melinda Gates Foundation, CEPI (Coalition for Epidemic Preparedness Innovations), FIND (Foundation for Innovative New Diagnostics), Gavi: the Vaccine Alliance, The Global Fund, Unitaid, Wellcome, the WHO, and the World Bank.

The ACT-Accelerator is consists of a four-pillar approach; diagnostics, treatment, vaccines, and health system strengthening. Each pillar is vital and operated in collaboration towards combating the pandemic. The Vaccine pillar of the ACT Accelerator is executed through the COVAX facility with the initiation of CEPI GAVI and WHO. It engages in the search for a vaccine, supporting the production of vaccines and buying for the distribution of vaccines under relief packages to countries ensuring fair and equitable access to the vaccine.

Norway's global health ambassador, John-Arne Røttingen, has amplified that the world is at a turning point to ensure equal access to the vaccine (Wintour, 2021). With several vaccines being manufactured and is starting to distribute around the globe, it is important not to discriminate among rich and poor nations as diplomats fear that if the issue of vaccine distribution is not resolved, it will result in years of resentment between rich and poor nations (Wintour, 2021). Therefore, it is expected to 1.8 billion doses to be available to the 92 economies of the Gavi COVAX Advance Market Commitment (AMC) in 2021" (CEPI, GAVI & WHO, 2021) These 92 economies/ countries can purchase vaccines by other means based as their preference but is it highly doubtful that they would be fiscally capable to fulfill vaccine needs.

## Vaccine Supply Under COVAX

The list of 92 Gavi COVAX AMC-eligible countries and economies (based on 2018 and 2019 World Bank Gross National Income data) are as follows; (Gavi the Vaccine Alliance, 2020)

- Low income: Afghanistan, Benin, Burkina Faso, Burundi, Central African Republic, Chad, Congo, Dem. Rep., Eritrea, Ethiopia, Gambia, The Guinea, Guinea-Bissau, Haiti, Korea, Dem. People's Rep., Liberia, Madagascar, Malawi, Mali, Mozambique, Nepal, Niger, Rwanda, Sierra Leone, Somalia, South Sudan, Syrian Arab Republic, Tajikistan, Tanzania, Togo, Uganda, Yemen, Rep.,
- Lower-middle income: Angola, Algeria, Bangladesh, Bhutan, Bolivia, Cabo Verde, Cambodia, Cameroon, Comoros, Congo, Rep. Côte d'Ivoire, Djibouti, Egypt, Arab Rep., El Salvador, Eswatini, Ghana, Honduras, India, Indonesia, Kenya, Kiribati, Kyrgyz Republic Lao PDR, Lesotho, Mauritania, Micronesia, Fed. Sts., Moldova, Mongolia, Morocco, Myanmar, Nicaragua, Nigeria, Pakistan, Papua New Guinea, Philippines, São Tomé and Principe, Senegal, Solomon Islands, Sri Lanka, Sudan, Timor-Leste, Tunisia, Ukraine, Uzbekistan, Vanuatu, Vietnam, West Bank and Gaza, Zambia, Zimbabwe
- Additional IDA eligible: Dominica, Fiji, Grenada, Guyana, Kosovo, Maldives, Marshall Islands, Samoa, St. Lucia, St. Vincent and the Grenadines, Tonga, Tuvalu.

Additionally, 80 other self-financing countries have joined with the COVAX facility who will be purchasing their vaccine needs through COVAX (Gavi the Vaccine Alliance, 2020).

So who will pay for the vaccines procured through COVAX Facility for small economies? It is set to be largely funded through Official Development Assistance (ODA) of larger economies. Nonetheless, the 92 eligible countries will require to bear some of the cost owing to delivery and it is estimated to be up to US$ 1.60 – US$ 2 per dose (Berkley, 2020).

Distribution forecasts have been formulated by WHO categorized by regional offices. And the forecast for Asia is as follows;

*Figure 8. COVAX supply forecast to South East Asia Region*
*Source: Coalition for Epidemic Preparedness Innovations, Gavi the Vaccine Alliance & World Health Organization, 2021*

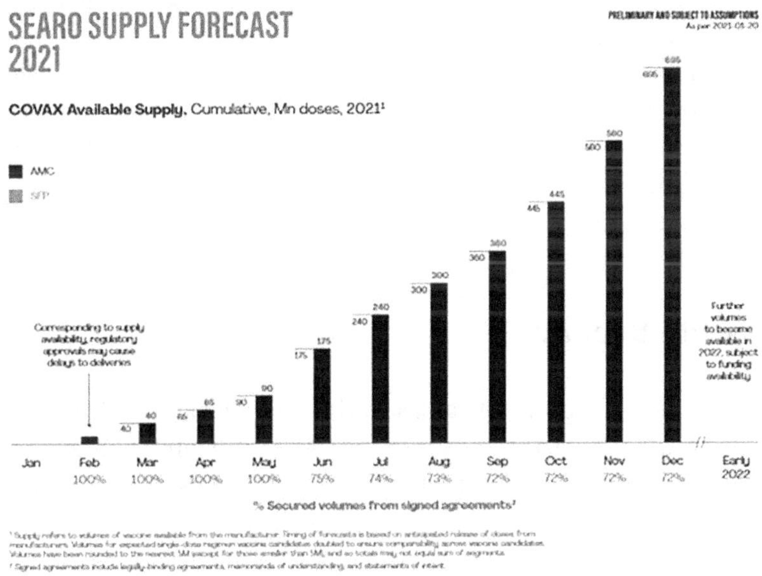


Accordingly, by mid-2021 (June), only 175 million doses will be made available for AMC countries. AMC countries of the African region will acquire only 140 million doses by June and the Pan American region will acquire only 20 million doses by June for their AMC countries (Coalition for Epidemic Preparedness Innovations, Gavi the Vaccine Alliance & World Health Organization, 2021)/ (Wintour, 2021). Accordingly, only 27% will be vaccinated in 2021 of AMC countries in other words, low-income countries (Coalition for Epidemic Preparedness Innovations, Gavi the Vaccine Alliance & World Health Organization, 2021)/ (Wintour, 2021).

The inadequacy of the COVAX facility is therefore evident and proportionally shows drastic contrast with that of doses purchased and available to high-income countries. Samantha Power, the USAid director, has admitted that the scheme is not on track. Røttingen further highlighted the challenges faced in executing the COVAX facility in its full potential; differences in timing and roll out in different country vaccine administration timeline, approval is only available for few vaccines for distribution and they are proving to be too expensive, approval for AstraZeneca vaccine is still awaited as COVAX is unable to distribute vaccines not approved by WHO, and rich countries exercising vaccine nationalism and over purchasing vaccines (Wintour, 2021).

Therefore, small powers will not have the global safety net to fall into, and provided that the global approach overcame the challenges mentioned above, it will take years for effective vaccine administration. While the global initiative should be admired for its collective action taken the logistical shortcomings and political background of the international system must be taken into account in understanding the degree of inefficiency.

The regional approach therefore again becomes applicable and is validated further in acquiring enough vaccinations for small powers through relief programs as well as through monetary provisions. At the same time, planning the rollout process can be addressed regionally similar to the African region mentioned. However, in a regional engagement, the small powers will require to balance the regional political, geopolitical, and economic implications.

## Risk to Health Security

The study analyses the impact on health security through vaccine distribution based on the vaccine availability to regions through COVAX facility juxtaposed with the country and number of population that require the vaccines. A number of vaccines arranged through COVAX is taken as a parameter as logistical and purchases of vaccines apart from the facility are still ongoing and numbers are not available.

The table highlights two regions as a microcosm to all six regions under World Health Organization namely, Regional Office for Africa (AFRO) - African region and South East Asia Region (SEARO). The above table reveals the shortage of vaccine doses secured to be provided to countries under the COVAX initiative in mid-2021 in comparison to the population (as of the second month of the year 2021). In AFRO, while AMC's country population presents approximately 1049 million citizens, only 140 million doses are available. And in SEARO, for a total population of approximately 1951 million of AMC countries only 175 doses are available.

The supply chain of the vaccine has thus drawn attention from production to distribution that of human resource, finance and logistics involved. Shortages caused in each of the stages will lead to a weakened vaccine deployment. At such a juncture, discussions have come to light on global public goods especially on health. As mentioned earlier since tools to diminish the pandemic are non-excludable

*Table 2.*

| Region | Vaccines Available (doses in million) by mid-2021 | | AMC Countries in the Region | | SFP (Self Financing Participants) Countries in the Region | |
|---|---|---|---|---|---|---|
| | AMC Countries | SFP Countries | Country | Population (million) | Country | Population (million) |
| AFRO – Africa Regional Office | 140 | 05 | Algeria | 43.8 | Seychelles | 0.09 |
| | | | Angola | 32.8 | South Africa | 59.3 |
| | | | Benin | 12.1 | Mauritius | 1.2 |
| | | | Burkina Faso | 20.9 | Botswana | 2.3 |
| | | | Burundi | 11.8 | | |
| | | | Cameroon | 26.5 | | |
| | | | Cabo Verde | 0.5 | | |
| | | | The central African Republic | 4.8 | | |
| | | | Chad | 16.4 | | |
| | | | Comoros | 0.8 | | |
| | | | Congo | 5.5 | | |
| | | | Côte d'Ivoire | 26.3 | | |
| | | | Dem. Repub. Of Congo | 89.5 | | |
| | | | Eritrea | 3.5 | | |
| | | | Ethiopia | 114.9 | | |
| | | | Gambia | 2.4 | | |
| | | | Ghana | 31.1 | | |
| | | | The Guinea | 13.1 | | |
| | | | Guinea- Bissau | 1.9 | | |
| | | | Kenya | 53.7 | | |
| | | | Lesotho | 2.1 | | |
| | | | Liberia | 5 | | |
| | | | Madagascar | 27.6 | | |
| | | | Malawi | 19.1 | | |
| | | | Mali | 20.2 | | |
| | | | Mauritania | 4.6 | | |
| | | | Mozambique | 31.2 | | |
| | | | Eswatini | 1.1 | | |
| | | | Niger | 24.2 | | |
| | | | Nigeria | 206.1 | | |
| | | | Rwanda | 12.9 | | |
| | | | São Tomé and Principe | 0.2 | | |
| | | | Senegal | 16.7 | | |
| | | | Sierra Leone | 7.9 | | |
| | | | Togo | 8.2 | | |
| | | | Uganda | 45.7 | | |
| | | | Tanzania | 59.7 | | |
| | | | Zambia | 18.3 | | |
| | | | Zimbabwe | 14.8 | | |
| | | | South Sudan | 11.1 | | |
| | | | Total population | 1049 | | 62.89 |

*continued on following page*

*Table 2. Continued*

| Region | Vaccines Available (doses in million) by mid-2021 | | AMC Countries in the Region | | SFP (Self Financing Participants) Countries in the Region | |
|---|---|---|---|---|---|---|
| | AMC Countries | SFP Countries | Country | Population (million) | Country | Population (million) |
| SEARO | 175 | 0 | Bangladesh | 164.6 | | |
| | | | Bhutan | 0.7 | | |
| | | | Korea, Dem. People's Rep. | 25.7 | | |
| | | | India | 1380 | | |
| | | | Indonesia | 273.5 | | |
| | | | Maldives | 0.5 | | |
| | | | Myanmar | 54.4 | | |
| | | | Nepal | 29.1 | | |
| | | | Sri Lanka | 21.4 | | |
| | | | Timor-Leste | 1.3 | | |
| | | | Total population | 1951.2 | | |

Source: Author. Derived from Worldometer, 2021/ Gavi the Vaccine Alliance, 2020 and Coalition for Epidemic Preparedness Innovations, Gavi the Vaccine Alliance & World Health Organization, 2021.

health tools must be then available as a public good. However, these health tools are accessible based on human intervention across three main areas mentioned earlier; financing, human resource, and logistics. Therefore, in making it (vaccines) a public good, global collective action is much needed.

China as early as May 2020, announced that they will be treating Coronavirus Vaccine as a global public good and Xi Jin Ping reiterated that "COVID-19 vaccine development and deployment in China, when available, will be made a global public good" (Wheaton, 2020). At the same time, earlier mention of New Zealand taking initiation of providing vaccines for the region could also be read in terms of a responsible leadership ensuring access to the vaccine as a public good. However, the regional approach in the provision of public goods also must be noted.

WHO director-general too, speaking at the Peace Paris Forum in November 2020, stated that "As global public goods, COVID-19 vaccines, therapeutics, and diagnostics must be available based on equitable and affordable access for all, especially for health workers, the elderly, and other at-risk groups" (Adhanom, 2020).

While WHO in a multilateral approach has initiated the project; "Covid-19 Tools Accelerator" as a response to elevate these tools as public goods, the inclusion of developed countries, as well as private entities working together with public entities, must be pursued in better manufacture, distribution of the vaccines. The leadership of countries such as France, Germany, South Africa, and also the European Commission in creating the political platform for the ACT Accelerator and engagement of public-private entities such as Bill and Melinda Gates Foundation (BMGF), CEPI, Gavi, Globa Fund, UNITAID, Wellcome Trust, Bill and Melinda Gates Foundation, and

Vaccine Manufacturers has led to the execution of COVAX initiative in the present magnitude.

## RECOMMENDATIONS

### Strengthening Regional Forums

The regional approach has appeared to be much efficient than a global approach. Therefore strengthening regional forums could take the initiation forward. For example, the South Asian Association for Regional Cooperation (SAARC) that of South Asia is dormant at present. Regional platforms such as those become significant as vaccine support, distribution can be handled through them and it presents a further opportunity to overcome regional politics as well.

### Strengthening Multilateralism Globally

Global initiatives such as WHO must be integrated more into other public and private partners to overcome challenges in keeping up with research and development, vaccine production, funding, distribution, and governance. As new variants surface, it is important to continue research and following up with vaccine production and then the rest accordingly. Therefore engagement of each significant link must be enabled efficiently through international multilateral platforms.

### Treating Covid-19 Tools as Public Goods

In pursuing a goal of achieving economic and social stability, vaccine access to every human on earth is vital. Therefore, health facilities especially vaccines must be elevated to a position of public good available to everyone at least under reasonable pricing. However, to attain it, human resources, logistics, finances must be sorted out.

### Providing Incentives for Countries, Partners to Involve in Funding for ACT Accelerator

In such a time where each country is experiencing economic issues, countries appear to be reluctant to provide monetary assistance to global funds. Therefore, incentives such as positive reciprocity from the international system, providing priority in vaccine rollout can be ensured as incentives for partners. At the same time, repercussions of protectionism must be highlighted for states and awareness must be made that economy, social activities, politics will not gain normalcy unless the region/ world together gains immunity.

### Strengthening Public-Private Partnership

As mentioned earlier, partnerships are very important to each and every step of the way from manufacturing to distribution. Being a link between government officers, health officers, in the execution of vaccine distribution is well needed.

### Expanding R&D Regionally

At the same time, vaccine production facilities should be expanded regionally. For instance, at least 2 facilities per region could be established for research as well as vaccine production. Thus, the regional dynamics of the virus with its population, culture, and politics can be grappled closely and relatively.

## FUTURE RESEARCH DIRECTIONS

Measures taken in response to COVID-19 must be analyzed on its efficiency state by state. As every state is different in economy, political system, social and cultural spheres must be analyzed in relation to COVID response. Global Health Security Index 2019 can be considered a guideline of measurements to be taken by each country to ensure that necessary mechanisms are met. Findings and learned lessons must be incorporated into the pandemic response programs and policies from each country accordingly.

Based on Health Security Index 2019, the following parameters can be utilized for analysis.

1. Prevention- Prevention of the emergence or release of pathogens
2. Detection And Reporting- Early detection and reporting for epidemics of potential international concern
3. Rapid Response - Rapid response to and mitigation of the spread of an epidemic
4. Health System- Sufficient and robust health system to treat the sick and protect health workers
5. Compliance With International Norms- Commitments to improving national capacity, financing plans to address gaps, and adhering to global norms
6. Risk Environment- Overall risk environment and country vulnerability to biological threats

## CONCLUSION

While it must be understood that Covid-19 vaccination is perhaps the largest vaccine program to date and it will require months and even years to complete global vaccine rollout, more effective and efficient pathways must be cleared and followed to achieve economic, social, and political stability preferably close to the pre-Covid era. Therefore, countries are provided with approaches; manufacturing their own vaccines, purchasing their own vaccine doses, obtaining through global initiative (COVAX), and following a regional approach. For small powers manufacturing or purchasing their own vaccines appears challengeable, therefore, advisable to approach global initiative and regional initiative. While the global initiative will require time, regional approach in terms of obtaining free doses, financial support will require less time, logistical requirements. Therefore, the regional approach proves to be much efficient and feasible. However, regional power politics, using leverage on smaller powers by big powers in the region has inevitable in a regional perspective.

As the pandemic has reached every nook and corner of the world, the need for responsible leadership is emphasized more than ever. Global, regional, local leadership and governance and their applicability is on judgment, and the multilateral tools that have originated to serve this purpose are also under high scrutiny. World powerful countries in exercising vaccine nationalism are blamed for hoarding vaccines thus responsible leadership is questioned worldwide. Countries such as Canada, New Zealand, and France have executed relief and relief packages even though few of them are blamed for hoarding. However, the extent of leadership undertaken is criticized.

While financing is a key in supplying health tools, it has led the richer and developed countries in the present context of Covid-19 health tools accessibility, to overpower small nations to acquire vaccine doses more than necessary. While the pandemic will not cease to exist with ensuring immunity in single countries alone in an interdependent world, a global outreach is needed thus endorsing Covid-19 mechanisms as Public Goods have become significant.

## REFERENCES

Adhanom, T. (2020). *WHO Director-General's speech at the Paris Peace Forum Panel: ACT-A: Covid-19 Vaccines, Tests and Therapies, the Global public good Solution - 12 November 2020*. World Health Organization. Retrieved December 05, 2020, from https://www.who.int/director-general/speeches/detail/who-director-general-s-speech-at-the-paris-peace-forum-panel-act-a-covid-19-vaccines-tests-and-therapies-the-global-public-good-solution---12-november-2020

Arden, J., Woods, M., Hipkins, C., & Little, A. (2020). *Two new vaccines secured, enough for every New Zealander*. The Official Website of New Zealand Government. Retrieved January 12, 2021, from https://www.beehive.govt.nz/release/two-new-vaccines-secured-enough-every-new-zealander

Artigala, A. (2021). *Cartoon* [post update]. Facebook. Retrieved January 26, 2021, from https://www.facebook.com/photo.php?fbid=263055201834012&set=pb.100043886031837.-2207520000.&type=3

Bekerly, S. (n.d.). *The Gavi COVAX AMC Explained*. Gavi the Vaccine Alliance. Retrieved January 26, 2021 from https://www.gavi.org/vaccineswork/gavi-covax-amc-explained

Belluz, J. (2021). *Rich countries are hoarding Covid-19 vaccines*. Vox. Retrieved February 01, 2021 from https://www.vox.com/2021/1/29/22253908/rich-countries-hoarding-covid-19-vaccines

Bland, A., & Davis, N. (2021). *Will Novavax and Johnson & Johnson Covid vaccines work against variants?* The Guardian. Retrieved February 01, 2021 from https://www.theguardian.com/society/2021/jan/29/how-effective-novavax-covid-vaccine-variants

Buzan, B. (1983). *People, States and Fear*. University of North Carolina Press.

Buzan, B., & Weaver, O. (2003). *Regions and Powers; The Structure of International Security*. Cambridge University Press. doi:10.1017/CBO9780511491252

Centre for Disease Control and Prevention. (2021). *Different COVID-19 Vaccines*. Retrieved February 02, 2021 from https://www.cdc.gov/coronavirus/2019-ncov/vaccines/different-vaccines.html

Coalition for Epidemic Preparedness Innovations, Gavi the Vaccine Alliance & World Health Organization. (2021). *COVAX Global Supply Forecast*. Author. Retrieved February 03, 2021 from https://www.gavi.org/sites/default/files/covid/covax/COVAX%20Supply%20Forecast.pdf

Cook, S. A. (2021). *America's Vaccine Diplomacy Is AWOL in the Middle East*. Foreign Policy. Retrieved January 10, 2021 from https://foreignpolicy.com/2021/01/08/americas-vaccine-diplomacy-is-awol-in-the-middle-east/

Diaz, J. (2020). *New Zealand Will Give Free Coronavirus Vaccines To Residents, Neighboring Nations*. NPR. Retrieved January 03, 2021 from https://www.npr.org/sections/coronavirus-live-updates/2020/12/17/947403839/new-zealand-will-give-free-coronavirus-vaccines-to-residents-neighboring-nations

Economic Times. (2020). *Scientists identify 8 strains of coronavirus*. India Times. Retrieved January 03, 2021 from https://health.economictimes.indiatimes.com/news/industry/scientists-identify-8-strains-of-coronavirus/74931204

Gallagher, J. (2021). *Covid vaccine: Single-dose Johnson & Johnson jab is 66% effective*. BBC. Retrieved January 30, 2021 from https://www.bbc.com/news/health-55857530

Gallagher, J. (2021). *Covid vaccine update: Those that work - and the others on the way*. BBC. Retrieved February 05, 2021 from https://www.bbc.com/news/health-51665497

Gavi the Vaccine Alliance. (n.d.). *92 low- and middle-income economies eligible to get access to COVID-19 vaccines through Gavi COVAX AMC*. Retrieved February 05, 2021 from https://www.gavi.org/news/media-room/92-low-middle-income-economies-eligible-access-covid-19-vaccines-gavi-covax-amc

Hertz, F. (1944). *Nationality in History and Politics*. Oxford University Press.

Hussein, H., Chams, N., Chams, S., Sayegh, S., Badran, R., & Raad, M. (2015). Vaccines through Centuries: Major Cornerstones of Global Health. *Frontiers in Public Health, 3*. Advance online publication. doi:10.3389/fpubh.2015.00269 PMID:26636066

Jaishankar, S. (2021). *Opening Remarks by External Affairs Minister at the Joint Press Conference with Foreign Minister of Sri Lanka*. Ministry of External Affairs: Government of India. Retrieved February 05, 2021 from https://mea.gov.in/SpeechesStatements.htm?dtl/33368/Opening_Remarks_by_External_Affairs_Minister_at_the_Joint_Press_Conference_with_Foreign_Minister_of_Sri_Lanka

Kecmanovic. (1960). *The Mass Psychology of Ethnonationalism*. Plenum Press.

Kretchmer, H. (2021). *Vaccine nationalism – and how it could affect us all*. World Economic Forum. Retrieved January 08, 2021 from https://www.weforum.org/agenda/2021/01/what-is-vaccine-nationalism-coronavirus-its-affects-covid-19-pandemic/

Louis, L. (1964). *The Dynamics of Nationalism: Readings in Its Meaning and Development*. D. Van Nostrand Company.

Marcus, B. M. (2021). *Ensuring Everyone in the World Gets a COVID Vaccine*. Duke Global Health Institute. Retrieved January 25, 2021 from https://globalhealth.duke.edu/news/ensuring-everyone-world-gets-covid-vaccine

Miglani, S., & Karunatilake, W. (2021). *India sends free AstraZeneca vaccines to Sri Lanka for Friday roll-out.* Reuters. Retrieved January 30, 2021 from https://www.reuters.com/article/health-coronavirus-sri-lanka-vaccine-idUSKBN29X1M6

Our World In Data. (2021). *Statistics and Research Coronavirus (COVID-19) Vaccinations.* Retrieved January 29, 2021 from https://ourworldindata.org/covid-vaccinations

Smith, R. D. (2003). Global public goods and health. Bulletin of the World Health Organization. *The International Journal of Public Health 2003, 81*(7).

Sytas, A. (2021). *Enthusiasm over COVID-19 vaccines tempered by talk of protectionism and hoarding.* Reuters. Retrieved January 30, 2021 from https://www.reuters.com/article/health-coronavirus-vaccines-int-idUSKBN29V2B4

The Economist. (2021). *More than 85 poor countries will not have widespread access to coronavirus vaccines before 2023.* Retrieved January 30, 2021 from https://www.eiu.com/n/85-poor-countries-will-not-have-access-to-coronavirus-vaccines/

The Hindu Business Line. (2021). *Sri Lanka to procure 2 to 3 million doses of Covid-19 vaccine from India: Official.* Retrieved January 28, 2021 from https://www.thehindubusinessline.com/news/world/sri-lanka-to-procure-2-to-3-million-doses-of-covid-19-vaccine-from-india-official/article33675032.ece

The World Health Organization. (2014). The immunization programme that saved millions of lives. *Bulletin of the World Health Organization, 92*(5), 314–315. doi:10.2471/BLT.14.020514 PMID:24839319

United Nations Development Program. (1994). *Human development Report 1994.* Oxford University Press.

Upadhyaya, S. (2013). *Country Grouping in UNIDO Statistics.* United Nations Industrial Development Organization.

Wheaton, S. (2020). *Chinese vaccine would be 'global public good,' Xi says.* Retrieved January 05, 2021 from https://www.politico.eu/article/chinese-vaccine-would-be-global-public-good-xi-says/

Wintour, P. (2021). *World's poor need action, not Covid 'vaccine nationalism', Say Experts.* The Guardian. Retrieved January 25, 2021 from https://www.theguardian.com/world/2021/jan/22/worlds-poor-need-action-not-covid-vaccine-nationalism-say-experts

Worldometer. (2021). *Countries in the world by population.* Retrieved January 25, 2021 from https://www.worldometers.info/world-population/population-by-country/

## KEY TERMS AND DEFINITIONS

**COVAX Advanced Market Commitment:** An AMC is a legally binding agreement for several funds to be subsidized in purchasing vaccines, at a given price, produced for specific disease-causing mortality in developing countries.

**Globalist Perspective:** It transcends the statist perspective and accepts the view usually labeled 'globalization'. It is rooted mainly in cultural, transnational, and international political economy approaches.

**Neighborhood First Policy:** Foreign Policy initiated by India's Prime Minister Narendra Modi's government in maintaining diplomatic relations with India's neighboring countries.

**Neo-Realist Perspective:** It is a state-centric, power-political understanding of international system structure.

**Vaccine Diplomacy:** Utilizing Vaccines to strengthen diplomatic, bilateral relations with other countries as well as influence their national sphere.

# Chapter 7
# Ideational Understanding of the Indo-Pakistan Nuclear Rivalry:
## The Way Forward

**Kasuni Ishara Ranasinghe**
*University of Melbourne, Australia*

## ABSTRACT

*Most of the existing discussions of the nuclear ambitions of states have neglected hidden ideational factors of nuclearisation. This chapter attempts to fill this gap by analyzing prevailing literature on the Indo-Pakistan nuclear rivalry. India and Pakistan have had a history of conflict with each other since the partition in 1947. The conflict is based on divisions of two religious groups, Hindus and Muslims, and extended to an identity crisis which later turned to a bilateral conflict between two nations. The nuclear test in 1974 diverted the conflict into a novel dimension. The study conceptualizes the factors of nuclear ambitions (material and ideational) of two nations using the model of the iceberg. A constructive psychological theory to analyze the moral orders of social actions and duties of participants to act in certain issues is given. Constructivism is used as the foundation of the proposed ideational framework.*

## 1. INTRODUCTION

The world experienced the deadliness of nuclear weapons at the end of World War II, after the two nuclear attacks on Japan; one in Nagasaki and the other in Hiroshima.

DOI: 10.4018/978-1-7998-7904-6.ch007

In the post-World War II period, the nuclear accidents at Chernobyl and Fukushima gave sufficient experience for mankind about its deadliness. Therefore, most of the countries with nuclear power ratified various treaties against using nuclear as a military power (United Nations, 2020). For that matter, India and Pakistan are not exceptions. They developed nuclear weapons and then signed such treaties.

However, the danger of the possession of nuclear power with India and Pakistan emerged with numerous tensions between the two nations, and on some occasions, they also threaten their rivals with nuclear attacks if the war continues. The Kargil War in 1998, the border confrontations in 2001 - 2002, the Mumbai attack in 2008, the Uri army camp attack in 2016, and then again the 2019 attack on Indian CRPF personnel were the major incidents that took place between two Asian nuclear powers.

India has conducted a series of nuclear tests in 1998 by mentioning the purpose of the development of science, technology, and energy. Meantime they accused Pakistan of developing nuclear missiles to challenge their sovereignty and integrity. "One or two intelligence reports indicating that Pakistan Army personnel were noticed cleaning up artillery deployment areas and missile launch sites at the Tilla Ranges… we considered it prudent to take some protective measures some of our missile assets were dispersed and relocated" (Malik, 2006, pp. 259-260). In return, Pakistan's Foreign Secretary, Shamshad Ahmed stated that Pakistan does not hesitate to use any weapon to defend the territorial integrity of the state. Shared "enemy feeling" since the partition, has heightened the tension and caused both parties to experience periodic cuts of economic and military aids. However, with the international condemnation, both were obliged to sign the Treaty of Non-nuclear aggression in December 1988. "India and Pakistan do not play their dangerous nuclear game on another planet; they are affected by changes in the international social and normative environments. The Indo –Pakistani nuclear competition is not an immutable fact of international politics because both countries are vulnerable to external normative constraints..." (Carranza, 2016, p. 17). With respect to the concerns of the international community, as mentioned in India-Pakistan Non-Attack Agreement in 1988 both agreed to refrain from undertaking or participating in any activity (direct or indirect) which caused damages to any nuclear installation in each nation and also contracted to share information of the latitude and longitude of its nuclear installations and facilities if there is any change.

However, it is questing whether materialistic solutions (treaties and discussions) could prevent the nuclear war between these two nations so far. "Because with the NPT's newfound permanence, India wanted to test before the CTBT gathered too much momentum. In other words, Indian policymakers did not want to wait until they were clear norm violators: It is better to break the rule while it is still informal rather than formalized" (Rublee, 2017, p. 484). The ideational ambitions of stakeholders (elites, commoners, global and regional actors, etc.) are challenging the practicality of material solutions. Unfortunately, the ideational ambitions are not visible and covered by the layer of social norms, national interest, and domestic and international political interests, etc. Thus, the iceberg of the nuclear conflict between India and Pakistan will examine to fill the gap of literature on nuclear ambitions. The positioning theory is the bridge connecting the two layers of the iceberg, the upper layer of the iceberg represents the material ambitions and the latter part is the ideational ambitions. Five cases including the Kargil war, attacks on the Indian Parliament, Mumbai, Uri, and Indian CRPF personnel would lay the foundation for this extensive discussion. The mixed analytical model will be used to understand the psychological motives of the nuclear ambitions of the two states. The analysis explores the attitude of leadership, national identity issue, and perception of all stakeholders (leaders, the general public of India and Pakistan, and leaders from other related nations). Finally, the article would introduce an ideational framework to address the psychological motives of the conflict. The ideational framework consists of five (5) steps. Identification of issues is the first step which is called an exploration stage. Secondly, the proliferation mentality will be humiliated. Consequently, norm diffusion will be done. Then the transforming stage was letting two nations identify the drawbacks of harmful nuclear implementations, and finally the acceptance of two countries.

## 2. BACKGROUND

### a. Theoretical Background

In order to explore the nuclearization of the South Asian sub-region, three independently developed yet interrelated theoretical frameworks are used.

The key features of the iceberg theory are that only some symptoms of a bigger problem appear first. It is like a "tip of an iceberg". When this theory is applied to nuclearization, it is understood that what we noticed in the present discourse is a tiny element of a bigger issue for the world; the threat of nuclearization. There are many hidden dimensions of the issue. Therefore, the iceberg theory suggests exploring the entire story before drawing any conclusion or policy recommendation on it. According to this theory, most of the moral-based remedies for nuclearization such as signing treaties, etc. may use with limited use, but definitely not a complete solution. The reality of this hypothesis can be judged by observing the trends of nuclearization. Although the entire world is against the production of nuclear weapons, North Korea has tested a nuclear bomb in the recent past. No one can judge which country will be the next nuclear country.

One of the key implications of the iceberg theory on nuclearization is that it has several dimensions. One of the key dimensions is psychological factors. It is argued that the psychological states of leaders, as well as the socio-psychological factors (fear of the society), generate a politically conducive environment for national leaders to continue investing in nuclear weapon productions. Following aggressive reaction by Pakistan leader Zulfikar Ali Bhutto against the Indian nuclear experiment in the Pokhran test range is a clear example of it. "…if India makes the bomb, we will eat grass or leaves, even go hungry, but we will get one of our own…" (Khan & Khan, 2018) (NTI Nuclear Security Index, 2019).

The psychological factors in nuclear proliferation have been reviewed by Hymans (2006). Lantis (2006) is an excellent review of Hymans (2006). According to the review, the psychology of nuclear elites is about the "national identity conception" where Hymans (2006) has identified four types of national identities. This classification has identified four types of nationalist psychologies; Sportmanlike Nationalists, Sportsmanlike Subalterns, Oppositional Nationalists, and Oppositional Subalterns.

Hymans (2006) has conducted several country studies. His interpretation of Indian investments in nuclear weapons development is based on his own classification of Indian leadership as "Oppositional Nationalists". According to Hymans (2006), it was Prime Minister Atal Bihar Vajpayee who directed India for developing nuclear weapons.

In summing up the review of Hymans' book, Lantis (2006) proposes a "further development" of Hymans' theory of nuclear psychology to incorporate "cultural orientation" of the national politics. Hymans (2006) differentiates the two as the national identity as "individual perception" and cultural orientation as a group consensus.

Another dimension that researchers may focus on is the "gender-lens" on nuclearization. Using the positioning theory, it is also interesting to explore the nuclearization of India from a gendered perspective. At the outset, the social researcher would like to question whether gender has anything to do with the nuclearization of India and Pakistan.

There are two broader approaches to explore the "role of gender" in the nuclearization of India and Pakistan. In one extreme, positioning theory [See *inter alia* Harre (2012)] suggests that the role and duties of women.

The iceberg module will be used to illustrate the motives of the Indo-Pakistan nuclear conflict. Material motives/factors such as treaties, laws, nuclear tests, etc are visible and demonstrated in the upper portion of the iceberg. Ideational or psychological motives are invisible to society and pictured in the latter slice of the iceberg. The top-down approach is adopted to evaluate the iceberg. According to the mainstream literature, material factors have been mostly addressed. Thus, evaluate the latter portion of the iceberg (hidden stories) is the main motivation of the article.

*Figure 1. Iceberg of the nuclear rivalry*

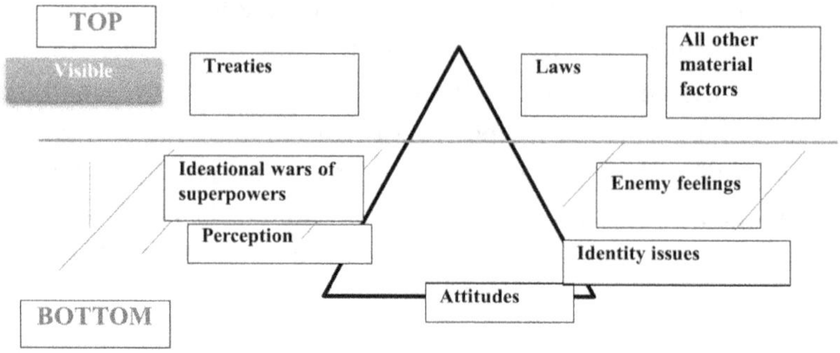


## b. Theoretical Approach

This study will focus on "Positioning Theory", social psychological theory, to understand the motives of two nuclear rivalries. The theory would analyze the social interactions of social groups, nations as well as institutions. As explained in the theory all interactions depend on the following three aspects: storyline, the social force of acts or speech, and position (Hirvonen, 2016). ***The storyline*** is described as the background of the particular issue or a group or nation and including ongoing interactions of the participants. ***The social force of act*** or speech refers to the social consequences of social activities or interactions. ***The position*** represented the moral aspects of those interactions (Van Langenhove and Harré, 1999). The extended constructivist approach would use for further analysis and develop the ideational framework to solve the nuclear dilemma. The constructivist approach was used mainly due to three features of the conflict: (1) two countries have already broken the trust of international society, (2) domestic opinion *"enemy feeling"* and political pressure of lobby groups owing to the hatred (3) Identity-based nature of the conflict (Carranza, 2016) (Rublee, 2017).

## c. Analysis

The positioning theory in line with constructivism is the basis of the analysis of the paper. The complete picture of the iceberg would analyze using the top-down approach. The storyline would reveal the material motives of the nuclear rivalry of two nations. The background of the journey of the nuclear proliferation of both nations and the role of stakeholders is discussed in the **"Story Line"**. The domestic and international political pressure from stakeholders is covered in the "**Social Force of Act".** The psychological motives of the conflict are analyzed under "**the position".**

## i. Storyline- Nuclear Proliferation

The nuclear journey of South Asia began with the studies of scientists and security strategists of Islamabad and New Delhi about atomic bombs in the 1950s. Global developments have influenced Prime Minister Nehru to focus on India's nuclear infrastructure which he broadly discussed in his four years plan (Ganguly, 1999). Parallel, India's defeat over China in 1962, China's first nuclear weapon test in 1964, and the blessings of non-regional actors received by Pakistan during the combats in 1947, 1965, and 1971 were motivated India to conduct a "peaceful" nuclear test in 1974 (Dalton & Perkovich, 2016). However, India never attempts to exercise nuclear weapons against any of its' neighbors until the mid-1980s. Afterward, the two nations continued with nuclear explorations in non-peaceful means. "Despite the tests, the two countries fought a short war in 1999 and came close to fighting a second war in 2002" (Joeck, 2008, p. 2) Consequently, the concept of nuclear energy has deviated to nuclear weapon productions. "The deteriorating relations between India and Pakistan after the 1971 war and the growing threat posed by a nuclear Pakistan, renewed India's resolve to continue its nuclear program designed to make nuclear weapons" (Jauhari, 2013, p. 44).

The nuclear weaponry program of Pakistan was initiated since the partition in 1947 and which was further promoted the defeat of the 1971 war against India that lead to the creation of Bangladesh. Subsequently, nuclear weapons became a way to deter future wars with its' neighbors. "Strictly speaking, Pakistan can be regarded as a proliferating country, particularly with regard to former activities of the Abdul Kader Khan network, but it can be observed that Islamabad's non-conventional effort, i.e. nuclear and ballistic, seems to be primarily aimed at national protection." (Foundation of Strategic Research, 2016, p. 10).

Islamabad managed to develop its weaponry with technological and equipment aids from some foreign nations, several from China. As stated by Senator S Brown USA, "China crossed limits of responsible behavior by supplying magnetic rings, other critical technologies to Pakistan... India faced a nuclear-capable Pakistan controlled by dictators with monkey mentality or unproductive and supported by equally unreliable China..." (Singh, 2012, p. 60). In the beginning, China has supplied the complete design of an atom bomb with uranium for another two bombs to Pakistan. Lately, M 11 missiles and further China has trained Pakistani scientists in the purification of uranium and Titanium gas for another 10 bombs (Singh, 2012). Subsequently, Pakistan has affiliated with North Korea in search of missile technology, presumably with the help of China.

However, Islamabad succeeded to develop both short-range (SRBMs) and strategic ballistic missiles (MRBMs) to counter the perceived threat from India. Nasr (Possibly Nuclear- 70 km), Abdali (Conventional- 180 km), Ghaznavi (Conventional-290 km) and Shaheen-1 (Conventional 600 km) are the exposed SRBMs. "Beside Nasr, Ghaznavi and Shaheen-1 are also offering some capacities to maneuver. Given its degree of technical difficulty, this particular capability could result from active collaboration with some more advanced actors or States" (Foundation of Strategic Research, 2016, p. 11). Strategic Missiles have developed to counterbalance the threats coming from India. Ghauri-1 (Conventional- 1200 km), Ghauri- 2 (Nuclear- 1200 km), and Shaheen-2 (Nuclear – 2200 km) are presently identified MRBMs in Pakistan territory. Apart Nodong strategic missile is acquired from North Korea to use under Ghauri designation. "Two versions are supposed to exist, one with conventional missions (probably with rather poor military efficiency due to lack of precision), and the other with nuclear missions. Ghauri being the workhorse of Pakistani deterrence, it is interesting to quote that it uses liquid propellants. Such constraints pose a problem regarding "pre-launch" operations due to the complexity of filling and preparation" (Foundation of Strategic Research, 2016, p. 11). Prithvi-1 (Conventional-150 Km), Prithvi-2 (Conventional-250 Km), Prithvi-3 (Unknown), and Agni-1 (Nuclear- 800km) are the short-range missiles belongs to India. Longer range BMs are: Agni-2 (Nuclear-2000 km), Agni -3 (Nuclear- 3500 km), Agni- 4 (Nuclear- 3000 km) and Agni 5- (Nuclear- 5000 to 5500 km). However, currently India access space with indigenous SLVs (LEO, SSO, and GEO). As explained in the Foundation of Strategic Research (2016) their satellites were developed with different capacities.

## ii. Social Force of Act

All five attacks including the Kashmir war have (directly or indirectly) threatened the sovereignty, peace, stability, and integrity of both states. The bomb lobby groups consist of powerful political, and religious elites, members of different religious and ethnic groups, and also other state and non-state actors amplified the nuclear ambitions. "This can be in the form of domestic elites who tangle with opponents, non-governmental organizations which influence elite opinion through the media, and mass movements that take to the street..." (Rublee, 2017, p. 484).

Carranza (2016) pointed out the absence of strong domestic opponents or alternative voices as the fundamentals for South Asia to be pronuclear. Further, he argued that elites in domestic lobby groups have a vested interest in continuing rather than ending the lethal conflict. "The nuclear hawks in each country do want to keep the nuclear competition 'frozen' in time and space" (p. 2). The opposition leaders of India have pressurized the ruling party to accept the failure of securing the borders and innocent civilians after every attack. Especially, after surgical sticks lobby groups of India have pressured the governing party for a military raid to punch Pakistan. Also, throughout the decades' politicians from rival states have exploited the frustration among victims by making undesirable promises in their campaigns "Amit Shah promised during the 2014 national election campaign that there would be no such intrusion under a BJP government…" (Sasikumar, 2019, p. 164). The desires of military leaders have further strengthened nuclear ambitions while the media profited by inflaming the sentiments of citizens.

The shadow of Islam heightens the danger of nuclearizing. The creation of Pakistan was Jinnah's contention that Muslims in undivided India require a separate nation and meanwhile separated Pakistan was declared as a "Muslim Nation". Islamabad managed to collaborate with Arab and other Muslim nations and became a member of the "Organization of Islamic countries" (OIC). However, Pakistan manages to use the OIC as an international lobby group to pressurize India about Kashmir. "Pakistan's concerted, over six decades-long anti-India in the OIC- and also outside, created substantial anti-India misunderstandings in the Muslim world..." (Singh, 2012, p. xxvii). Madrasas were radicalized with the funding of Muslim countries such as Saudi Arabia and Emirates. Eventually, Pakistan has converted to the breeding ground of Islamic fundamentalists in South Asia. Arms and finance from mentioned sources brought up international Islamic extremists' groups into the Indo-Pakistan nuclear emergence. The gold and narcotic smugglers converted to the ISIS members and later on the greed of money and Islamic doctrinarians got suppressed minorities in India as agents of sleeper cells to become active whenever signals came.

USA, China, and the Soviet Union were the main stakeholders of the nuclearization of the Indo-Pakistan conflict. In the beginning, the USA and China were backing Pakistan while the Soviet Union was with India. The USA withdrew its investments in the Bokaro steel plant by accusing India of the communist camp. Russia grabbed the opportunity. Indians were disappointed and doubted whether the USA backing the anti-Indian sentiments in Pakistan. As Singh (2012) explains, "Nehru had expressed his disappointment to Ambassador George Allen saying that he was not worried about the US motives but the internal feelings of Indians that were hurt and the boost that it would give to anti- Indian sentiments in Pakistan" (p. 60). India had to experience the nuclear capabilities of Pakistan, controlled and backed by "Monkey Mentality" United States and unreliable China. The USA turned a blind eye on the ganging up of Pakistan and China against India. Western powers treated Pakistan as the "favorite Child" while controlling supplies of critical equipment for nuclear proliferation in India. In the beginning, China has supplied magnetic rings, other critical technologies to Pakistan, and later M11 missiles, complete design of atom bombs and uranium for two bombs. Further, Pakistani scientists and technologists were trained on the purification of uranium and gifted Titanium gas for ten bombs. Later on, Pakistan has established its military affairs with North Korea with the help of China in search of missile technology.

However, India's refusal of ratifying the "Nuclear Non-Proliferation Treaty" (NPT) was considered seriously by the USA while not even questing Pakistan's denial of the inspection of its atomic plants by "International Atomic Energy Commission" (IAEA). "Since India does not plan to deviate from its principled approach towards the NPT and CTBT, the shadow of Western powers on the Indo-Pak relations shall continue to cast its influence in showing India as an obdurate and non-cooperative entity" (Singh, 2012, p. 64). USA- NATO and Afghanistan relations was given huge financial and military assistance to Pakistan as a cost of compensation for assisting the NATO. The military assistance included missiles and fighter planes. However, soon after 9/11, the US announced the "war against terror" and the "good Taliban" changed to the "evil Taliban". US perception of Indo-Pakistan nuclear relations has changed with the 9/11 attack and also with the economic growth of India as an emerging power. "At the same time, the US has shown in several dramatic steps that it is deeply unsatisfied with Pakistan's effects to stop the Afghan Taliban operating out of Pakistan. Last month it used a drone in Baluchistan province to kill Mullah Akthar Mansor, the Taliban leader, which led to Pakistan accusing the US of violating its sovereignty..." (Rashid, 2016). The 48 nation Nuclear Suppliers Group (NSG) was a battleground for India and Pakistan again on nuclear. After the USA visit of Indian Prime Minister Narendra Modi, Washington has manipulated all member countries and lobby groups to reserve a seat for India in NSG. Pakistan requested the same and but the request was denied by mentioning their records are not good as India. The Pakistanis are angry and asked China to veto the Indian bid. However, like the rest of the small countries complained neither India nor Pakistan can become members until they sign the nuclear nonproliferation treaty (NPT). Carranza (2018) argues that the USA is not only interested in nuclear weapons in South Asia, but indeed the Kashmir as well. That's because Kashmir is a breeding ground for regional also for international terrorism. Thus, continuous observations, engagements, and interventions of state and non-state actors on the Indo-Pakistan nuclear diplomacy will be experienced. The outcomes will further heighten the butanes of the conflict.

## iii. Positioning- Historical "Enemy Feeling" and "National Identity"?

The "enemy feeling" or "mutual distrust" is an outcome of colonization. The "Divide and Rule" colonial principle pitted the Muslims against Hindus. The growth of Muslim nationalism "Islam being danger" in Hindu dominating society has caused Islamic believers to demand a separate territory for them (Ganguly, 1986). An attempt by the Indian nationalist party of "Secular Indian nationalism" was failed and at the time of independence, old India has divided into two states. Hindu dominating India and Islamic Pakistan. British has drawn the Radcliffe Line on 17th August

1947 and since then officially India has divided with international borders. Further, the ideological and personality clashes between the two leaders had worsened the conflict (Cohen, 2002).

Seeded "enemy feelings" during British rule have continued till today. Meanwhile, the ideological-oriented conflict has converted to the "national identity conflict" between two nations over Jammu and Kashmir. The issue became crucial with the decision of the ruler of Kashmir, who was a Hindu believer. He signed the "instrument of accession" by expressing his will to be a part of India while the majority of the population of Kashmir was Muslim. However, Pakistan denies the accession and claimed that the will of the people was ignored when signing the accession agreement. Hatred has been planted in people's hearts which resulted in a war between India and Pakistan since 1947. "Pakistan may not have planned the raid, but supported it when the Pathans took up the Jihadi challenge. Between October 22 and 27, many thousands of Pathan mujahidin -some estimates go as high as 10,000 -murdered, raped, burnt and looted their way down the road from Muzaffarabad to Baramulla in the name of Allah and the newly emerged Muslim state of Pakistan" (Stenhouse, 2010). Then the war of 1965 which was also based on Jammu and Kashmir ended in an UN-mandated ceasefire. This is a seventeen days war but marked thousands of casualties and witness the largest engagement of armored vehicles after WW II (Higgins, 2016). The war of 1971 was another vital combat that happened between the two nations. The result of the combat was the division of West and East Pakistan and India plotted to separate East Pakistan as Bangladesh.

The Kargil war, 1988, was vital for both nations. Hatred of splitting the nation into two and challenging the integrity and sovereign rights of Pakistan was deep-rooted and resulted in continual tests of nuclear missiles. "In 1988, India and Pakistan conducted a series of nuclear tests, making evident to the world and each other that they had robust weapons capabilities" (Joeck, 2008, p. 2). Two nations entered the Kargil dispute as nuclear-powered nations. During the crisis, both parties announced nuclear threats. Pakistan was suspected of using Nuclear weapons (Malik, 2006).

Further, Robert Gates, the national security assistant to President Bush has claimed in his essay on "On the Nuclear Edge" to The New Yorker, March 29, 1993, that USA satellites identified heavy-armed trucks moving from Kahuta to Chaklala airport and further the F 16 with nuclear-capable bomb racks stood ready on the runway (Hersh, 1993). But, after three years of the tragedy, he denied the statement. The USA intervention has amplified the conflict. India has moved some missiles and conveyed the message of India's readiness for a counter-nuclear strike. However, Indians manage to handle the crisis and were praised by the United States as a "mature country". Pakistan's miscalculation on international reactions led Kargil into a tragic defeat.

The "mutual mistrust" between the two nations had evoked again with the futile terrorist attack to storm the Indian Parliament on 13th December 2001. "The actual Indo-Pakistan crisis began on December 13, 2001, when terrorists attacked India's parliament building, killing several guards but failing in their larger ambition of capturing and assassinating senior members of the Indian government..." (Joeck, 2008, p. 12). India accused the group of Jaish-e- Mohammed of carrying out the attack and believed that terrorists had been supported and directed by Pakistan. India demanded the extradition of several felons residing in Pakistan and the demand was backed up by deploying approximately half a million Indian troops to the international border for several months (ABC, 2020) (BBC, 2019). Abhorrence was further inflamed by the assault of the Indian military camp at Kaluchak in May 2002 which callously slain the families of military personnel (Sasikumar, 2019). Meanwhile, the general public pressurized the government of India to pursue a military attack against Pakistan. "Nuclear blackmailing" was visible in the ground. The head of Pakistan Strategic Plans Division, Khalid Kidwai, outlined four red lines that may provoke Pakistan to use nuclear weapons in his interview with two Italian scholars in January 2002. "They broadly repeated the two red lines Shashi, Sattar and khan had identified but added two more… in addition to the territorial and communications red lines, if India were to destroy a large part of Pakistan's land or air forces or destabilize Pakistan politically, Pakistan would be prepared to use its nuclear weapons..." (Joeck, 2008, p. 15). The Prime Minister of India, Vajpayee declared a defensive battle against terrorism on May 22, 2002 "the time has come for a decisive battle and we will have a sure victory in this battle..." (Sasikumar, 2019) (Chaudhury, 2004). However, Pakistan perceived the statement as threatening.

Islamic group Lahkar-e-Taiba which was banned by the Pakistan government in 2002 launched a series of coordinated shootings and bombing attacks from Karachi targeting public areas frequented by tourists such as hospitals, railway stations, and historical and religious sites across India's largest city Mumbai. Over 160 innocents were killed during the assaults. Tensions between the two nations were heightened with India's claim of Pakistan hand over the assailants while Karachi denied it. "The world feared that the Manmohan Singh government in New Delhi- a few months away from a tough general election- would retaliate with military action that could escalate to nuclear war…." (Sasikumar, 2019, p. 159). During the tense period, India has called some military personnel, former government servants, and media pundits to conduct *"limited military strikes"* across the Line of Control (Raghavan & Chaudhuri, 2008). India accused the possibility of disproportionate responses of Karachi including nuclear weapons if any chance of military actions. However, insurgences defused with the diplomatic mediations of the United States, China, and Saudi Arabia (Jauhari, 2013) (Joeck, 2008) (Nayak & Krepon, 2012) (Singh, 2012).

The hatred has evoked again with the attack on 18th September 2016 targeting the Indian army camp in Uri which is a garrison town close to the Line of Control. The terrorists killed 19 Indian soldiers and the Indian government claimed the militants who carried out the attack were bearing Pakistani identity (hindustantimes, 2016). Also, initially, New Delhi accused the Pakistan-based terrorist organization *"Jaish-e-Mohammad"* (JeM), and lately "Lashkar-e-Taiba" another Pakistan-founded group was identified for carrying out the attack. However, after ten days of the Uri attacks, India conducted simultaneous raids targeting *"launch pads"* or terrorist camps located in Jammu and Kashmir by crossing the LoC. As mentioned in Hindustan times (2016) "… Based on very credible and specific information which we received yesterday that some terrorist teams had positioned themselves at launchpads along the Line of Control with an aim to carry out infiltration and terrorist strikes in Jammu and Kashmir and various other metros in our country, the Indian army conducted surgical strikes last night at these launch pads….". However, Pakistan denied India's report of "surgical strikes" and conveyed that Indian troops had never crossed the LoC but had only skirmished with Pakistani militaries at the border. Further, Karachi refused India's report on casualties. "it is estimated that 70-80 men (both uniformed personnel and other not in uniform) were killed in these raids..." (Sasikumar, 2019, p. 160). However, two nations continued to exchange fire along the LoC in Jammu and Kashmir throughout the years (2016-2018) and which resulted in dozens of casualties on both sides.

India and Pakistan standoff has called again with the 14th February 2019 suicide attack on a convoy of India's Central Reserve Police Force (CRPF). "at least 40 CRPF personnel were killed on Thursday in one of the deadliest terror attacks in Jammu and Kashmir when a Jaish suicide bomber rammed a vehicle carrying over 100 kg of explosives into their bus in Pulwama district that also left many critical wounded, officials said…" (The Times of India, 2019). Condemning the terror attack, Prime Minister Narendra Modi said that "attack on CRPF personnel in Pulwama is despicable. I strongly condemn this dastardly attack. The scarifies of our brave security personnel shall not go in vain…" (Modi, 2019). Indian jets crossed the international borders to bomb and destroy the biggest training camp of "Jaish-e-Mohammad" (JeM) in Balakot Pakistan which was about 80 km from the LoC. After the incident, the army spokesman Major General Asif Ghafoor verified that the Prime Minister of Pakistan, Imran Khan has told his army and people to get ready for any eventuality and "now it is time for India to wait for our response. We have decided. Wait for it..." (Outlook Web Bureau, 2019). The nuclear threat was grounded with the wreckage of Indian aircraft fallen in Pakistan administrated Kashmir and while others in Indian administrated Kashmir (BBC, 2019). However, Pakistan denied India's claim of "one of its fighter pilots shot down a Pakistani F 16 fighter jet in an aerial battle between the two nuclear power..." (Seligman, 2019).

Islamabad managed to prove the fact by inviting US personnel to count F 16 and they found non-missing (Lalwani & Tallo, 2019).

## d. The Mindsets of Leaders

The human way of responding to threats, personally or collectively, may be evolved with their culture and experiences. Violence is acceptable and constant. In such a situation, the responses of both leaders and commoners are in the same equation at different levels. The historical "enemy feelings" planted with the partition, brutal three wars in 1947, 1965, and 1971 between two nations, insurgencies in Jammu and Kashmir, 2001-2002 standoff, 2008 Mumbai attack, 2016-2018 border skirmishes,2019 suicide attack on a convoy of India's CRPF and the historic cold war between Muslim and Hindu communities stimulated violent based responses continuously. Defeat and misery of the enemy, the neighbor, considered as the victory. President Ghulam Ishaq Khan and General Aslam Beg, one of them said to Robert Gates, the national security assistant to President Bush during his visit to Islamabad to defuse the Kashmir crisis "we are desperate enough to blow India to smithereens" (Hersh, 1993). The psyche of the leaders of the two nations was the foundation of the crisis; the arms race along with the development of military capacity has further strengthened this culture. Nuclear power has heightened the misfortune. Personality crashes, negative images of each other, and trust deficit created a huge vacuum between two social groups which resulted in the partition of India. "… the greed or personal shortsightedness of leaders on both sides of the border—in particular, Nehru's romance with Kashmir and his Brahminical arrogance (the Pakistani interpretation), or Mohammed Ali Jinnah's vanity, shortsightedness, and religious zeal (the Indian interpretation.)" (Cohen, 2002, p. 33). Consequently, Pakistan elites accused Indian leaders of threats to the existence of Pakistan. "From the very first day of independence, India has made a concerted attempt to crush the Pakistan state" (Cohen, 2013). Thus, the dominant elites in Islamabad presumed India as the only enemy "India is our enemy number one. There is no other threat to us" (Singh, 2012, p. 15). Thus as declared by General Khalid Kidwai, head of the strategic plan division Pakistan in his interview to an Italian NGO in 2002, that scenarios of Pakistan's nuclear use have been directly focusing on India "In case that deterrence fails (nuclear weapons) will be used if: (a) India attacks Pakistan and conquers a large part of its territory, (space threshold) (b) India destroy a large part of either its land or air force (military threshold)" (Lavoy, 2007). Eventually, Pakistan has developed a peculiar "anti-India mindset" vis-a-vis in India, which turned them to worrying about insignificant incidents into a "core one" at drop of a hat, without inquiring the reality.

The Indian leaders presumed that Pakistan has intents to insecure India and destroy the image of "Mahabharata" "they seem to have read a lot of our 'Mahabharata' and usurped the methodologies of Duryodhana and Sakuni in a monopolistically strange manner." (Singh., 2012, p. 2). Both fought three wars and experienced several standoffs and attacks throughout the preceding decades but still the culture of censuring each other entertains. Thus, the two nations continuously failed in addressing internal turbulence and terrorism. US President Barack Obama in his initial period of the presidency has been stressing to Pakistan that they should be more concerned on homegrown terrorist groups rather than India further Obama has reminded the same in Karzai joint press conference in 2010 "Cancer of terror, not India, a threat to Pakistan" (The Hindu, 2010). The psyche has fueled the fertile grounds of nuclear combats. The inherent danger of leaders seized and turning them into self-centric autocrats who ready to use nuclear weapons for survival. "So far, they have only learnt to love bombs..." (Rublee, 2017, p. 485). To begin with, since May 1998 nuclear tests, two nations have faced enormous difficulties to stabilize the bilateral relations. Narang security specialist has used the term "deep instability" to characterize post-test relations of two nations (Carranza, 2018). The Kargil war had brought two nations near to nuclear warfare and respectively the other mentioned insurgencies. But, luckily, none of them has used nuclear armaments and they practiced only "nuclear blackmanship" to make evident each other's capacities and prestige (Joeck, 2009).

Pakistan's foreign secretary, Shamshad Ahmed threaten nuclear use "We will not hesitate to use any weapon on our arsenal to defend our territorial integrity" (Ahmad, 1999) and India took the threat seriously and activated three types of nuclear delivery vehicles just to deliver the message of their readiness (Carranza, 2018). However, the statement of Indian former Prime Minister Vajpayee given to Kapur in 2006 "we never thought atomic weapons would be used, even if we had decided to cross the LoC", (Kapur, 2009, p. 396), verified that leadership of India had never wanted to use nuclear weapons in the Kargil same as their prejudice of not concerning Pakistani's nuclear capacity seriously. But Several security analysts argued that the two countries survived the Kargil war without a nuclear confrontation because none of them was aware of the capacities of each other. The possibility of nuclear attack, survival, and continuation afterward might terrify the elites of the two camps.

Democratic leadership of India with the attitude of civilian controls the military made the nuclear as a political weapon to blackmail the enemy "nuclear weapons are political weapons and will not be used in war-fighting" (Sood & Sawhney, 2003, p. 143) and further the "no first use" policy (Dalton & Perkovich, 2016) which remains strong among Indian politicians and strategists had counterbalanced the Pakistan "anti-Indian mindset" throughout the decades. The militant attitude of Pakistani' leaders, even though the country is in a democratic process, has heightened the nuclear tension since today. Pakistani journalist Ahmed Rashid wrote to The Washington Post in 2010 "Pakistan's military has virtually taken control of foreign policy and strategic decision making from civilian government… thus Pakistan's foreign policy reflects the military's obsession with India..." (Rashid, 2010).

The political and religious extremists in both countries had used fundamentalism and terrorism to maintain nuclear tension "they carelessly talk of destroying Mumbai and New Delhi to the ground or talking so-called Pakistan occupied Kashmir by force of arms, unmindful of the devastating effects on their population in the event of a nuclear exchange. They are ready to pay whatever price is needed to protect and promote their objectives. Religious animosity and the hysteria that can be built up around it have often resulted in irrational behavior by the extremists in both countries" (The News, 1998). The historical Hindu-Muslim hatred, unfortunately, continues in the minds of religious fundamentalists on both sides. Demolish of the historic Babari Mosque in Ajodhya by BJP wounded the hearts of the Muslim community which was carried by leaders motivated by narrow self-interest. The religious leaders in Pakistan use Islam as "national glue" and Islam has been employed as "the national doctrine" (Singh, 2012). According to the Rashtriya Sevak Sangh (RSS) in India, the possible solution for the tension is "dropping of nuclear bombs over Pakistan is a solution to the longstanding Pakistani hospitality and belligerence against India" (The Panchajanya, 1999). Lately, even the Pakistan Prime Minister Mr. Imran Khan "Demanded the international community take action, accusing Modi of an anti-Muslim agenda..." (New Straits Times, 2019). The terror attacks on the Indian Parliament in 2001, the Mumbai attack in 2008, Uri army camp and suicide attack on a convoy of India's CRPF further made evident the psyche of the elites (both civil and religious), entertaining the fundamentalists and terrorists. During the border standoff in 2001, India demanded the identified terrorists from Pakistan by issuing threat signals. Islamabad denied the request by declaring its readiness for an atomic bomb attack assuming the sovereignty of the nation was threatened. Domination of a militant perspective even among democratic leadership has been visible in the case. However, the motives of Indian leaders as "responsible and matured nuclear nation" has exchanged the navigational coordinates of their nuclear installations and facilities with Islamabad respecting the 1998 agreement. In addition, India informed Pakistan in advance about the test of "Agni" in accordance with the Lahore Memorandum of Understanding in 1999 (Chaudhury, 2004). The practice of New Delhi leaders of "nuclear-matured nation" has continued even after the Mumbai terrorist attack in 2008. The retaliation proposal from Indian Air Force to bomb terrorist camps crossing LoC was rejected by the civilian authorities (Singh & Chaudhuri, 2011). "India put diplomatic pressure on Pakistan both directly, and through the United States, China and Saudi Arabia" (Sasikumar, 2019, p. 159). Even, in the Uri terror attack, Indian Prime Minister Narendra Modi has criticized the responses of Pakistan "Sacrifices of our 18 Jawans won't go in vain. We will isolate Pakistan in the world" (Nath, 2016) (Sharma, 2016) as the leader of a responsible nuclear nation. He further mentioned that instead of fighting each other "let both the countries fight to end poverty, unemployment, illiteracy and see who wins..." (Nath, 2016). He has further emphasized the same after the 2019 suicide attack on a convoy of CRPF.

## 3. THE MAIN FOCUS OF THE CHAPTER

### a. Ideational Framework

It is a universal truth that can only come if the cause of conflict is removed. Indo Pakistan nuclear conflict requires a sustainable solution where both countries meet their equilibriums. At the minimum, prevision from nuclear war is essential. As the psychological ambitions of two nations are the key causes, the approach of the framework of non-proliferation should be ideational. The proposing framework consists of five steps. ***Identification or exploration*** of issues is the first stage. Secondly, ***the mentality of proliferation is humiliated***. Thirdly, ***norm diffusion*** and then the ***transformation stage***. Finally, ***acceptance*** and implementation.

As the first step, **identification** is essential to understand the gravity of the conflict. For that two nations should not be either friends or enemies, but cooperation and tolerance are compulsory. Continues bilateral strategic dialogues will provide a platform to gain a greater mutual understanding. The material and psychological ambitions of nuclear rivalry should elaborately discuss. Information sharing is mandatory to build confidence amongst the main stakeholders. Especially, the historical psychological battle "enemy feelings" should opening bring in to the table. Two countries should encourage to see arms rising as a vital threat to their own national security. The process of US and Soviet Union used after the 1962 Cuban missile crisis could implement. However, the discussions should be constructive and help India and Pakistan to build greater confidence about the non-proliferation framework while trusting the counterpart. Also, the issues should review from a regional angle rather than as individual nations. Participation of all eight South Asian members as mediators and victims must require.

**Humiliating the mentality of proliferation** is the second stage. After building confidence amongst the counterparts, identified ambitions modestly preview to understand the harmful ideologies. Optimistic ideologies must appreciate and encourage as "best practices". Passive causes such as "long term mutual distrust", "enemy feelings", and decisions of elites made with historical anger, religious fundamentalism, and unnecessary political pressure coming from lobby groups should be humiliated. Members of lobby groups mandatory to be part of the humiliation process.

**Norm diffusion** is the third stage of the framework. Humiliated customs and norms of the conflict must collectively diffuse. Ratifying Nuclear Non-Proliferation Treaty (NPT) is one way of rejecting those customs. Introducing peacebuilding programs or courses to the schools and university curriculums will be another successful model to eradicate the inherent angry feeling against each other. Recalling the experiences of nuclear explosions and World Wars can be a useful tool to discard the historic norms and customs on the nuclear proliferation of both nations.

**The transformation Stage** is the most vital step of the framework. After rejecting the customary beliefs, Pakistan and India should implement a proper mechanism to transfer their positions from the nuclear game. Nuclear should capable to use as a means of energy. Sharing technologies might enhance the bond of two nations as well it will ensure the security of the region. Viewpoints of individuals and groups should change and bomb lobby groups should voluntarily dismantle or participate in the non-proliferation process. The nuclear capacity of the two nations should be released and share the latitude of missiles and nuclear bombs amongst each other. Probably, the bilateral agreements on nuclear usage will prove the degree of transformation.

**Acceptance** is the final stage of the proposed solution. Two nations should individually accept their mistakes and best practices during the last decades of the conflict. Admission of guilt would heal the wounded hearts of victims of the ideological game. Proposing transformation methods should accept and implement by participating all stakeholders of the conflict. At the end of the process, each and every participant should ready to accept the guilt and the viewpoint of the conflict mandatory to transfer.

## 4. CONCLUSION

Aftermaths of the Kargil war, then-US president Bill Clinton announced South Asia as the most dangerous place on the earth. However, by analyzing five crises between India and Pakistan, the paper describes the material and ideational ambitions of the nuclear game of the two nations. The theory of iceberg used to analyze the nuclear ambitions and material factors reflect the visible portion of the iceberg while ideational factors are hidden. The positing theory has been used to understand the nuclear ambitions (both material and psychological) of these two countries. It is identified that the weight of the hidden ideational ambitions of the conflict is comparatively high. Thus, the solutions should address the phycology of the stakeholders. The ideational framework has introduced which consist of five stages: Identification, humiliation, diffusion, transformation, and acceptance.

## REFERENCES


ABC. (2020, June 20). *India seeks extradition of Mumbai attacks suspected mastermind Sajid Mir*. Retrieved from ABC News: https://www.abc.net.au/news/2020-06-29/india-seeks-extradition-of-suspected-mumbai-attacker-sajid-mir/12401608

Ahmad, K. (1999, July 3). *Kashmir horror insight*. Retrieved from The Lancet: https://www.thelancet.com/journals/lancet/article/PIIS0140-6736(05)75331-9/fulltext

BBC. (2019a, February 27). *India Pakistan: Kashmir fighting sees Indian aircraft downed*. Retrieved from BBC: News: https://www.bbc.com/news/world-asia-47383634

BBC. (2019b, February 14). *Kashmir attack: Bomb kills 40 Indian paramilitary police in convoy*. Retrieved from BBC News: India: https://www.bbc.com/news/world-asia-india-47240660

Carranza, M. E. (2016). *India-Pakistan nuclear diplomacy: constructivism and the prospects for nuclear arms control and disarmament in South Asia*. Rowman & Littlefield.

Carranza, M. E. (2018). Deterrence or taboo? Explaining the non-use of nuclear weapons during the Indo-Pakistani posttests nuclear crises. *Contemporary Security Policy*, *39*(3), 441–463. doi:10.1080/13523260.2017.1418725

Chaudhury, R. R. (2004). *Nuclear Doctrine, Declaratory Policy, and Escalation Control*. Washington, DC: STIMSON. Retrieved from https://www.stimson.org/2004/nuclear-doctrine-declaratory-policy-and-escalation-control/

Cohen, S. P. (2002). India, Pakistan, and Kashmir. *The Journal of Strategic Studies*, *25*(4), 32–60. doi:10.1080/01402390412331302865

Cohen, S. P. (2002). India, Pakistan, and Kashmir. *Journal of Strategic Studies*, *25*(4), 32-60. Retrieved 0140-2390, from doi:10.1080/01402390412331302865

Cohen, S. P. (2013). *Shooting for a Century: The India-Pakistan Conundrum*. Brookings Institution Press.

Dalton, T., & Perkovich, G. (2016). *India's Nuclear Options and Escalation Dominance*. Carnegie Endowment for International Peace, Publications Department. Washington, DC: Carnegie Endowment for International Peace. Retrieved from https://calhoun.nps.edu/bitstream/handle/10945/48706/CP_273_India_Nuclear_Final.pdf?sequence=1&isAllowed=y

Foundation of Strategic Research. (2016). *Understanding The Ballistic Missile Proliferation: Issues Of Today, Challenges For Tomorrow*. Foundation of Strategic Research.

Ganguly, S. (1986). *The origins of war in South Asia: Indo-Pakistani conflicts since 1947*. Westview Press.

Ganguly, S. (1999). India's Pathway to Pokhran II: The Prospects and Sources of New Delhi's Nuclear. *International Security*, *23*(4), 148–177. doi:10.1162/isec.23.4.148

Gokhale, N. (2017). *Securing India the Modi Way: Pathankot, Surgical Strikes and More*. Bloomsbury India.

Hersh, S. M. (1993, March 22). *A Reporter at large*. Retrieved from The New Yorker: https://www.newyorker.com/magazine/1993/03/29/on-the-nuclear-edge

Higgins, D. R. (2016). *M48 Patton vs Centurion: Indo-Pakistani War 1965*. Osprey Publishing Ltd.

Hindustan Times. (2016, September 29). *India's surgical strikes across LoC: Full statement by DGMO Lt Gen Ranbir Singh*. Retrieved from Hindustan times: https://www.hindustantimes.com/india-news/india-s-surgical-strikes-across-loc-full-statement-by-dgmo-lt-gen-ranbir-singh/story-Q5yrp0gjvxKPGazDzAnVsM.html

India-Pakistan Non-Attack Agreement (1988).

Jauhari, A. (2013). India-Pakistan Relations: International Implications. *Asian Social Science*, *9*(1), 42–51. doi:10.5539/ass.v9n1p42

Joeck, N. (2008). *The Indo-Pakistani Nuclear Confrontation: Lessons From The Past, Contingencies For The Future*. Center for Global Security Research. Retrieved from http://www.npolicy.org/article_file/The_Indo-Pakistani_Nuclear_Confrontation.pdf

Joeck, N. (2009). The Kargil War and Nuclear Deterrence. In S. Ganguly & S. P. Kapur (Eds.), *Nuclear Proliferation in South Asia: Crisis Behaviour and the Bomb* (p. 251). Routledge.

Kapur, A. P. (2009). South Asia's Unstable Nuclear Decade. *Strategic Analysis*, *33*(3), 393–403. doi:10.1080/09700160902790068

KhanM. A.KhanA. Q. (2018). Retrieved from https://www.atomicheritage.org/history/pakistani-nuclear-program

Lalwani, S., & Tallo, E. (2019, April 17). *Did India shoot down a Pakistani F-16 in February? This just became a big deal.* Retrieved from The Washington Post: https://www.washingtonpost.com/politics/2019/04/17/did-india-shoot-down-pakistani-f-back-february-this-just-became-big-deal/

Lantis, J. (2009). Strategic Culture and Tailored Deterrence: Bridging the Gap between Theory and Practice. *Contemporary Security Policy*, *30*(3), 467–485. doi:10.1080/13523260903326677

Lavoy, P. (2007). *Pakistan's Nuclear Posture: Security and Survivability.* Arlington: The Nonproliferation Policy Education Center (NPEC). Retrieved from http://npolicy.org/article.php?aid=291&tid=30

Malik, V. P. (2006). *Kargil from Surprise to Victory.* HarperCollins Publishers India, a joint venture with the India Today Group.

Modi, N. (2019, February 15). *@narendramodi*. Retrieved from Tweet: https://twitter.com/narendramodi/status/1096035566670565376?ref_src=twsrc%5Etfw%7Ctwcamp%5Etweetembed%7Ctwterm%5E1096035566670565376%7Ctwgr%5E&ref_url=https%3A%2F%2Fwww.india.com%2Fnews%2Fsacrifices-of-our-security-personnel-wont-go-in-vain-assures-prime-

Nath, J. A. (2016, September 24). *Prime Minister Narendra Modi Hits Out At Pakistan After Uri Terror Attack. The Top-10 Quotes.* Retrieved from News: https://www.indiatimes.com/news/india/prime-minister-narendra-modi-hits-out-at-pakistan-after-uri-terror-attack-the-top-10-quotes-262330.html

Nayak, P., & Krepon, M. (2012). *The Unfinished Crisis: US Crisis Management after the 2008 Mumbai Attacks*. The Henry L. Stimson Center. Retrieved from https://www.stimson.org/wp-content/files/file-attachments/Mumbai-Final_1_1.pdf

New Straits Times. (2019, August 8). *Pakistan to expel Indian envoy, suspend trade over Kashmir.* Retrieved August 11, 2020, from New Straits Times: https://www.nst.com.my/world/2019/08/510959/pakistan-expel-indian-envoy-suspend-trade-over-kashmir

Nuclear Security Index, N. T. I. (2011). *India-Pakistan Non-Attack Agreement.* Retrieved from https://www.nti.org/learn/treaties-and-regimes/india-pakistan-non-attack-agreement/

Nuclear Security Index, N. T. I. (2019, November). *Pakistan.* Retrieved from NTI Nuclear Security Index: https://www.nti.org/learn/countries/pakistan/nuclear/

Outlook Web Bureau. (2019, February 26). *Pakistan Army Confirms Indian Jets Dropped 'Four Bombs'.* Retrieved from Outlook: https://www.outlookindia.com/website/story/india-news-pakistan-army-confirms-indian-jets-dropped-four-bombs/326185

Raghavan, S., & Chaudhuri, R. (2008, December 30). *Unlimited damage.* Retrieved August from DNA: https://www.dnaindia.com/analysis/main-article-unlimited-damage-1217693

Rashid, A. (2010, April 27). *Afghan crunch time: Obama must decide whether to talk to the Taliban.* Retrieved from The Washington Post: https://www.washingtonpost.com/wp-dyn/content/article/2010/04/26/AR2010042603020.html

Rashid, A. (2016, June 14). *World Asia.* BBC News.

Rublee, M. R. (2017). India-Pakistan nuclear diplomacy: Constructivism and the prospects for nuclear arms control and disarmament in South Asia. *Contemporary Security Policy, 38*(3), 483–490. doi:10.1080/13523260.2017.1312075

Sasikumar, K. (2019). India-Pakistan Crises under the Nuclear Shadow: The Role of Reassurance. *Journal for Peace and Nuclear Disarmament*, 151-169. doi:10.1080/25751654.2019.1619229

Seligman, L. (2019, April 4). *Did India Shoot Down a Pakistani Jet? U.S. Count Says No.* Retrieved from Foreign Policy: https://foreignpolicy.com/2019/04/04/did-india-shoot-down-a-pakistani-jet-u-s-count-says-no/

Sharma, V. (2016, September 25). *Mann ki Baat on, to Pak.* Retrieved from The Tribune: https://www.tribuneindia.com/news/archive/nation/sacrifice-of-18-soldiers-won-t-go-in-vain-will-isolate-pak-pm-300160

Singh, R., & Chaudhuri, P. P. (2011, May 6). *Can India pull off a covert strike?* Retrieved from Hindustan Times: https://www.hindustantimes.com/delhi/can-india-pull-off-a-covert-strike/story-yeeFCRlawj1KUPugz6b05K.html

Singh, U. V. (2012). *Indo-Pak Relations Glamour, Drama or Diplomacy.* Pentagon Press.

Sood, V. K., & Sawhney, P. (2003). *Operation Parakram The War Unfinished.* SAGE Publications Pvt. Ltd.

The Hindu. (2010, May 13). *'Cancer' of terror, not India, a threat to Pakistan: Obama*. Retrieved from The Hindu: https://www.thehindu.com/news/international/lsquoCancer-of-terror-not-India-a-threat-to-Pakistan-Obama/article16300628.ece

The Times of India. (2019, February 16). *Jaish terrorists attack CRPF convoy in Kashmir, killing at least*. Retrieved from The Times of India: https://timesofindia.indiatimes.com/india/37-crpf-jawans-martyred-in-ied-blast-in-jks-pulwama/articleshow/67992189.cms

United Nations. (2020). *Office for Disarmament Affairs*. Retrieved from The United Nations: https://www.un.org/disarmament/wmd/nuclear/npt/

# Section 3

# Chapter 8
# Zipato:
## A Risk Assessment for Smart Homebuyers

**Terrence Frost**
*Security and Cyber Security Reporting and Investigation Team (SCSRIT), USA*

**Michael P. Nolan**
*Cyber Living, Thailand*

## ABSTRACT

*The authors were presented with the task of reviewing a product by Zipato, which has a sizable user base (20,000 households by Zipato according to an article from TechCrunch). The Cyber-Living team is assessing products in the smart home and cybersecurity realms to help consumers make more informed choices. This is the first part of their risk assessment series on Zipato's smart home solutions. It also expands upon existing reporting by other security researchers. Two articles were found most informative out of what is out there for similar products by Zipato. Some of these articles have appeared multiple times because they were picked up by news sites. They often refer themselves to other researchers' discoveries. Part 2 and 3 are for education and research particularly focusing on firmware update vulnerabilities and possibilities of man-in-the-middle attacks that exploit devices. That will be the authors' contribution to the work. They will review other teams in this first part.*

## INTRODUCTION

The first article came from Andrey Muravitsky, Vladimir Dashchenko, Roland Sako and we found it on the Kaspersky website. In this article what popped out at me

DOI: 10.4018/978-1-7998-7904-6.ch008

first was: "we also think there can't be too many IoT (Internet of Things devices) investigations" and have been doing their own investigations for quite a long time. In a community spirit, we ride on the coattails of each other's discoveries which are shared to help people reveal flaws and hope these are fixed before they bring bigger problems to the users who employ these solutions. This team reported that "users are under significant risk" and they went on to detail how they broke into the device physically and observed how the device synchronizes with cloud server setting updates. We found a Zipabox teardown online so we could see that they were working on Zipabox hardware even though they didn't mention that detail. This team is working with Kaspersky Labs – an anti-virus provider I've known for many years. The team gave an assessment of many attack vectors and vulnerabilities that they reported to Zipato before releasing this report to the public. (Muravitsky A, 2019)

## PART ONE: OTHER TEAMS FIND VULNERABILITIES

### Disclaimer

We will probably sound pessimistic, but we are not saying don't buy Zipato, instead, we are trying to research for you. It is up to you to read onward to get a measure of the risks of using a Zipabox or other product that could easily be worse – like an RPi (Raspberry Pi) based one for example that is probably even easier to attack. The more you know the terminology the better you can search the internet for keywords to see if the company is on its game and transparent about security flaws or countermeasures. Zipato does support several types of devices and IoT (internet of things) related communication modules, so one might assume they have a very comprehensive investment in their own research and development. We began to wonder if Zipato is spreading themselves very thin to win by the "feature-rich" category or have the "most supported devices". Maybe you have a diverse set of IoT devices you want to manage and Zipato has come to your attention because of this. If you are building a new system you might only need a very simple setup and want to find a product with best practice for your needs.

### Issues, Controversies, Problems

The title says how to break a smart home "...again" which apparently means this is not the first time this team went through a hacking study and wrote it up to warn users of such risks. Teams like this are working towards keeping smart home providers challenged to remove vulnerabilities or perhaps even be honest about their smart home solution security claims. Another team has been even more successful in discovering security issues with Zipato. Zipato is just the next product in line for Cyber-Living to assess at this time. An aspect of community hacking and vulnerability reporting is to demonstrate that advertised claims and reality are not a match. We don't want to reveal how to use these vulnerabilities, but we have to reference what can or has already been done to educate our readers. It is still a new field, some kind of score system that spells out a number out of ten is yet to be developed.

The Kaspersky article does link to their previous "IoT lottery: finding a perfectly secure connected device" article. In that research, you don't find Zipato referenced but they were giving advice "*When it comes to the vendors of IoT-devices, the advice is simple: collaborate with the security vendors and community when developing new devices and improving old ones.*" Could it be that they felt engagement with Zipato since then has not progressed? Kaspersky has a product that scans the network for IoT devices and gives reports on the level of security … so they are not free of commercial interest, but they point out that security should be considered an important feature rather than a bothersome after-thought that is costly to implement.

Vulnerabilities the Kaspersky team revealed:

1. Firmware is downloaded via an unsecured HTTP (HyperText Transfer Protocol) … We verified this and acquired the firmware, which enabled me to verify other claims.
2. There are conceivable and testable man-in-the-middle attacks that can be made against the Zipabox.
3. If your serial number is known (via physical inspection perhaps) then "remote attackers with the possibility of downloading data to access the user's web interface account, which doesn't have any additional security layers, such as 2FA (Two Factor Authentication). As a result, attackers can take control over someone's home "

Now for some more recent revelations found in this article by INIT_6 and Charles Dardaman: and later used as the basis of a further article by Zack Whittaker for TechCrunch:

Vulnerabilities the INIT_6, Charles Dardaman team revealed:

4. Zipamicro Z-wave controller had 3 vulnerabilities – some enabled attackers to just unlock a door via an API (Application Programming Interface) endpoint URL (Uniform Resource Locator) using a value stolen from the file system which in that case was on a removable media card. Our research is on a different product, but we will verify if these methods are common to the Zipabox 2 equipment we were checking.

a. Embedded SSH (Secure Shell) private key for Root stored in the device file system (very bad – called CRITICAL)
b. Pass-the-Hash Local API Authentication CRITICAL
c. Pass-the-Hash Remote API Authentication CRITICAL

Critical is a risk rating term – it doesn't explain if the attack is simple, it just demonstrates that the attack is high risk and serious. We want to go further than this and make it more accessible by normal computer users trying to navigate through and find out how to buy a smart home hub/controller and understand if it is secure or not. (Dardaman C. 2019)

This second team is quite serious about ethical hacking and sharing information which is, unfortunately, deemed necessary to give a strong pressure for the company to improve their software to remove these vulnerabilities. Did they admit or fix these? It is more our duty to reveal risks and for Zipato to be more transparent about knowing and attending to what is revealed by security researchers. Eventually, as organizations mature they become less foolish and tend to open up that they have become aware of and are doing something about security flaws rather than try to divert attention.

Zipato has replied to these security researchers stating that "we've disabled user passwords on Zipamicros and ----Hubs for ------- pretty much the same day as we got the report. We've also released a new firmware for --------- devices with the following changes:

locally created SSH host key, disabled local API, a different root user key, disabled serial console, no root password.

They are still rolling the firmware upgrade out. …". This excerpt is copied from an image of the response email (from Darko …. ----@zipato.com) shared on the black marble.sh report. They ----- are words that were blacked out in the image.

The Techcrunch follow up on this includes reveals a little more

*"Zipato's chief executive Sebastian Popovic told TechCrunch that each smart hub now comes with a unique private SSH key and other security improvements. Zipato has also since discontinued the ZipaMicro hub in favor of one of its newer products."*

The most important point here is that they discontinued a product completely and we are guessing this is because that device is too physically vulnerable to reading its files. It also means we want to confirm if the SSH key is vulnerable even if it is "unique" by getting into the device via downloading the firmware which we feel must be built as custom for each device to ensure this "unique" key. Some fixes don't bypass systemic vulnerabilities. (Whittaker Z. 2019)

## Conclusion

Given that IoT and Smart Home devices are often found to have many vulnerabilities there is leeway to test if these claims are true. We expect that it might be more difficult to find or test vulnerabilities if what was already being revealed has in fact been addressed. We expect that software and devices using other communication protocols remain to be tested and could have the same flaws. We don't see any references to the hash passing API being fixed other than being disabled locally. That is a pretty big change in functionality, if the local API is re-enabled does it comes back still flawed and vulnerable?

In **Part 2 – Zipato Firmware analysis** we are going to explain more about attacks based on research we have done with this new firmware update that Zipato released, how it was still available to be acquired by Cyber-Living associate researchers. What does Zipato explain to the public about this firmware? The firmware seems to have been released as a reaction to being informed of many flaws by the INIT_6 team. How can we piece this Zipato vulnerability puzzle together when assessing risk? You might also just think this research is enough and you want to look elsewhere because CRITICAL and vulnerable disturbs you. That risk really depends on what you use Zipato equipment for. Cyber-Living wants to provide verified and accurate research to consumers so we will dive deeper. However, we did confirm so far that what has been revealed by security research is correct. The reply from Zipato is an additional sign of confirmation of the flaws of the design.

## PART 2: FIRMWARE ANALYSIS

In this second part, we extend and update progress since Zipato product vulnerabilities were discovered and exploited by other security research teams. Cyber-Living has completed an initial firmware analysis and finds it necessary to provide these interim assessments due to the ongoing critical status of certain vulnerabilities. Further investment into proof of concept that leverages the vulnerabilities has not been planned to date. Even though there are patches many users will not have applied them and may even be at risk at the time they do apply them if a man-in-the-middle attacker is lurking.

In this part we include some of the firmware analysis … but you know we don't have to be the one saying bad things about Zipato's coding because it's already out there, where Kieren McCarthy is really mocking them as appalling internet of S**t; Just in case you wonder why people are interested to see what is in their newer firmware. It references material already covered in part 1 of this risk analysis. What we found useful from that to know is that:

"The danger of hardcoded and default passwords is so significant that California passed a law last year that legally requires smart home manufacturers selling products in the state to include "a preprogrammed password unique to each device manufactured" or "a security feature that requires a user to generate a new means of authentication before access is granted to the device for the first time." It will come into force in January 2020." (McCarthy K. 2019)

So that explains why Zipato has claimed that their new firmware makes a unique key for each device. What we see is that Dropbear start will initialize (create) the RSA key (RSA is a public-key cryptosystem that is widely used for secure data transmission) if it doesn't exist now. So, it does not come pre-programmed, the key locations are empty on the fresh firmware.

Let's talk about the way Zipato uses Mender for software updates. Mender is a platform that offers a "secure and robust over-the-air (OTA) software update process". Sounds great but is it secured? Mender representatives explain that while software developers can cobble together some kind of updated script, they often underestimate the complexity and requirements to be able to secure their devices with regular updates and security patches.

Previous white-paper Cyber-Living released on Raspberry Pi devices emphasizes that lack of updates is one of the big weaknesses that gets exploited as new vulnerabilities are discovered by IoT devices remain in service unpatched because … they must be manually applied assuming there is even a new firmware release. There are firmware directories within the Zipato firmware itself assumingly for updating certain devices that really need firmware updates and where it could be managed by the smart home hub … but, that also means they could be patched badly by a compromised smart home hub. So the biggest risk concerned about in our analysis is this pathway to initiate or receive updates.

In the case of the Zipato products, we see no signs they have utilized the security features to ensure their server is signed and gives signed, nor encrypted images. That is typical when security is not a high priority over sales-related features.

The process of acquiring the firmware itself had flagged this risky Zipato firmware. We followed up by going through the Mender documentation and checked all documented locations in the Linux file system that run Zipato products (i.e. the firmware) to inspect wherever Mender stores its settings in the Linux file system and there were no keys or server signatures. Mender provides the client and server aspect of updating so we can assume it was a probably mender server. The researcher received the update file via packet capture by just asking for the file in a web browser without making any kind of secure connection. We could do that because the URL is revealed by the update process connecting via HTTP.

A predictable risk exists if this Mender firmware update system isn't secured and not attended, we'll see Zipato hacks that don't seem to be traced to any obvious vulnerability because compromised updates will find their way into devices either via a local network attack or a broader internet hijacking. If the honey pot is big enough someone will do the math and it will happen. We'll be happy if Zipato contacts us to let us know things have changed but the firmware we analyzed says it all – this is still their latest firmware. The main purpose of the research was to discover feasible attack vectors rather than assume the vendor's claims of being secure. Their centralized management of devices is a structural vulnerability that attracts attackers due to the scale of control if their management website is compromised.

Zipato seems to be aware of man-in-the-middle attacks and the need to encrypt communications now because on their previous firmware there was an update note explaining that they force encrypted HTTPS (Hypertext Transfer Protocol Secure) communications since their previous firmware version 0.9.999.8 includes a fix "- General: forced https connections ". This also reveals a very poor unsecured phase suggesting myriad flaws remain to be exploited.

In the raw and generic language of IoT safety standards I've found this type of threat: "Exploiting the lack of, or inappropriate security checks that, if properly implemented, would detect the actions that are, or likely to be, misleading or deceptive".

So, this seems to be a very wide-open gap … where we cannot assume "if properly implemented". There are keys and systems to verify the provider of the malware, but it was not an encrypted file … so security was clearly not a design priority. Rather just getting something to work first and leave security to the future where the company may choose not to fund such development without pressure from security researchers such as ourselves.

Zipato would do well to share some kind of roadmap since they have been caught out with a few bad security gaps. This would show they are aware of their shortcomings, but this is of course unlikely and not the way most businesses think. Securing the settings after the firmware is downloaded is too late so we can exclude that idea. We haven't observed that level, but if a forged update is downloaded then anything goes. Kaspersky didn't name Zipato but they revealed enough information about their research to demonstrate it was a Zipato product, such as a Zipabox. Since then, Init_6 who has released reports on vulnerabilities in Zipato devices has to find these through a reverse engineering process we call "Firmware Analysis".

## What Cyber-Living Discovered

Once you find the point [within packet capture] where the update was initiated by the user on the Zipato website you can read text directly from the packet and find the URL for the HTTP as plain text. So you can download the firmware. The fact that its gzip-compressed file is visible even if the filename is "zipabox2-image-mender". If you own the hardware and a license to use the software, there is no reason you should be able to read through what is written in the storage of your own copy of the product. Especially if you are doing it to check for risks to your own network security.

*Figure 1.*

```
extracted from this packet

0000   d8 cb 8a ef 63 a6 e4 95 6e 45 35 d5 08 00 45 00    ....c...nE5...E.
0010   00 b8 ac de 40 00 3f 06 e0 c4 c0 a8 08 72 36 4d    ....@.?......r6M
0020   ae 35 d9 e2 00 50 10 41 30 a1 91 22 87 ad 80 18    .5...P.A0.."....
0030   03 91 dd 1d 00 00 01 01 08 0a 59 2d 0f ae ef aa    ..........Y-....
0040   d2 5c 47 45 54 20 2f 7a 69 70 61 62 6f 78 32 2f    .\GET /zipabox2/
0050   [illegible] 2f 7a 69 70 61 62 6f 78 32 2d 69 6d 61    [illegible]/zipabox2-ima
0060   67 65 2e 6d 65 6e 64 65 72 20 48 54 54 50 2f 31    ge.mender HTTP/1
0070   2e 31 0d 0a 48 6f 73 74 3a 20 75 70 64 61 74 65    .1..Host: update
0080   [illegible] 63 6f 6d 0d 0a 55 73 65    [illegible].Use
0090   72 2d 41 67 65 6e 74 3a 20 47 6f 2d 68 74 74 70    r-Agent: Go-http
00a0   2d 63 6c 69 65 6e 74 2f 31 2e 31 0d 0a 41 63 63    -client/1.1..Acc
00b0   65 70 74 2d 45 6e 63 6f 64 69 6e 67 3a 20 67 7a    ept-Encoding: gz
00c0   69 70 0d 0a 0d 0a                                  ip....
```

Next, we'll go through what is known and what we've observed in the file system of the firmware as well as by watching data we capture as it talks to the Zipato cloud servers.

- **Risk Analysis –** ***Medium High Risk – Multiple IoT Vulnerabilities***

When there are active vulnerabilities then we consider the product "vulnerable" and the firmware update is at high risk of failing to observe standards in securing this class of device by not installing the key management needed. So, the Zipabox2 is definitely vulnerable and not just at the local network level. However, because the user has to initiate firmware upgrades (see the image from console), at least the way the system is set up now they could be aware of the risk. We like that the user can go with the previous firmware – except for the fact that the previous firmware, or what we got out of the box, is riddled with exploits including a common SSH key.

So, the basic risk assessment for now is"

*"The Zipabox2 out of the box needs attention to reduce multiple vulnerabilities and needs some extra confirmation that updates are authentic – which is a currency not available other than by assuming the update is from the real Zipato source and not a hijacked server giving modified firmware."*

Many users never upgrade firmware unless advised of the risks of not upgrading. The Zipabox web management console does recommend upgrades in various ways.

*Figure 2.*

- **SSH/ Keys –** ***Medium Risk Until Upgraded Firmware Applied***

So far, we haven't found any SSH-related private keys, just the public key that is set up as authorized. We can't confirm there aren't any that could be found, yet this is inconclusive. We suspect some key will be there though because they only said they will use a unique set of keys per device rather than the same one for all devices. It is just a matter of discovery.

Also depends if the key is generated with sufficient randomness at the device, or with a good enough random seed. If the key is pre-generated at the time the firmware is packaged for your unique device then it would already be passed by someone who listens and captures the firmware download URL. This would be investigated in a future follow-up. This is the point of standards … IoT standards need to be sufficiently compressible rather than just comprehensive or people can't take the time to read and follow them.

- **Mender Image Limitations -** ***Not Secure or Signed Update System***

*The mender file format is very easy to read – after unpacking, de-archiving then you can mount the file system image (an EXT3 Linux partition) and go through the directories looking for software, configuration, stored passwords, or keys.* Part of the file name from the Mender Artifact file is downloaded as firmware.

"zipabox2-image-zipato-box-1.3-zipabox2.ext3"

- **SSH Key –** ***Some Signs of Progress***

Analysis still in progress. There is a lot of https-related code … so securing communications with their API at the cloud seems to be a priority. The SSH key is generated or initialized in the operating system set up – it is not pre-configured. Drop bear does the usual key generation procedure if no key file is made. We couldn't find the SSH key file discovered by other teams in the previous firmware.

- **Did Zipato Abandon Their Own Firmware Update Software for Mender?**

We used JAD (JD is a decompiler for the Java programming language. JD is provided as a GUI tool as well as in the form of plug-ins for the Eclipse and IntelliJ IDEA integrated development environments.) to decompile their Java binaries and there was an upgrade. We did find that despite the mender security features missing there is software that will apply a signature check "gpg –verify" and that .md5 and .asc type files are supposed to be downloaded during the new firmware upgrade. Class file (among many files that were decompiled and read through). It isn't clear if this upgrade process is implemented or not – there may be multiple pathways for firmware upgrades. We are including this because in part 3 we concluded that there is a risk based on the observation that Zipato has not encrypted the updated firmware files it is less certain they have sufficient checking to reject unauthorized firmware upgrade files.

Here is a decompiled code fragment – this is not sourced code, it is just reconstructed code from (downloadAndCheckFirmwareFile(String server path, String fileName, String workDirPath):

```
"downloadFile(url, (new StringBuilder()).append(saveLocation).
append(".tmp").toString());
            downloadFile((new StringBuilder()).append(url).
append(".md5").toString(), (new StringBuilder()).
append(saveLocation).append(".md5").toString());
            downloadFile((new StringBuilder()).append(url).
append(".asc").toString(), (new StringBuilder()).
append(saveLocation).append(".asc").toString());
            LOG.trace("Verifying signature of {}",
saveLocation);
            builder = new ProcessBuilder(new String[] {
                "/usr/bin/gpg", "--verify", (new
StringBuilder()).append(saveLocation).append(".asc").
toString(), (new StringBuilder()).append(saveLocation).
append(".tmp").toString()
            });
            builder.directory(workDir);
            Process process = builder.start();
```

```
            process.waitFor();
            if(process.exitValue() != 0)
                throw new IOException((new
StringBuilder()).append("Error while verifying signature
").append(saveLocation).append(".asc").toString());
```

This would potentially be a safeguard against downloading fake firmware … but we believe it's not implemented in this version. There is no /usr/bin/gpg installed in this firmware – and so this doesn't appear to function yet and is likely an option they have for when they do have the keys and gpg in place. Mender is in place, so it seems that is their system for upgrading, and this is another pathway they have developed alongside mender. Possibly one that didn't work that led to a change to using mender. Mender exists because writing software to handle firmware updating over the air is complex and developers often underestimate the task. We have to speculate but the lack of the gpg software indicates a gap here.

We also found a hard-coded password in the key generation software, so this was concerning but not critical without other relevant information. The password name indicated code that is still in progress … but that is also speculation.

We are not trying to reverse everything in there – just find notable aspects that answer the previous design flaws or indicate new vulnerabilities.

1. They knew and had simply not considered these bugs critical enough to be a high priority
2. They rushed some changes and accelerated the release of their post version 1. firmware. Up to that point, their firmware was all beta 0.9xxx or lower numbering

**• Using a Serial Number to Request Settings Including Usernames and Passwords**

The previous firmware (or out-of-the-box firmware) has a type of secure VPN (Virtual Private Network) connection that does encrypt communication but it is also known to be compromised. That changed to something else after the upgrade … this will take time to confirm but we believe there is more security so we can't say this is still a threat to security unless the firmware is never updated from pre-version 1 Zipato firmware.

- **Local API – Exploits Exist in Previous Firmware – Awaiting Zipato to Patch**

The major hack from INIT_6 that enabled door locks to be opened remotely on Zipato equipment used calls to a local API. Zipato emails a reply them they disabled that, but it is listed as a version 2 added feature in this new firmware. *"General: added local API for /v2/systems and /v2/abilities"* but also *"General: added option to disable local API"* so it would potentially be this local API turned on if needed and then it needs to be retested for vulnerabilities.

Having reverse-engineered the java code one can study how the api is called and what keys are used so they can begin to probe or read communications. Many API attacks are likely to be possible based on typical IoT security oversight in the industry. The Zipabox becomes associated with an account and downloads configuration information and usernames, passwords, or anything else it needs to manage IoT devices it will manage. These are likely cached inside the device but once an attacker knows the serial number of the device he could use some kind of buildout of this software that poses as a zipabox. It appears it just depends on skill and determination because the software is an open book, java is easily decompiled into readable code as you can see in an example we created from the firmware's upgrade class file.

## Conclusion

Zipabox uses a Mender client to apply downloaded firmware upgrades. Zipato has the capabilities to secure software at their disposal, but they have either decided against or not gotten around integrating the certificates that would recognize if someone was posing as an upgrade server and they downloaded hacked firmware.

They used sub v1 "beta versions" of their firmware up until they responded to vulnerability reports by swiftly releasing a 1.3.59 version. A system like Mender is essential to automate or simplify user-initiated upgrades. Mender appears to be missing its "secure OTA update" security features that are part of a complete solution. By omitting that confirmation, the Zipato firmware doesn't meet IoT security standards – even if they are unofficial and optional – which are there to guide manufacturers.

The SSH key issue has changed and new laws in some parts of the USA will force smart home and IoT manufacturers to not make terrible security oversights by hard-coding a single key in all devices simplifying intrusion attempts.

The more complex or feature-rich your product gets the more attack vectors to need to be secured. Man-in-the-middle attacks by redirecting the device's firmware download request to a hijacked DNS (Domain Name Server) are a serious threat. We invested time to read firmware download software code to determine if they were, in fact, using certified software certificates. This could happen globally, regionally, or locally. DNS servers themselves are an important part of security.

Cyber living is researching the potential for modified firmware that exposes the Zipato by pre-installing backdoors and other remote tools into a forged firmware image. Part 3 - "Thoughts on "man in the middle" attacks" will explain or visualize a variety of types of man-in-the-middle attacks and associate information gathering techniques. This is intended to help people consider risks inherent in products like this where there seems to be a lot of delays releasing firmware with better security.

*Many comments written above refer to the latest firmware on the Zipato website. We found the release notes to be very vague and opaque.*

*https://community.zipato.com/knowledge-base/article/1-3-59 – the firmware was released on 3/17/2019 according to their documentation.*

*The zipato documentation of changes in the latest firmware is quite obscure to understand. Security researchers have increasingly powerful tools to study firmware and reveal possible gaps or actively test exploits to prove the issues are real.*

## PART 3: THOUGHTS ON "MAN IN THE MIDDLE" ATTACKS

In the 3rd part of our research on risks impacting Zipato products, we evaluate the specific risks of man-in-the-middle type attacks. This analysis is written for users – it attempts to simplify the complex and open up the unknown. The question we ask ourselves here is – Is this Zipato product "Zipabox", and indeed their whole range susceptible to man-in-the-middle attacks? What are those, how and why are Zipato products (and many other IoT-type embedded system products) vulnerable. Finally, you take this to make whatever decisions about risk relevant to how you choose or operate the equipment you have. Cyber-Living will eventually try to compare various products but for now, IoT products and smart home hubs which aggregate and manage these are both vulnerable and increasingly targeted.

Let us get started by explaining some types of conditions that are prone for man-in-the-middle attacks to be developed by hackers. Once the most obvious ways of gaining root access to modify or search a device have been patched the hacking doesn't stop. What is known about a Zipabox in this case is the address where it will download its firmware update. What may be useful to know is if the device can be triggered to do this or if it will do it automatically. How can the hacker masquerade as the authentic source an over-the-air firmware update is loaded from? A successful attack is where a product requests a file from a server the hacker is in control of (rather than Zipato's server). Thus, downloading the change which gives access to this Zipabox and overwriting its current firmware. You could create a server that just gives the firmware you want regardless of what filename is requested – but there is R&D involved in testing this just like there is for the manufacturer. It may also be very simple, just rewrite a key or change a configuration, introduce a backdoor. So a security feature where one has assumed only an authentic manufacturer firmware will be downloaded becomes a vulnerability.

Firmware analysis, searching through the files, software, and configuration of the system, is part of this process that takes deeper and deeper searches for both the known and unexpected. Most developers leave a backdoor to give certainty of how they can reset or regain access. They don't realize that finding where the device has "login" text in its code and tracing how it checks a username/password is relatively simple.

A similar fail-safe is a device that has a button you hold for 10 seconds so if a person can hard reset the device it will then reboot on previous firmware and its known SSH exploit. In part 2 we searched the updated firmware for signs that the mender updater client configured to use encryption features – but we found no signs. We downloaded unencrypted firmware ourselves and studying what we found apparently with no other security in the update process. Thus, we feel the same as the Kaspersky team who mentioned the man-in-the-middle attack possibilities for a product they did not identify – which we saw to be a Zipabox – we feel confident that a man-in-the-middle vulnerability continues to exist with the newer version Zipabox2. Who knows what levels of misuse of Zipaboxes are already in the works? It is conceivable that the mender (OTA over the air) update system could be the target itself and, if exploited, a method could be developed to reload persistent hacks into future firmware updates. Firmware update man-in-the-middle exploitation remains "what can go wrong, will go wrong" murphy's law. Bot networks are always looking for ways to invade and abuse new classes of devices and a smart-home hub will be a valuable, always-on, addition.

## Is Zipato Keeping on Top of Vulnerabilities?

Offensive security involves building tools that prove a weakness that can be exploited – small programs to prove what an analyst has discovered to be a critical vulnerability. The industry doesn't necessarily publish or demo the best of these. We can't confirm or deny what is possible beyond spelling out that it is possible. The ball is back in Zipato's court to either wait for another security team to do their work for free OR publish what they really did to limit the vulnerabilities that persist in their equipment and infrastructure.

*"Nevertheless, one concerning part of this story is how smart hubs such as the Zipato seem to be spreading to apartment complexes. That's not an issue when they*

*work as advertised but means that one unpatched hub could potentially be used to expose numerous homes as a single point of security failure.*

*Zipato claims it has issued patches for the three CVEs mentioned above, which as far as we can tell means applying v1.3.60 or later, which appeared in March after the company was told of the issues." (Dunn J. E. 2019)*

One of the CVE {CVE-2018-15123 284} says

*"Insecure configuration storage in Zipato Zipabox Smart Home Controller BOARD REV - 1 with System Version -118 allows remote attacker perform new attack vectors and take under control device and smart home."*

The *v1.3.60* update is in fact optional, and in the users' hands to initiate. Some additional exploits were reported less formally before and after these. 3 CVE were published on the same date. See above "one unpatched hub could potentially be used to expose numerous homes ...".

There is a timeline on one of the advisory CVE published by Kaspersky Labs

2018.01.12 – Vulnerabilities reported
2018.01.29 – First feedback from the vendor
2018.06.06 – Vendor notifies that some vulnerabilities are fixed
2018.07.07 – Reminder sent to the vendor. … (SEE CARTOON frame 3 and 4)

## Working With the Security Community

It isn't good enough to say Ethical hacking to attempt to report vulnerabilities to improve the security model and features. There are certain advances made across the industry thanks to the security research community but when there is a communication breakdown it seems some manufacturers just move on to new products. Without bounties to find and report vulnerabilities, there is no open channel to make discoveries right through to proof of concept and there is even the threat of legal action limiting research to what might appear as speculative open questions. If buyers don't have a number of watchdog services to keep an ongoing study going it is easy to hide risks. We need best practices that reveal whatever progress or lack of such the manufacturer has made. Without this companies may just dump old designs and focus on new products which they represent as secure.

*Figure 3.*

The true price of a product is often higher when the company is committed to R&D and security features. A lower-priced product gathers a lot of market share, but that business model may not survive damage to its reputation if security updates can't keep up. Confidence in security is diminished by the way companies like Zipato give the appearance of a serious producer but don't have the development team or investment capital to keep regularly updating vulnerable products? Nor is there any real public face of security staff beyond the CEO doing damage control.

*The API also makes the https://my.zipato.com website a bit of a target for a man-in-the-middle to capture user logins. A Trojan horse is like a human interface illusion to capture information, but an API means you can just get it directly at the time the device wants to connect. So, this is a bit of a honey pot – especially if a local API is in place. Zipato switched that off but apparently it is back.*

***Zipato***

*Figure 4.*

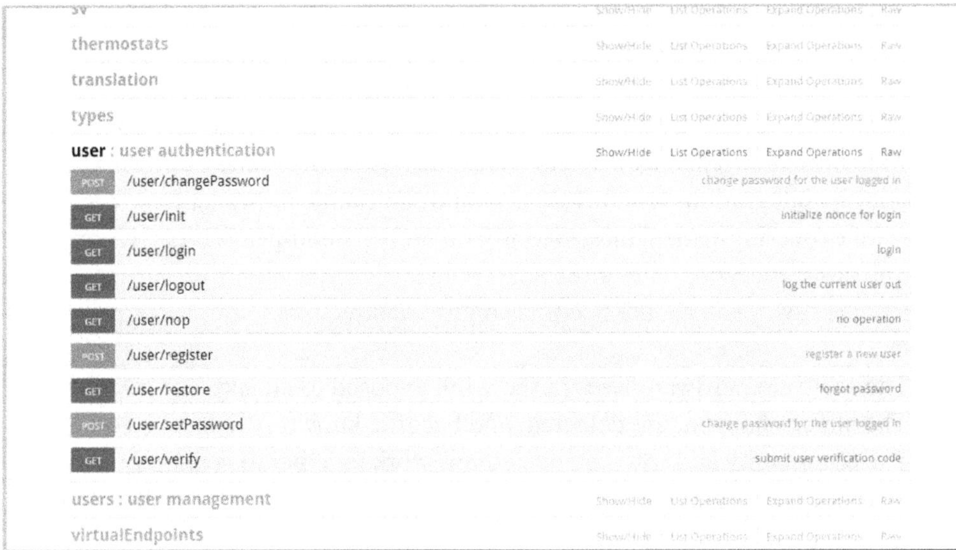


The point here is that once you notice a major gap in security like the updates and servers being unencrypted it is worth expanding the implications. Zipato's Zipabox does use encrypted communication but not at the time of firmware updates. Zipato is doing the usual software engineering life cycle of having flaws pointed out to them and releasing newer software. There remains still a lot of scope for security gaps and vulnerabilities to be discovered. Another specialty in security testing is to attack product API features which help integrate other products to remote (see image above) – an interface that takes direct commands - which is a whole new realm to dive into for security analysts to discover exploitable vulnerabilities. So, using what is in the firmware, or previous one man-in-the-middle attacks can listen in on API interactions between IoT equipment and the smart hub.

Sometimes the design process itself leases to repeating patterns of the same flaws to be found again and again because code is re-used and there is a lot of different IoT devices that Zipato supports. A recent back and forth between Zipato and one security group who demonstrated the ease of opening an exploited smart lock resulted in Zipato taking a "ZipaMicro" product with a removable memory card off the market after the most recent security expose demonstrates to us that Zipato products are going to continue to present vulnerabilities to security researchers. That should be no surprise – it is typical for hundreds of vulnerabilities to be present in IoT devices according to experts.

What is really resonating with us is the way leaving a mender update security vulnerability longer-term invites bigger threats. So, after our team noted several vulnerabilities published in the public domain, we wanted to look into how Zipato was responding and adapting to previously revealed vulnerabilities including this same category of man-in-the-middle attack susceptibility. Do Zipato decision-makers feel that threats like this are "unlikely" or unavoidable or merely theoretical? One factor that suggests this might be true is the lack of progress in simply configuring their infrastructure. This seems odd given that Zipato products offer extensive compatibility integrations with IoT devices and communication adapters. The attack surface for extracting critical information by merely listening in is broad if you don't apply the basic encryption defenses at all points.

There are 3 ways a product becomes highly secure

1. The software/hardware lives in the wild, exposed to attacks
2. The attacks happen, are detected, and become known
3. The community and software custodians work together to *genuinely* fix rather than give the illusion of fixing the vulnerabilities, bugs, or unstable code.

Smart home hardware and software are often stored in a network where one assumes it is safely behind a firewall. We assume that either attacks are not happening or that that they have become known and fixed. Writing for the Cyber-Living website is about bridging the gap between security news and user education without dumbing it down to the point where you can't explain what a user needs to google for themselves. It will require users to read articles, such as this, to know/understand if your target product security is hardened or vulnerable. Trusting the product description alone we keep making the same mistakes when we decide which products to buy and install at home, or work.

## The Life Cycle of a Hack

Anatomy of an attack given by experts in IoT security

1. Reconnaissance --- Discover vulnerabilities
2. Intrusion --- Initial Access
3. Insert back-door --- Ongoing Access
4. Clean up --- Avoid Detection

once they detect what you have installed. Then you often find the research has been done and are applying known exploits (those match vulnerabilities) that give them access. People don't give away the best tools though – if someone builds a fake update host or adapted firmware images … they don't tend to share that so openly. These are the black-hat types (*Black Hat hackers* are criminals who break

***Zipato***

*Figure 5.*

| Type | Domain Name | IP Address |
|---|---|---|
| A | my.zipato.com | 52.49.238.44<br>Amazon.com, Inc. (AS16509) |

into computer networks with malicious intent.) – and they are often the very same people who say they are ethical hackers. They want to have a long-lasting relationship with your smart-home hub. The entire attack might be pre-scripted into a botnet (A **botnet** is a collection of **internet**-connected devices infected by malware that allow hackers to control them.) once they get it working on a new product. (Habibi E. 2019)

Zipato employs a cloud-based service provider and they disable local web services to some of their products. You cannot manage the setup of Zipabox without using their website. They have products like Zipatile, which we have not yet investigated. Zipabox seems more popular in the smart property rental space a box where a non-descript white box that resists tampering seems to be popular. This enables property managers to save money and time by automating access to renters. The Zipato products are managed from virtual servers hosted by Amazon web services (AWS). This design has advantages because Zipato must connect to home where the server can more safely (in theory) integrate with mobile phones and web browsers. Connecting to the cloud service means the device does open port forwarding rules at the firewall or router that expose it to be discovered by internet scans.

Unfortunately, this cloud server just means that Zipato has moved the target to where hackers will be able to study and probe it for weakness. With enough time attackers can pose as an authorized device and collect all the access information they need to manipulate your "smart home". We can confirm via this graphic that AWS address space is used by users (and devices) connecting to my.zipato.com. AWS servers with much more sensitive data like cryptocurrency wallets have had the DNS hijacked so users all logged into a trojan and gave away the keys … it was done before and you don't know that it isn't happening already. Hackers will spend time gathering what they need before they risk giving away what they know. Search "Cryptocurrency exchange EtherDelta gets hacked

*"for that DNS hijack example – briefly "the attacker managed to take over EtherDelta's DNS server and serve a fake version of the site to visitors. (Wilmoth J 2019)*

*Amazon owns the IP address that your Zipato console web application resolves to indicate the website is hosted by their "cloud computing service AWS"*

Let us assume you have very good wireless LAN security, or you own a large number of devices and they are for example using 3g or 4g to connect to Zipato's cloud structure independent of your local home network.

If your first line of defense is your router and/or firewall – assuming you even have something that justifies the term "firewall" installed. What attack vectors remain. In fact, a DNS hijack can impact you because attackers are attacking the cloud server or setting a firmware man-in-the-middle that targets the whole internet or certain segments, ISPs (Internet Service Providers) as soon as anyone downloads the firmware and gets the wrong network address.

This is a classic man-in-the-middle attack that requires hijacking the IP address and that does not have to be at your location … if your Zipabox goes looking for its firmware update using a domain name and a rogue DNS server is in play …

*"A rogue DNS server translates domain names of desirable websites (search engines, banks, brokers, etc.) into IP addresses of sites with unintended content" (Wikipedia 2019)*

Indeed, most update servers are secured and use HTTPS. Yet many websites still use HTTP because it is simpler or difficult were upgrading to a certificate or host using HTTPS. Big companies like Microsoft, or even Red Hat Enterprise Linux suggest all driver software should be signed and authenticated wherever possible but in practice, smaller companies don't manage to get through the process of qualifying their software.

Does Zipato have countermeasures to prevent this? Features to improve security with update procedures are well known and documented in the very product they use. Mender is a commercial operation suggesting that "OTA updates can also address currently unknown vulnerabilities" but of course they will not suggest their OTA updater itself is a vulnerability because it is a necessary component but to be fair, they did design it to use encryption.

A system might try to avoid DNS hijacking by using hard-coded IP addresses. That won't really provide safety either unless those addresses point at verifiably signed servers. If an attacker has already intruded, they might assign themselves the IP address of what should be an external server. We note that Zipato may be attempting to use this as a simple solution and continue to avoid signing the update server. Of course, the attack can come from within your LAN too.

## Is Your Zipato Safe From Your Own Computer if It Carries Malware?

So, we are concerned that most of Zipato's users are exposed to a network-wide (all products) risk of this kind of attack. Does Zipato employ any built-in anti-virus to detect malware and back-doors, hooks installed by this kind of attack?

In fact, if any computer in your network is compromised it is likely that a DNS-changing trojan "invisibly switched the automatic DNS server assignment by the ISP to manual DNS server assignment for rogue DNS servers." You might say that DNS abuse is a specialty of any network administrator and for many years doing that type of work we have seen a plethora of security update man-in-the-middle attacks come into existence that needed to be patched. Often these were automated by malware that infected someone and turned their computer into a man-in-the-middle server or redirected updates as described above.

So, anyone, including the user who belongs in that LAN can execute a man-in-the-middle that automates redirection of your next firmware update. Then your Zipato potentially joins a bot-net such as Mirai, Hajime, Brickerbot to become a spam relay, digital currency miner, ransomware/malware delivery agent, or just for hire to people who want to use a botnet.

This kind of malware, man-in-the-middle updated the firmware or software is already a whole business model, so they don't even need to see your home as a target. They may just want your Zipato because it is so reprogrammable. These attacks exist for Microsoft OS and it was fixed by higher levels of encryption. *See **MS16-072: ...** "The vulnerability could allow elevation of privilege if an attacker launches a man-in-the-middle (MiTM) attack against the traffic passing between a domain controller and the target machine."* and after that, all updates first required such fixes installed. These attacks also go for SIP phones, routers, web cameras, and internet TV-related equipment. (Microsoft 2019)

## Getting in Between Zipato Controllers and IoT Devices in the Home

A lot of the other attack vectors involve getting in the middle of the communications between your smart home hub such as a Zipato and the smart lock, lightbulb, or whatever IoT device. Your Zipabox once configured can switch over to use the wifi – but this might enable evil twin wifi [wifi phishing] attack.

Say you have secure wifi... well it is fine, we can use the "evil twin wifi" attack. *"WiFi will auto-connect to the best Access Point which shares the same name as the user selected (with security settings and all). If you know an access point's password or if they aren't using a password it's trivially easy to set up an evil AP."* - What is interesting is that this attack is best defended by proactive and offensive means to disable the attacker. The same goes for 3G and 4G if you are organized enough to dare to interfere – the stronger local signal will initiate the products to all log in to the stronger signal if the ISP hasn't set up countermeasures and then … you can do the rogue DNS. To the device, it stays on the internet, but it is getting compromised information about where to source updates. The "evil wifi" is designed to act as you authenticated but it possibly even captures your details and accepts whatever password you use. Yet another man-in-the-middle type of attack – in fact, a lot of exploits are simply about misrepresenting yourself.

We brought up this Evil Twin wifi to reinforce that your Smart Hub must assume it is being watched and its data captured. It should be using encrypted communication at all times. This is why users are turning to the virtual private network, so their communications are encrypted at home, traveling, using public wifi. Locks and IoT devices will have to be doing the same or they will reveal something that opens up further attacks or the ability for unauthorized tampering and manipulating your smart home devices. Encryption will also be something that gets broken and needs to be improved – this has already been happening for many years. 64 bit, 128 bit, 256 bit 1024 bit, and so on as fast computers attack encrypted passwords to reveal the original input used to make the encryption – the password.

Your door is attached to the smart network hub, but once you build a modified Zipato you could start to masquerade if you have an exploit where the IoT device, such as the lock, trusts a password hash (rather than the authentic password). That was the exploit with the local API and the door lock that Dardaman and INIT_6 wrote "They found that the smart hub uses a "pass-the-hash" authentication system, which doesn't require knowing the user's plain text password, only the scrambled version. By taking the scrambled password and passing it to the smart hub, the researchers could trick the device into thinking they were the home-owner." If there is an unencrypted link between devices … or trust that can be abused opportunities present themselves.

## No Network Is to Be Trusted, Especially the Internet or DNS Names

So, your device can't just rest on an assumption such as "it is ok we are in a safe network". No network is always as it appears to be. Everything involved in smart home technology has to be using encryption or you are exposed to these risks. Now granted this can happen with the full gamut and not just your smart home products. The point here is that you are leaving a small computer on all the time and there is plenty of information that can be gathered as we and others have done that exposes everything. The addresses, there are keys we found inside the latest firmware that may enable a modified version of the Zipato java application to do a man-in-the-middle – that is for further research to check. Certainly, if the source code gets acquired that will be easier again … but an unpacked JAR from the firmware has a lot of binaries that can be tested to log into the cloud server.

## FUTURE RESEARCH DIRECTIONS

With the advancement and dependence on IoT devices, the age of the digital home is truly upon us. Thus, opening us up to a new kind of home invasion. If the information security portion of technology contained in homes is not regularly reviewed, this will leave homeowners open for attack. The main goal is to stay one step ahead of the virtual burglars by implementing security reviews of existing technology with software patching & Firmware updates. Looking to the future Cyber Living is creating an in-home custom configuration Perimeter Firewall based on Linux Free BSD called www.siteblock.us. We at Cyber Living feel that the perimeter is always our most significant point of attack for hackers trying to infiltrate today's Smart Home. The elusiveness and sophistication of today's dark web hacker and each private home having a public IP address at the perimeter to the internet accessible to outsiders. This is the primary area of concern and something that needs to be addressed with a sense of urgency. Public awareness and the availability of such a technology should be as mandatory as setting one's alarms or physically locking the front door. We at Cyber Living are bringing to the market a solution to prevent perimeter attacks and make sure in this digital age we are at the forefront of our home's security, adding protection to the homeowner & peace of mind to protect digital information security.

## CONCLUSION

Man-In-the-middle attacks are an area of concern that needs to be 1$^{st}$ understood and secondly investigated. Even patching of devices can still leave a smart home for a more sophisticated attack. If a hacker or cyber-criminal is performing a dedicated attack on a home, a man-in-the-middle-style attack would be a definite avenue to infiltrate somebody's private home network. Bot Networks are always scanning looking for ways to find man-in-the-middle exploitation on firmware or software updates for devices such as Zipabox. It would be certainly possible to masquerade as the 'internet server' from which the Zipabox gets its updates by emulating its IP address and for the BOT to then install its own firmware as part of the update which could give total control to its nefarious developer.

If a vulnerability is exposed in a multifamily building where Zipato Hubs exist that transmit data to Zipabox client devices contained in different apartments, for example, this could leave many residents open not just from their client device in their dwelling unit but they can be hacked from a higher level at the Hub which could trickle down and allow an attack to open doors or disable alarms, etc. on multiple dwellings at the same time. The old 'lock and key' is now entirely controlled by these devices and disastrous consequences could be experienced if it fails, due to software manipulation of the devices that control these instruments. Security patching is shown to be optional so even if a vulnerability is known by the manufacturer the devices don't just do automatic updates. These would have to be kicked off by an administrator and there's no telling when that might happen. So known vulnerabilities would still exist ad infinitum. If manufacturers wait for the internet security community to let them know what vulnerabilities exist on their devices this falls way short of in-house offensive hacking and penetration testing. If buyers don't have a watchdog community to report such shortcomings to manufacturers it's easy for them to ignore the problem.

We found that it is typical for 100's of vulnerabilities to be present in IoT devices.

Malware can be used to change your DNS server's addresses to their own, emulating known web addresses but with an underlying fake website designed to hack (gleam) information from your personal computer.

Given that IoT and smart homes are such new technologies and the stabilizers have not come off yet, like any information technology discipline it will take time to mature and grow. From a Law Enforcement standpoint, these devices would need to be administered by a trained professional and at this juncture of their early development, Cyber Living does not recommend their use for this purpose.

## FUNDING INFORMATION

This research received no specific grant from any funding agency in the public, commercial, or not-for-profit sectors.

## REFERENCES

Dardaman, C. (2019). *Breaking and Entering with Zipato SmartHubs*. Black Marble. Accessed from https://blackmarble.sh/zipato-smart-hub/

Dunn, J. E. (2019). *Open Sesame! Zipato's smart hub hacked to open front doors.* Naked Security. Accessed July 4, 2019 from https://nakedsecurity.sophos.com/2019/07/04/open-sesame-zipatos-smart-hub-hacked-to-open-front-doors/

Habibi, E. (2019). *Anatomy of an Attack on the Industrial IoT.* Dark reading. Accessed July 4, 2019 from https://www.darkreading.com/vulnerabilities---threats/anatomy-of-an-attack-on-the-industrial-iot-/a/d-id/1331097

McCarthy, K. (2019). *Here's a great idea: Why don't we hardcode the same private key into all our smart home hubs?* The Register. Accessed July 3, 2019. from https://www.theregister.co.uk/2019/07/03/zipato_hardcoded_key/

Microsoft. (2019). *MS16-072: Security update for Group Policy: June 14, 2016.* Microsoft. Accessed July 12, 2019 from https://support.microsoft.com/en-us/topic/ms16-072-security-update-for-group-policy-june-14-2016-7570425d-d460-3003-b2ac-a464c874725d

Muravitsky A. (2019). *IoT Hack: How to break into a smart home again.* Securelist by Kaspersky. Accessed July 2 2019 from https://securelist.com/iot-hack-how-to-break-a-smart-home-again/84092/

Whittaker, Z. (2019). *Security flaws in popular smart home hub let hackers unlock front doors.* TechCrunch. Accessed July 2, 2019 from https://techcrunch.com/2019/07/02/smart-home-hub-flaws-unlock-doors/

Wikipedia. (2019). *DNS Hikacking.* Wikipedia. Accessed July 7, 2019 from https://en.wikipedia.org/wiki/DNS_hijacking

Wilmoth, J. (2019). *Cryptocurrency Exchange EtherDelta Hacked in DNS Hijacking Scheme.* CNN. Accessed July 5, 2019 from https://www.ccn.com/cryptocurrency-exchange-etherdelta-hacked-in-dns-hijacking-scheme/

## KEY TERMS AND DEFINITIONS

**API:** Application programming interface. Any software or hardware mix can be integrated using an API that uses a common communication protocol to pass specific calls/requests and retrieve or monitor the resulting output.

**CVE:** Common vulnerabilities and exposures. This is a numbered standard for documenting exploits and attack vectors, hacks, weakened security, etc. for software, operating systems, etc.

**IoT:** Internet of things. Small microcontrollers or microcomputers generally single-board small factor aimed at being teamed with devices to make a smart home or smart factory device that can be queried, probed, or controlled via LAN or WAN. The small computer may use ethernet/TCP-IP to be native internet or one of many other protocols via an IoT Hub that translated internet communications to other wireless management protocols. It is a loose term - more of a buzzword.

**Mender:** A software toolkit for downloading and applying updates and patches "over the air" - it is a client-server architecture.

**MiTM:** Man in the middle. A term for some software or hack that redirects sensitive communications to a spoofed or masqueraded service (computer, node) for the purposes of a hack or crack or simply for monitoring. If one routes the data onward as expected by the originating programs and doesn't block returning information, then a compromised system can continue to function without awareness of the existence of the man in the middle. The MiTM attack would involve changing or switching data to enable further compromise and control of a target computer or device.

**SSH:** Secure shell. A remote shell that has a lot of features and is security minded. Typically used in Linux/Unix system environments.

# Chapter 9
# Raspberry Pi Inappropriate for App Hubs in Smart Home and Security Installations:
## Risk Analysis 2019/20

**Terrence Frost**
*Security and Cyber Security Reporting and Investigation Team (SCSRIT), USA*

**Michael P. Nolan**
*Cyber Living, Thailand*

## ABSTRACT

*With the advent of IoT (internet of things), our homes are becoming more dependent on technological devices to perform everything from basic to advanced tasks. In this paper, cyber living delves into the realm of home security and the use of Raspberry Pi compute devices to secure our homes. Raspberry Pi is an educational 'system on a chip' that sells for anywhere from $30 and up. Companies have been taking these basic devices, rebranding them, and turning them into the computers that drive a home security system. They operate everything from digital locks, cameras, thermostats, fire and CO2 alarms, and more. The authors take a deep dive and look under the cover at the security and viability of Raspberry Pi as a controlling device for home security.*

DOI: 10.4018/978-1-7998-7904-6.ch009

## INTRODUCTION

Running a Smart Home or Security Software on a Raspberry Pi invites bigger threats. Criminals and hackers will seek, discover, and likely take control of your devices.

The US and global home Security Market is opening up as new start-ups leverage open hardware and open software to assemble products that replicate existing security and home automation products. SCSRIT research into the markets reveals evidence of the serious limitations of design. It is easy to reveal numerous vulnerabilities, flaws, and scope to exploit Raspberry Pi applications and operating systems using attacks including "zero-day hacking exploits" and standard attack methods which bypass network access controls. Entrepreneurs compete for market share by re-purposing educational products such as the Raspberry Pi {R.Pi} or newer clones, Banana Pro, Intel Computer Stick, etc. Of these, the key product we explored was the range of Raspberry Pi products. Typically new start-ups are utilizing or building upon free software from the RPi community of "builders" that offer alternative solutions that emulate matured security marketplace systems. However easily and cost-effectively one might, for example, be able to get their camera feed running using an RPi project kit they typically lack awareness of how many risks are associated with this hardware or their software which lacks secure engineering design considerations.

This white paper exposes the categories of threats (via an attack surface analysis) that will be avoided by favoring commercial and proprietary solutions over RPi and similar DIY hardware tools and related security applications. This advice is offered on the balance of the experience of the researchers and the state of the market and widespread hacking activity one must proactively prevent. We mention both consumer and hobbyist installations of open community project software for the RPi. The best practice is to choose the least risky installation one can afford. So we offer some criticisms of commercial providers who are building their solutions with RPi or the home DIY user but marketing them without proof of their typical claims of security being managed appropriately or warning their customers adequately of such risks.

### The Solution

SCSRIT researchers, as enthusiasts of computing solutions and security, have themselves a long familiarity with RPi and open-source software. This paper seeks to simplify that familiarity objectively to give a balanced warning as to why we don't consider RPi security software equivalent to commercial designs. Of course one still has to find a provider that has a proven track record of offering secure smart home and security products. It is beyond the scope of this paper to review and compare commercial products such as RPi and turnkey or proprietary hardware-based alternatives. Instead, we introduce terms you need to know to make your own inquires leading to a more informed decision. What we recommend you look for when shopping for a security system is to have a relationship with a company that will be able to enact the security framework (Identify, Protect, Detect, Respond, Recover) on your behalf when you are away or busy out of the home or even if you are home and there is a detectable intrusion event. Without experience and adequate cover the ability to detect and respond, the recovery aspect of security can fall down if you use an insufficient plan or provider.

Make an informed choice by assessing risk and removing high threat platforms or avoiding them where they will expose your network and compromise privacy and access.

This paper is designed to highlight the ways products that seem to offer a cost-effective advantage yet typically fail to address a broad spectrum of new dangers and intrusions made possible when supplying an RPi or similar hardware-based product. In the worst cases, common criminals will simply be able to enter undetected and there will be a diminished capacity to respond to the breach. This paper is not alone in its premise and conclusions – other white papers exist that warn of IoT Solutions in general and how they must be separated from the enterprise network.

## SECTION A: MAIN FEATURES OF ELECTRONIC AND COMPUTING SOLUTIONS FOR HOME SECURITY

In the last decade, people have become accustomed to having paired security management applications (apps) for their mobile devices and remote management tools. Such access and monitoring capabilities that were once uncommon and found mainly in medium to large scale businesses have hit mainstream users as smart home and security hub consumer products.

Such products are selling the capability to log in and check up on conditions, view cameras, or unlock areas for visitors or family on request has become affordable. Not only that, but some business operation models for rental property management activities focus on smart home automation. The idea is that by emailing access codes or credentials rental and AirBnB business cuts costs by enabling access to the tenant remotely rather than in person. Such a change represents a potential "disruptive edge" dramatically reduce costs of hospitality and management staff. As most key appliances in the home now have features that enable monitoring or alerts and even direct control users may also look to unify access and management into a software console or "hub". Smart devices such as televisions (often with cameras for communication), refrigerators, lights, and locks can be integrated into a control console or hub along with traditional security sensors and automation devices.

With the introduction of the educational product, Raspberry Pi people began to home-cook their own solutions for as little as $30 to $100 of computer hardware I set and forget "hub" or "server" can be installed. Previously the investment of the management computer may have made such a choice seem prohibitively expensive. Some users have an abundance of time or experience to build up a system in a DIY or "maker" approach. Others receive pre-installed packages when paying for a fully delivered smart home or security solution. I call the former enthusiast solutions – as they are often installed just for the person to prove to themselves that they could accomplish the task using some free open-source Linux-based software. Likewise with the later commercial products in each case the free software that fills out such small computer products like RPi are often not maintained, upgraded, or secured. Researchers in the business of security and smart homes such as Lesley Carhart have suggested that cheap and quick will exclude "secure".

*"I often tell people that, in terms of [multifamily smart home] security, things can be quick, cheap, and secure,* **but not all three at once.** *" -[***Lesley Carhart, security researcher, and blogger** ] *(Carhart, 2019)*

## A-1: Turnkey or Proprietary Designs

A turnkey system is a box that has standard hardware which has been assembled, installed, and customized to work as an appliance like a product rather than as a generic computer. A system will typically boot right into the application and shut down or reboot without the need for a user to interact with the operating system. Security firms have been installing PC systems packaged and ready to run for as long as home computers have been able to run security software. A turnkey system may prevent a user from being their own worst enemy by installing additional software which may interfere with the performance of the product.

Typically turnkey systems run into the $1000s of dollars due to development, testing, and hardware costs and require hardware integration that is compliant and supported to link to smart home or IOT devices, sensors, locks, and cameras. One example of a turnkey system is a digital phone system … essentially just a computer and some communications interfaces but it might be sold for 20x the price of what you actually get due to the work making it fulfill its required purpose. This is why you might also pay a huge multiple of the actual cost of the hardware to get a working solution but yet receive a very low-cost set of hardware – as long as it does perform as intended most people are satisfied. People can and do make their own phone systems but they tend to be associated with failures and issues and lack of up-time. So in the home, only a very few specialists will install their own smart home as a "do it yourself" solution. The question is – will it run reliably without a team maintaining it the way a turnkey system is upgraded and standardized to stay more secure and stable.

What if you are paying for what seems to be a professional turnkey smart home or security system? You may feel you are getting state-of-the-art technology only to later discover that Raspberry Pi hardware has found its way into the commercial chassis of what you purchase and install on-site. Some providers are likely not even aware of the challenges or necessity of configuring the OS to be security hardened. It is, therefore, important to consider what is under the chassis of these turnkey products and if it is indeed an RPi you should deem the risks unacceptable due attack surface demonstrated by this research. This paper is might arm a purchaser with evidence to counter the arguments that products are equivalent to more traditionally secure or enterprise-class solutions. The company selling the product will no doubt claim they have taken all precautions but penetration testers and security researchers tend to certainly disagree unless the builder was made completely aware of the attack vectors (that successfully intrude and bypass access restrictions) and how to defend against them.

Small compute units with a full OS attack surface installed are capable but generally not appropriate, in terms of security for many levels of install:

- Class 1: Sensor or actuator
- Class 2: Edge platform
- Class 3: Platform
- Class 4: Enterprise platform

Solution providers are using RPi platforms for all classes from managing an individual sensor through to Enterprise platforms. The low power consumption of RPi has made them interested to do odd jobs throughout the computing world. Once an intruder can scan your network they may well tag the RPi as an easy target and move in to enable stronger forms of network attacks or listening. Unless you are able to identify a promiscuous mode network interface capturing data you might be infiltrated for many years before paying attention to that RPi you put in simply to measure temperature and send warnings for example. All the worse if it runs the locks and cameras.

The hardware in the graphic (below Fig 1.) appears to be RPi by the port positions and dimensions of the case shown. If you don't notice this is a general-purpose educational hardware the owner might then assume the product to be appropriate and secure hardware of a much higher value. They might also assume it is custom hardware that is part of a long process or R&D rather than just an educational project toy re-purposed into a "platform" possibly with free-ware merely customized with company logos.

*Figure 1. The image clearly looks to be the form of an RPi computer with USB power – yet they prefer perhaps you don't know you have a $30-50 hardware device with a free educational OS opening your home to hackers, worms, and scripts when you plug it into your router.*
*(Dwelo, 2019)*

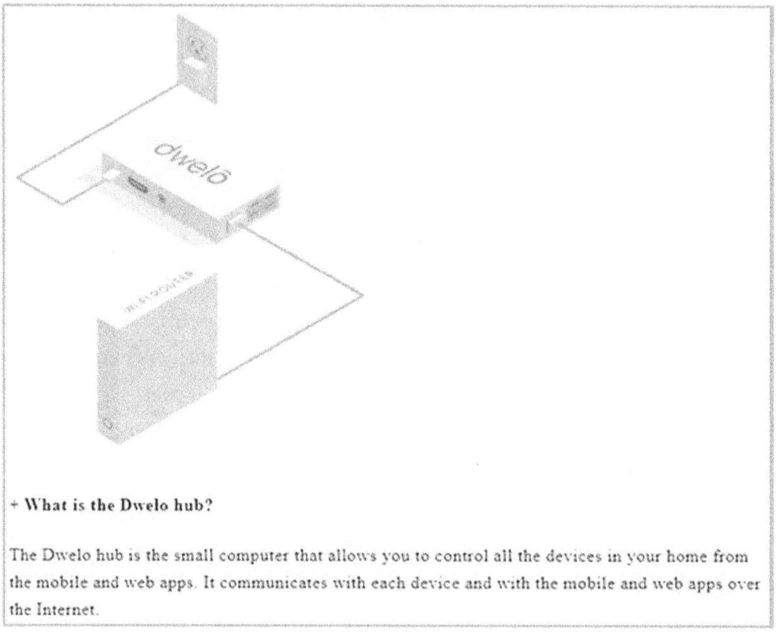


## A-2: Open Hardware

By mass-producing a design, the price of minimally functional computers has hit a new baseline for the economy. Single chips that hold a SOC or "system on a chip" can be deployed in phones or in small circuit boards read to plug and play additional hardware. Via and Intel are also manufacturing SOC solutions that are widely used but the ARM chip used in a Raspberry Pi was particularly accessible and ready to play full-resolution HD video. While there is no avoiding of these small-scale systems there is also no reason why one of many designs and systems that are designed for security should be selected. Look at the crypto-currency hardware wallet industry and you'll see a pure focus on security and yet you'll also see completely random lightweight designs on generic hardware masquerading as equivalent. The takeaway is that unless you can look into the provider and its investment and commitment to the product then you can just be swallowing misinformation and marketing white-lies or worse. Independent security reviews are a key indicator of commitment to real security enhancement and best practices.

A Raspberry Pi is not a commercially featured computer but it does have a lot more physical interfaces working than typical small hardware put inside phones, tablets, and media players for example. It is extensible and supported by a community that maintains Raspbian Linux tuned and customized, or as the front page for this software states *"Raspbian is a free operating system based on Debian optimized for the Raspberry Pi hardware."*

Many Linux variations and even a cut-down Windows 10 IOT have been delivered as partial or full compatibility for Raspberry Pi 3. See *section B-8* for a more exhaustive list of OS or "distributions". Typically these are distributed as an SD card image that one flashes and plugs in. Many if not all of these OS have been targeted for hacking and intrusion and exploit knowledge sharing. Some have known vulnerabilities that just don't get fixed until major version upgrades which in turn bring new weaknesses to be discovered and exploited.

This white paper represents an important cautionary stance due to a run-away industry taking advantage of the strategic price-cutting involved when building "solutions" with the Raspberry Pi and similar low-end computing units. Some businesses represent a home project kit now reintegrated commercially as an install hub for their products. This may seem to be the way of the world to some but it bypasses decades of experience and appropriate hardware design requirements. So it is logical that the RPi is on less than equal footing with established security system providers. There are reports of companies deploying solutions that use a Raspberry Pi such as SmartRent.com, Dwelo.com, Zego.io, IOTAShome.com (IoT is a reference to the Internet of Things). I found the websites of these companies disturbingly generic and rushed as I looked for signs of security expertise I found little to nothing with details or substance.

A company will typically boast:

*"We take every precaution in protecting your data through encryption and the installed devices we use in units are also held to those same standards." (Smartrent, 2019)*

Such a statement, however, is immeasurable without a review by an independent security review or equivalent which lack conflict of interest. Precautions are known to be increasingly expensive such that 99.999% secure would be 1000s of times more expensive than 99% secure and such numbers are not so meaningful.

This is why Open Hardware that has no basis in design for security would be contrary to such an intention. Generically capable of running the software will always require more investment and layers of engineering to prevent tampering and intrusion.

## A-3: Security Design Features

Commercial hardware. While less efficient in terms of price, custom hardware is still the basis for many commercially built electronics and computing products. In terms of the security space, the details of the internal parts are often private and thus it is more difficult for the open-source community to reverse engineer and document because of difficulty working with or acquiring such a product. By comparison, open hardware has a captive community of users, programmers, and hackers – an extension of the programmers and users. Commercial hardware hackers are more clandestine and unlikely to give their solutions or tools away for free for anyone to utilize.

The industry is highly competitive but as we see with many growing industries a start-up may flourish, get venture capital, and yet they are barely into their first product before they pivot. Gozego.com "Zego drives engagement and efficiency across residential real estate communities. With our mobile-centric engagement platform, communities manage their resident-facing tasks within a single app.

"so it is more likely that marketing is running the show in terms of boasting the product as "secure enough". The attitude is that as long as you can make the software appear to service customers, they can go on in ignorance to the fact that they didn't get commercial grade secured hardware but potentially a mere $30-50 shelf component and an educational operating system. (Gozego 2019)

For these Smart Home and IoT-based security companies using RPi, we couldn't locate evidence that a red team or pen-tester had been engaged to secure or manage the device. Even if they had they may as well be boasting that they can secure a widely known OS when they know it's likely they will get hacked. In a world full of commercial and government hacking agencies your apartment might automatically be housing anyone who can unlock it and bypass any payment of rent. Very similar to the crypto-currency industry which has huge start-up firms operating software that is merely copied and re-branded. Start-ups have been known to demo projects that look promising but never deliver a fully developed solution – hoping they can gain momentum and popularity first and fix the problems when the sales and investors are in.

The Zego.io hub and software were produced by developers who describe themselves as "*a group of real estate owners, managers, and investors who are technology enthusiasts*" and not so much security and automation engineers.

# SECTION B: ATTACK SURFACE STUDY OF RPI CLASS DEVICES

## Lightweight Linux vs. Commercial Security

### B-1: Internet Direct Connection – Open Ports, Open Access, Wi-Fi Exploits

We can make several assumptions if someone chooses lightweight hardware and Linux OS such as a Raspberry Pi to install low cost or face value "freeware" projects that provide device security monitoring with cameras or other detectors, zone alarms.

#### *SSH and Tunneling*

SSH keys are a known weakness even though they offer somewhat strong encryption. Everyone is so reliant that these ports are typically open (on a known port number) and give a serious attack vector. (Bisson D. 2019)

A system may have default keys or not very random new keys generated. Other ports like FTP, HTTP(s) may be running soon after a new install in order to test and provide upload access. A professional security device would be pre-configured with a relatively strong key and run on an uncommon access port but a fresh Linux typically uses default ports that are assumed and probed. So the following staged sets of attacks typically penetrate deeper and deeper into your network.

#### *Exploiting Predictable Mistakes (Making Educated Assumptions)*

These assumptions are that typical oversights will happen in the "whatever can go wrong will go wrong" fashion that engineers come to know through experience (aka Murphy's Law). So we assume that hackers will accelerate penetration by working with common oversights. One or more mistakes give them a vector to access the LAN from the internet or locally. Exploits are based on mistakes being distributed with the software and operating system such that it is a known way to bypass the need for or gain root access.

**Assumption 1:** Exposed during setup time.

Having installed Linux an internet direct connection will be needed to acquire and update packages. Most of the users who work with a Linux operating system are prone to leave internet access on for potentially days or weeks before the device gets re-purposed and security gaps are closed off.

**Assumption 2:** Password not changed fast enough, or well enough

It takes a high degree of focus to secure and prepare your Linux OS of any type but particularly for a "quick and inexpensive solution" to bring it up to a low level of security. The guidelines of the Raspberry Pi are to change the password from the default set up password image flashed onto the SD card as pre-defined. So from the start, the system comes online with a default password. If the device is probed then it might be compromised immediately.

**Assumption 3:** Trusting your own LAN – no DMZ

A significant percentage of users will likely have a new threat that they don't manage lurking in their homes as a result of the first two assumptions. At some point, if they have mobile or PC devices in the same network that get compromised they will likely have the intruder discover and move into their Linux laptop or other servers that have any weakness. Pen testers do these scenarios where they take over more and more assets on the network once they enter. They assume people feel their home network is safe and weak passwords are acceptable.

**Assumption 4:** Trusting your workstation security

Once LAN access is established and local computer crack has been accomplished further penetration is likely simplified. The main workstation or personal computers will have stored passwords in browsers that help an intruder get into devices protected with better passwords or mac-address restricted access lists. From here where convenience, lets us all down the intruder will further install malware and other packages, rootkits that may be undetectable or customized so they are not known.

**Assumption 5:** Worms exist because we create conditions for them to breed

There is a continuous probing for exactly these weaknesses often enabled by worms (*An Internet worm is a type of malicious software (malware) that self-replicates and distributes copies of itself to its network*) spreading wherever an exploit works. A virus tends to require some interaction like a replug or power cycle that triggers the payload but a worm runs autonomously. Once caught the system will "phone home" and hackers will manually engage the discovered network. The thief/hacker/system cracker is likely to leave a payload that will periodically probe the local network and report back to the new secret users of the "zombie" device information about equipment that is accessible in your local network. Even after you cleansed everything a payload may be a Trojan horse that you run accidentally. The anti-virus that you expect to warn you of the types of rewriting of sensitive files might even be disabled by the Trojan before it does its dirty work. Antivirus, anti-malware is a necessity that happens because … it has to for the Trojan to spread widely. That is why we label these assumptions rather than problems … we know they happen predictably in the wild. We assume they will keep happening due to human nature.

These assumed potential vulnerabilities are all relevant to an RPi installation – particularly due to the pre-installed SD flash with the standard password and the use of a home network and smart home, IoT devices, sensors – the kind of installation where an RPi seems to be a cost-effective add-on. In reality, this network becomes all the more in need of risk management. Additionally business's we might rent or buy products from – if they get hacked or the access discovered then you will get owned by the trusted side. If they are willing to use RPi then I assume they are less aware of the attack surface analysis that makes it (potentially) so undesirable and obvious low hanging fruit.

These assumed vulnerabilities are very common to find in-home enthusiast computer user installations. So many devices may be operating on a home network. It is easy to overlook or just lack awareness of security guidelines due to a lack of time to complete the work. Quick is obviously a typical hope for the project, get it up and running as fast as possible. The apps themselves will beg to have internet access and it is unlikely the home user will use a proxy or local cache to prevent direct ports from being opened by network NAT port settings that require the RPi OS install to be exposed directly to the internet at least by a few ports required for external access of camera feeds and other remote access desires. With growing commercial sales of products that are essentially home enthusiast products under the veneer of commercial-grade security, there is a growing honey pot incentivizing more hacker activity to specialize in breaching these systems?

One company that was researched was IOTAShome.com (IoT)and this whole internet of things philosophy is referring to a vision. Unfortunately, the vision can be delivered in such a way that you have an internet of hackable things that you lose control of.

### *Open Access and Wi-Fi (802.11a/b/g/n)*

If a deployment involves cabling, it is possible that some sensors will merely use Wi-Fi instead to get around the difficulties of hard wiring. This means that the threat is dual, the internet can expose the device to be "captured" by a breach or the device can be captured via Wi-Fi at the location, bypassing the firewall and exposing the local network once it has been rewritten. The power could be cut and during a reboot, a less-developed product might be in a "discovery mode" or even join a network spoofing the Wi-Fi access name to name a couple of more obvious attacks. Typically, an RPi has the cheapest Wi-Fi onboard as part of its experimentation-oriented function. If someone does join a Wi-Fi network (let us assume they know-how or the password was weak) they can listen and record enough information to know what types of hardware and which exploits are worth attacking. These devices could also become hubs installed just to capture sensors and be forgotten and left unsecured after installation even if the hub was somehow kept configured and defended. After all, salespeople will realize they can sell many of the inexpensive hub units to give the customer the solution and expand the threat to many R.Pi. An open port for a probe or sensor can be attacked just like any network port that has interrogated/response, buffer, malformed data, and other potential weaknesses. These sensor deployments may have new network services that have never been developed with security in mind and may even be insecure because they are not considered in need of defense (deadly assumption).

## B-2: Internet Via Gateway, Firewall, and NAT

If your device is protected by being in a local network behind an internet access device you will mostly eliminate that security benefit as soon as you forward a port. It is normal to open up access to your web applications for your own ability to view them from the internet side. Redirecting can be made slightly less obvious using unusual port numbers that may be scanned less often. The issue is you are also letting anyone get through that "gateway" to attack relevant network ports (and services) of RPi. With some installs, the security feeds and monitor cameras are not yours to view and doors can't be unlocked for visitors when you aren't at home unless you open the device to access. This basically reduces you to B-1 type exploits and attack vectors listed above. It can be abated somewhat by using tunneling and VPN access but these tend to run on more heavyweight network security installations. Consumer internet IP ranges with weaker low-cost internet gateways will get attacked as flaws with their hardware being discovered.

Open source projects and security applications tend to focus first on providing services. Then often they have left security and testing to be an afterthought even if the application is related to the security industry. Those same services aren't easily turned into an asset of the hacker or thief trying to compromise your property or home. The applications may use UPnP (universal plug and play) to automatically open themselves a port if your internet router/firewall has this option switched on so some users. We can't assume they are secure or insecure … but we know there are a lot of RPi and IOT getting leveraged by hackers so we have evidence that bugs and flaws will always exist and be found. This is basic to computing science – that code always has bugs and side effects. Any system to verify code runs precisely with no side effects or bugs becomes impossibly complex as the code base scales up. Testing these truths are for example network attacks that use malformed URLs or scripts to overload or create side effects at the network service port and yield unexpectedly big successes. Once discovered the knowledge spreads and what was once considered secure needs an update.

Once a port is available for attack … be it XML, HTTP, FTP, SQL … there are systems to confirm if vulnerabilities are present which enable access or execution of commands at the destination. This pasted graphic lists a tiny portion just for one type of user interface offering web services. Testing systems use language such as "Assertions are used to assess if the responses for the Security Scan requests contain some kind of content that indicates if the target system has a corresponding vulnerability"

*Figure 2. pg11*

SQL Injection
XPath Injection
Fuzzing Scan
Invalid Types
Boundary Scan
**Malformed XML**
XML Bomb
Cross-Site Scripting
Malicious Attachment

The process of finding the best provider who has answers to these attack surface topics is one way to choose a capable product. How do they avoid open port risks – do they have locked down port source/destination, or server/slave access rules and firewall software standards to ensure these can be maintained. Software engineers may have designed the system to offer access to the security devices by enabling connections through the firewall. This means ports are not exposed and the connection is made from the inside of your network to the trusted external server giving access to their smart home and cameras. The security provider's design may notify the user if their account is being accessed from a new location so there can be more warning if their account is used without authorization.

It is also likely they will provide devices that are locked to exclusively communicate with their servers at the security website so that threats are limited by design from turning into attack assets to probe and break further assets in your local network once one device is compromised. On the other hand, devices that advertise "not talking to" are assuming they can't be upgraded so one has to be sure the upgrade or rewriting of the local software has been made as difficult as possible.

## B-3: Physical Direct Access, Tampering Detection, USB Attacks

The Raspberry Pi has a USB/SD card storage system making it exceptionally easy to tamper with or just shut off, remove, copy and re-plug a compromised replacement. Keeping a system that boots from an SD card encrypted is more difficult on an RPi than on a conventional PC so if you can pull the card then likely you can find some usable hack or secret by copying it and returning it. (See B-4 for more detail) An attacker could also plug in a USB device that automates an attack to compromise the device – keyboard simulators can be built into tiny USB modules and feed a series of attacks – that attempt to execute commands or download payloads and execute those. Here is only a list of one single category of USB attacks just to expose the reader to the vastness of this attack vector. (Catalin Cimpanu 2019)

### Reprogrammable Microcontroller USB Attacks

1. Rubber Ducky - a commercial keystroke injection attack platform released in 2010. Once connected to a host computer, the Rubber Ducky poses as a keyboard and injects a preloaded keystroke sequence.
2. PHUKD/URFUKED attack platforms - similar to Rubber Ducky, but allows an attacker to select the time when it injects the malicious keystrokes.
3. USBdriveby - provides quick covert installation of backdoors and overriding DNS settings on an unlocked OS X host via USB in a matter of seconds by emulating a USB keyboard and mouse.
4. Evilduino - similar to PHUKD/URFUKED, but uses Arduino microcontrollers instead of Teensy. Also works by emulating a keyboard/mouse and can send keystrokes/mouse cursor movements to the host according to a preloaded script.
5. Unintended USB channel - a proof of concept (POC) USB hardware Trojan that exfiltrates data based on unintended USB channels (such as using USB speakers to exfiltrate data).
6. TURNIPSCHOOL (COTTONMOUTH-1) - a hardware implant concealed within a USB cable. Developed by the NSA.
7. RIT attack via USB mass storage - attack described in a research paper. It relies on changing the content of files while the USB mass storage device is connected to a victim's computer.

8. Attacks on wireless USB dongles - a category of attacks first explored with the release of the KeySweeper attack platform by Samy Kamkar, a tool that covertly logs and decrypts keystrokes from many Microsoft RF wireless keyboards.
9. Default Gateway Override - an attack that uses a microcontroller to spoof a USB Ethernet adapter to override DHCP settings and hijack local traffic. (Catalin Cimpanu 2019)

Raspberry Pi is obviously just a raw part that a designer can take and build into a computing application. The point here is that the generic purpose of RPi doesn't make it difficult to tamper with or slow down such work – it makes it as easy as possible. Many home designers won't consider that their device will end up exposed to such a threat. A chassis or product can be made tamper-proof or have tamper detection and alarms … if you use a company that thinks of and has such a device manufactured to mitigate this attack vector.

## B-4: Physical Storage Media Vulnerabilities

While some solutions in security software make modification and tampering difficult an educational product using an SD card or USB flash drive for storage offers easy access, encryption challenges, update and hack vectors. What is great for ease of use is also a serious attack surface and pulling, copying or accessing, and rewriting the system to have new back-doors or malware is made all the easier because RPi and its low-cost storage system were not designed with commercial use in mind. The system makes it very difficult to install an encrypted storage mode … it requires advanced techniques to modify and keep data encrypted.

*Figure 3.*

Security anecdotal evidence and other research reveal that novice security software suite developers leave important lock codes stored locally where they can be copied and read directly. Best security practice is very far down the developmental road map. So rough software tends to expose data to easily be copied. Data is often left in obvious 'config' files or databases that lack encryption. Leaving unencrypted "access codes" where they are easily accessed by a simple copy of the SD card or USB "disk" of the R. Pi is a typical "you aren't going to need it" rapid development approach that enables these free products to be produced on a low budget. See the peer review section where developers have given code a look over and found many shocking issues with the security of products that are recommended highly by users who are possibly just happy it works at any level at all. The bar can be quite low when it comes to setting up and operating open-source software.

RPI supports booting "bare-metal code" (from SD card)which means it is possible to do highly sophisticated tricks if one knows how to work with the device – this is less secure perhaps than just having a BIOS at boot time. Some security experts explain a pathway to modifying the SoC firmware:

*"The GPU mounts the SD card, loads GPU firmware and brings up display/video/3d, loads a kernel image, resets the SD card host, and starts the ARM. You could replace the kernel image with a bootloader image, and that would work fine." (Elinux 2019)*

This means that an SD card could do things you just don't understand or see if tampered within a highly specialized way.

To avoid devices being a source of sensitive data there are different ways to store the crucial information – places that are harder to find or access in possession of the property owner. Lock codes could be far more difficult to access stored in smartphones and cloud-based security consoles behind password/authentication walls. Encryption keys are often irrelevant if someone is able to log in and recover an operating system that was cloned, this is due to recovery tools in design that essentially render some types of security ineffective just so the data won't be lost.

## B-5: System Updating Reliability

Securing a Linux-based PC for personal use is one thing but leaving a hub running and potentially unable to update without intervention means that fresh "zero-day" exploits will mean your security hub becomes a candidate for being hacked/cracked at some random time in the future. As mentioned above open-source OS are very broad and general purposed and so there are huge amounts of software installed that can yield vulnerabilities. That is why updates are ongoing and endless. Some RPi will have a very small SSD disk that makes downloading and upgrading impractical without a complete re-flash. A provider is unlikely to be shipping you updated SSD to re-plug, many systems are left in older versions until the customer pays for upgrades or accesses them manually. Meanwhile, you forget about updates and get on with life – until the day you get a breach.

### *An Uncharted Vulnerability*

A zero-day attack happens once that flaw, or software/hardware vulnerability, is exploited and attackers release malware before a developer has an opportunity to create a patch to fix the vulnerability.

Though some security vendors sell defenses against zero-day attacks it is also generally the best we can do to simply patch our system when a patch that removed the vulnerability is released. So there two layers of updates – the operating system and the applications themselves. Within those, some distributions may neglect to keep their repositories updated. The most professionally maintained repositories are typically commercial subscriptions and unlikely to be utilized on an RPi.

## B-6: Operating System Attack Surface Scope – Local Device Threats

This point is mentioned throughout section B but to summarize. Raspian is an academic/educational OS and is not sold hardened for security. Nor do the companies that I reviewed mention anything about hardening Raspian to attacks. It is likely many services should be not just shut down but blocked fully by a firewall in case they do start for some unexpected reason (such as a hacking attempt). Many ports will directly open your router via Universal Plug and Play such that they are exposing their ports directly to attack and this is done for ease of use and convenience and such things are only the start of being well configured at the distribution level. Should you upgrade to the latest version of Raspian to be "more secure" it is possible that attempts to harden are just overwritten. So unless the OS is maintained by your provider as hardened and they maintain upgrades from their own servers you could be switching on everything one day unexpectedly that needs to be turned off to maintain any hope of security from exploits and hacking. This is why so often you will see pictures on Twitter of people's smart locks being simply and easily "taken ownership of" every time a new trick is figured out and a gap in security shared by the hacker community for bragging rights.

Discussions on forums reveal that the Raspberry Pi is not practical for locking in a read-only (locked) boot image. Automated restarts require storing passwords/passphrase on the device. That means that as per the topic on physical media access – it is simple to pull and copy your SD card if anyone is visiting your location. Encrypting the system is reported to be problematic for the same reasons – so security basics are lacking as a priority for the Raspian OS community.

## B.7: Novel Attack Vectors – Bluetooth Keyboard and Mouse

Just for completeness – it should be noted that attack systems are engineered to come near the device and masquerade as its keyboard – then begin attacking via the console directly. It may be that new Wi-Fi has such a range that one can access the console remotely through a door or wall. The console could even be insecure assuming only local access is possible via a physical keyboard.

USB attacks described in section B-3 are likely to be adapted for Bluetooth keyboard device mode. These may be common problems with all computers but the utility of the RPi does tend to suggest people will find Bluetooth convenient and pair a device and possibly leave their RPi exposed. Bluetooth is often involved in security challenge/response dongles (smart car keys for example) but these are the kind of devices that can be sniffed, a listening or interrogation technique, to reveal codes. Further research into these attacks may yield new vectors.

## B.8: Community Interest In Exploiting and Hacking Low-Cost Compute Units Such As R.Pi

The RPi is considered by many as an invaluable tool for hacking itself – there are YouTube videos and "ethical hacking" OS and tools that train people how to use an RPi to learn to hack. Suffice to say they will be very aware of their own RPI attack surface and vulnerabilities when learning this way. We will be investigating what can be learned via the online hacking community that lends itself to updates on the risks of using an RPi in home security and so forth.

*Figure 4. Hacking the RPi is even an event/conference and hackathon see hackrpi.com even though "hacking" doesn't only mean trying to break security (crack) it does mean taking advantage of unforeseen uses and exploits of hardware and software.*

HACK RPI

To demonstrate the extent of community and educational use and how many sub-communities have ported their OS distributions to RPi here I'm including a list.

What I'm pointing out is how much knowledge of what is weak and exploitable is available to the hacking community. Note that some distributions are application-oriented and surveillance-oriented. Windows as an IOT install is possible rather than a fully functional Windows 10. In fact, a hacking study group can use these group devices to create affordable environments to practice their techniques and become more familiar with OS or and network service vulnerabilities.

### *Supported Linux Distributions*

As of 2019-2020, few Linux distributions that aren't ported to the ARM processor family and tested for Raspberry Pi 1,2,3 and 4. You can easily get a list from distrowatch.com and see a very long list there. Notably, Kali Linux runs on RPi which is based on Debian and that shows that the hacking community has embraced the Raspberry Pi which means its attack surface is all the more exposed versus a proprietary platform that has a barrier of time to research and reverse engineer unknown software.

## C. NEWS AS EVIDENCE

The structure of this section is simple – the source URL and a quote that we find relevant to help the reader confirm the sentiment and recommendation expressed in this white paper. At the time of this chapter being written, several researchers were confirming the premise the authors make in this document.

*"PrivateEyePi is a home automation and monitoring project for the RaspberryPi. I saw some articles about PrivateEyePi and saw that they even have their own store on their website. Since I am the author of alertR (another open-source alarm system), I thought I take a closer look at what they are doing. Before we started with alertR, we looked briefly at some open-source projects to see if some projects were doing what we wanted to do. In most cases, it was sufficient to only look at the website of the project. PrivateEyePi was quickly dismissed by me because they only work with one host. Hence, I never took a closer look into it. And I know that it looks a little bit pitiful that I am writing an article about "how insecure this project is". But after taking a closer look, I have to say that from a security perspective I strongly discourage anybody to use it. " (Squall, 2019)*

*"We've seen cybercriminals leverage connected devices for destructive purposes before.*

*Last year, the Mirai botnet took control of smart home devices, like security cameras, all over the world, effectively turning them into zombie machines directing web traffic to take down popular websites like Netflix and Twitter." (Larson S. 2019)*

*"Building management systems says Clacherty, are not built with internet connectivity and security in mind. Many of the devices have IP interfaces and installers often enable internet access with little consideration for the security implications."*

*Note: A building management system and a smart home are essentially the same. AND*

*"For example, a hardware developer might choose to use a processor technology that comes with an older Linux distribution. That hardware is integrated with the solution and sold with little consideration given to how that software will be updated."' (Clacherty, 2019)*

*"Experts caution consumers to research carefully and move diligently when adding smart devices to their home network. "If one device gets compromised, it could be the same as allowing an attacker to plug into the entire network," giving the criminal control over all devices, warned Mr. Henderson." (Henderson, 2019)*

## D. CONCLUSION AND RECOMMENDATIONS

This white paper does not recommend any brand or company – but was written to assist a buyer in selecting a product appropriate for their needs. If people are aware of risks and ask questions that expose vulnerabilities in a product that is being considered, they can say they have done their research and if that means using an RPi – then so be it. Maybe an RPi gives more security than one has without it – be sure to install it with the understanding of its potential to be taken over.

A buyer should simply be able to express that "I don't wish to use a Raspberry Pi-based installation" if the seller is concealing the use of such hardware. One can ask questions if they aren't sure and use this report to match up what I consider an unacceptable attack surface and unreliable data protection model. I am not reviewing the software but generally stating that software installed on this product Raspberry Pi – let the buyer beware of the risks. From a Law enforcement perspective, it may be risky to deploy Rpi-based systems, given their many vulnerabilities.

You may be a corporate or home buyer, but you can represent your own need to do due diligence by asking some questions. Simply tell the salesperson that all prospective sellers need to answer these questions. That is what I would do and have done for similar types of system acquisition working as a CIO.

1. Due Diligence Questions for sales/technical:
2. Does the product use Raspberry Pi hardware? Why?
3. Does the product have tamper-proof or secure storage, encryption?
4. Does the product login to an online portal instead of hosting a website that opens ports to a router/firewall at the installation location?
5. Is the product running on the secure or hardened OS and is the repository maintained or updated regularly?

**Alternative products** are beyond the scope of this white paper. A prospective buyer of a turnkey system should be suspicious of those products that don't say what is "inside the box". Be curious and investigate to see if there is in fact a generic compute unit and OS being used to operate a security hub or smart home host device.

## Addendum: Notes and Links of Interest on Raspberry Pi

Details on the construction of the Raspberry Pi B (the model that has been sold most)

### Notes from the Manufacturer Website

RS Electronics mention the *endless possibilities* for RPi – which is just saying "it's a computer" with interfaces. However, it should be noted they don't list security as the main strength when they describe home automation. In fact, they reduce it to benign and limited examples of appliances. Perhaps knowing that it is likely to get attacked and misused in many situations where the user exposes the RPi to the internet, Wi-Fi, or even Bluetooth attack vectors.

RS Electronics does push some of the applications that have been developed for the RPi

"Home Automation" - enter the generation of the Internet of Things by setting up automated lighting, appliances, or temperature control systems throughout your home. (Andrew Rassweiler 2019)

## E. TERMS AND DEFINITIONS

This section is a selection of terminology (or terms) and a brief introduction and context are given to assist the reader in following the body of this white paper.

## Terms 1: Security Framework – Scope of Security Solutions

A security framework such as this 5 category approach as advised by NIST (National Institute of Standards and Technology) gives us an overview. A framework structure to understand limitations, weaknesses, and threats of insufficient or inexperienced installations.

- **Identify** – Risk Assessment and Risk Management are relevant here (Section A and B speak to new risks of RPi solutions).
- **Protect** – Delivery of critical services (for example managing and defending smart locks, power, and telecoms connectivity to advise police, local security, or emergency services) such that they remain available and work as intended. Sections B1, B2, and B6 are related.
- **Detect** – Develop and deliver strategies to capture evidence that enables the response immediately and for review to breaches. Lighting, infra-red, audio, motion sensors, camera motion triggering, door opening, and even malfunction reporting such that detectors are off-line or need attention.
- **Respond** – Apply rules and requirements possibly choose silently summoning or sonic alarm deterrents, lockdown as appropriate in an automated and managed system. Cutting costs often make it difficult or unstable to get automated attention and response. Generally, without a commercial partner and standards related to installation, it is only a basic post-event re-active rather than an immediate and proactive response that is associated with DIY solutions. It is possible to integrate with police or security services but this would make the user equivalent to a security expert building a commercial grade system. Some home or site automation is related to response, to interact with an intruder a professional is preferred.
- **Recover** – A plan and system to restore services or facilitate assisting external activities to recover financial loss or compensate the user in the event of a breach or harmful act. It is possible that insurance or police will be unable to accept or deal with homegrown installations and so there is an additional threat that recovery will be hindered by systems that are not verified and engineered to comply with standards that may be required by insurance and investigative authorities. *(NIST, 2019)*

## Terms 2: Raspberry Pi (RPi) as a Problematic Hardware Foundation in Home Security

This white paper is, above all, a risk analysis of using the Raspberry Pi for Home Security and Smart Locks, Smart Home automation or to gather sensor and camera feeds. The risk is high because the attack surface is considered, in our opinion, unmanageable by the companies or home users who use a Raspberry pi as a platform for installing proprietary or open-source software related to this industry. Commitment to managing risk would mean developing one's own hardware or sourcing a lower-risk platform.

As an educational or normal computer tool, the Raspberry Pi is what it is, low cost and quite excellent for proof-of-concept projects and connecting to electronics for testing. This white paper is offered to improve consumer awareness of the way high-risk internet-connected devices enable intruders the potential to unlock or tamper with your premises.

Used as a set and forget part of your building a Raspberry Pi will create new security gaps. See section C for evidence of how hackers harness many home security devices as part of their "Botnet" taking control of small always-on computers with custom scripts that exploit and take over Raspberry Pi. Raspberry Pi and its essentially free software is likely the basis on which many new start-ups competing with the incumbent security industry. Knowing about this hardware one can ask questions (as seen in section D) to salespeople who may want to hide what is under the hood of their solution.

*Figure 5. One can identify a Raspberry Pi by the small footprint, HDMI and audio jack, and SD card slot that typically acts as your 'disk' for the OS.*

To be fair the Raspberry Pi is also a solution-making tool as much as it is a problem but this is contextual and the negative stance we demonstrated hereafter with the attack surface study of the device explains.

Commonly held to be "Intended as an inexpensive educational platform for comp sci" https://electronics360.globalspec.com/article/4013/teardown-raspberry-pi-b

Total cost (from 2014) (direct materials and manufacturing): $19.83

Major components:

- Apps Processor, ARM117JZ-F CPU, Dual Core VideoCore GPU, 1080p30 Video, PoP - MFG: BROADCOM CORP - MPN:
- BCM2835RIPPG - (Qty: 1)
- SDRAM, Mobile DDR2, 4Gb, PoP - MFG: SAMSUNG SEMICONDUCTOR INC - MPN: K4P4G324EB-AGC1 - (Qty: 1)
- Ethernet Controller / USB Hub, 10/100Base-TX, USB 2.0 - MFG: SMSC - MPN: LAN9512-JZX - (Qty: 1)
- 6-Layer, FR4 - (Qty: 1)
- Jack, RJ45, Right Angle, w/ Metal Shielding - MFG: EDAC INC - (Qty: 1)
- SD Card Slot, Push-Push - MFG: TOBY ELECTRONICS - MPN: 412D02F-09PC003-SV Series - (Qty: 1)
- TVS Diode Array, 5V, 150W, 4-Line, Unidirectional, .30pF - MFG: SEMTECH CORP - MPN: RClamp0524PATCT - (Qty: 2)
- FFC / FPC, Vertical, w/ Lock - (Qty: 2)
- Jack, USB, Type A, Dual Stacked, Right Angle, w/ Metal Housing - MFG: TE CONNECTIVITY LTD - (Qty: 1)
- Jack, HDMI, Type A (Female), Right Angle, w/ Metal Housing - MFG: TE CONNECTIVITY LTD - (Qty: 1)

The newer RPi B+ has upgraded capabilities but is very similar.

[Ed: Since 2019 the RPi 4 has introduced improved specs including more RAM – 2GB, 4GB, and soon 8GB options]

## Terms 3: Attack Surface Definition

"Attack Surface Analysis is about mapping out what parts of a system need to be reviewed and tested for security vulnerabilities. The point of Attack Surface Analysis is to understand the risk areas in an application, to make developers and security specialists aware of what parts of the application are open to attack, to find ways of minimizing this, and to notice when and how the Attack Surface changes and what this means from a risk perspective." - Definition quoted from the Attack Surface Analysis Cheat Sheet

## Terms 4: IoT (Internet of Things)

Internet of things a new jargon referring to small, generally cost-effective compute units (such as R.Pi) purposed to give an interface for an appliance such as your TV and audio systems, refrigerator, lights, doors and locks, and other items that one might not expect. A white paper on security risks of IoT in the enterprise network says *"the diversity of IoT devices leaves enterprises vulnerable. A recent CEB, now Gartner, the* survey *found that nearly 20% of organizations observed at least one IoT-based attack in the past three years."*

## Terms 5: SOC (System on a Chip)

System on a chip refers to very-large-scale integration which not only puts a microprocessor on one silicon chip design but all the related communications, video graphics, and peripheral devices that were previously separate chips or even daughter cards in computer hardware. SOC devices are typically small and specialized but in the case of the RPi, they can be made into a General Purpose computing unit. An RPI has video and processing but there are still additional chips for communications on the small form factor circuit board.

## Terms 6: ARM (Advanced RISC Machines) as a Category of CPU Type

A series of Reduced Instruction Set computer designs that has, over the last 20 years, gained more and more market share and developed into many cutting edge designs. These typically work well for mobile devices or light, small computers due to their minimal power consumption in particular. See reference: https://en.wikipedia.org/wiki/ARM_architecture

## Terms 7: SSD Solid State Disk Drive

A solid-state drive is a solid-state storage device that uses integrated circuit assemblies to store data persistently, typically using flash memory, and functioning as secondary storage in the hierarchy of computer storage.

## Terms 8: What Is Rasberry Pi

The Raspberry Pi is a low-cost, **credit-card-sized computer** that plugs into a computer monitor or TV, and uses a standard keyboard and mouse. It is a capable little device that enables people of all ages to explore computing and to learn how to program in languages like Scratch and Python. It's capable of doing everything you'd expect a desktop computer to do, from browsing the internet and playing high-definition video, to making spreadsheets, word-processing, and playing games.

What's more, the Raspberry Pi has the ability to interact with the outside world and has been used in a wide array of digital maker projects, from music machines and parent detectors to weather stations and tweeting birdhouses with infra-red cameras. We want to see the Raspberry Pi being used by kids all over the world to learn to program and understand how computers work. https://www.raspberrypi.org/help/what-%20is-a-raspberry-pi/ Accessed May 2nd, 2019

## REFERENCES

Bisson, D. (2019). *SSH keys are a known weakness even though they offer somewhat strong encryption. Everyone is so reliant that these ports are typically open (on a known port number) and give a serious attack vector*. https://www.venafi.com/blog/top-4-risks-weak-ssh-key-management

Carhart, L. (2019). *Do renters have the right to reject smart-home technology?* Accessed March, 3rd, 2019 from https://www.marketplace.org/shows/marketplace-tech/do-renters-have-right-dumb-apartment/

Cimpanu. (2019). *Here's a List of 29 Different Types of USB Attacks*. https://www.bleepingcomputer.com/news/security/heres-a-list-of-29-different-types-of-usb-attacks/

Clacherty. (2019). https://www.cso.com.au/article/600538/building-management-systems-afraid-very-afraid/

Dwelo. (2019). *Documentation for Dwelo hub*. Author.

Elinux. (2019). *The GPU mounts the SD card, loads GPU firmware and brings up display/video/3d, loads a kernel image resets the SD card host and starts the ARM. You could replace the kernel image with a bootloader image, and that would work fine*. https://elinux.org/RPi_Software

Gozego. (2019). *Zego drives engagement and efficiency across residential real estate communities. With our mobile-centric engagement platform, communities manage their resident-facing tasks within a single app*. https://www.gozego.com/platform/zego-smart/

Henderson. (2019). https://www.nytimes.com/2019/01/22/business/smart-home-buyers-security-risks.html

Larson, S. (2019). *A smart fish tank left a casino vulnerable to hackers.* https://money.cnn.com/2017/07/19/technology/fish-tank-hack-darktrace/index.html

NIST. (2019). *Cyber Security Framework 2014 version.* National Institute of Standards and Technology. https://www.nist.gov/cyberframework

Rassweiler, A. (2019). *Teardown: Raspberry Pi B*. https://electronics360.globalspec.com/article/4013/teardown-raspberry-pi-b

Smart Rent. (2019). *We take every precaution in protecting your data through encryption and the installed devices we use in units are also held to those same standards*. http://org.smartrent.com/data-security-privacy/

Squall. (2019). *Security Issues in PrivateEyePi Home Alarm System: Why I would not use it!* https://h4des.org/blog/index.php?/archives/353-Security-Issues-in-PrivateEyePi-Home-Alarm-System-Why-I-would-not-use-it!.html

# Chapter 10
# The Significance of STEM Education for National Security

**Tianxing Cai**
*Lamar University, USA*

## ABSTRACT

*Reaffirming America's role as the global engine of scientific discovery and technological innovation has never been more critical. Challenges like climate change, pandemic disease, and resource scarcity demand innovation. Meanwhile, the nation that leads the world in building a clean energy economy that will enjoy a substantial economic and security advantage. That is why the administration is investing heavily in research, improving education in science and math, promoting developments in energy, and expanding international cooperation. This chapter is aimed to provide the introduction of the significant role of STEM education for national security. The chapter will provide an introduction to integrating the awareness training of national security into higher education with the demonstration of the practice of our education module of DHS CFATS in the chemical engineering course of plant safety and security.*

## INTRODUCTION

Reaffirming America's role as the global engine of scientific discovery and technological innovation has never been more critical. New developments in science and technology (S&T) play a key role in predicting and addressing threats to our national and economic security. When threats are unavoidable, S&T is critical to minimizing negative impacts and helping our Nation recover as quickly as possible.

DOI: 10.4018/978-1-7998-7904-6.ch010

At the same time, international cooperation in S&T plays a key role in meeting transnational priorities that improve the quality of life and global security.

The Office of Science and Technology Policy's National Security and International Affairs (NSIA) division is committed to advancing policies that apply S&T in the following areas:

- **Cybersecurity:** Facilitate Federal research and development (R&D) efforts to develop innovative technological tools that can thwart cyber threats.
- **Biological Threats**: Promote S&T for a robust global biological surveillance enterprise, a strong response and recovery capability in the case of a biological incident, and forensics techniques to identify the source of a biological attack.
- **Nuclear Threats**: Strengthen the Nation's capability to detect and control the transfer of nuclear explosive devices and weapons-usable nuclear material.
- **Intelligence Capabilities**: Apply S&T to help address the Nation's most pressing intelligence challenges.
- **International S&T Cooperation**: Enhance international S&T initiatives and strengthen global S&T cooperation in priority areas such as energy, environment, health, cybersecurity, and advanced manufacturing.
- **National Security and Emergency Preparedness**: Leverage technology and innovation to improve the Nation's resilience to both man-made and natural disasters, especially with respect to communication systems.
- **National Security R&D Enterprise**: Strengthen the health and sufficiency of the national security R&D enterprise, including its workforce, infrastructure, and other resources.
- **Transborder Security**: Strengthen S&T initiatives to improve transborder security in key areas such as aviation security, countering improvised explosive devices (IEDs), narcotics interdiction, and identity technologies.

## BACKGROUND

Provide broad definitions and discussions of the topic and incorporate views of others (literature review) into the discussion to support, refute, or demonstrate your position on the topic.[1] The Associate Director of the National Security and International Affairs Division at OSTP is co-chair of the National Science and Technology Council's Committee on Homeland and National Security (CHNS). The National Science and Technology Council (NSTC) is the principal means within the executive branch to coordinate science and technology policy across the diverse entities that make up the Federal research and development enterprise. The CHNS supports the NSTC's efforts to increase the overall effectiveness of S&T related to the homeland and national security. The CHNS also addresses significant national and international policy matters that cut across agencies and promotes interagency policy coordination and collaboration.

The nation that leads the world in building a clean energy economy will enjoy a substantial economic and security advantage. That is why the Administration is investing heavily in research, improving education in science and math, promoting developments in energy, and expanding international cooperation. As President Obama declared in the National Security Strategy, "Simply put, we must see American innovation as a foundation of American power. America's long-term leadership depends on educating and producing future scientists and innovators. We will invest more in STEM education so students can learn to think critically in science, math, engineering, and technology; improve the quality of math and science teaching so American students are no longer outperformed by those in other nations; and expand STEM education and career opportunities for underrepresented groups, including women and girls. We will work with partners – from the private-sector and nonprofit organizations to universities – to promote education and careers in science and technology."This chapter is aimed to provide the introduction of the significant role of STEM education for National Security. We will provide an introduction on how to integrate the awareness training of national security into higher education with the demonstration of the practice of our education module of DHS CFATS in the chemical engineering course of Plant Safety and Security.

## STEM SUBJECTS AND STEM EDUCATION

The nation that leads the world in building a clean energy economy will enjoy a substantial economic and security advantage. Science, Technology, Engineering and Mathematics (STEM), previously Science, Math, Engineering and Technology (SMET)(Hallinen, 2015). The science in STEM typically refers to two branches of science: natural sciences, including biology, physics, and chemistry, and formal sciences, of which mathematics is an example, along with logic and statistics.

In the United States/ United Kingdom education system, in elementary, middle, and high schools, the term science refers primarily to the natural sciences, with mathematics being a standalone subject, and the social sciences are combined with the humanities under the umbrella term social studies. The change was, in part, instigated at an interagency meeting by Peter Faletra the director from the Office of Science division of Workforce Development for Teachers and Scientists. The acronym was adopted by Rita Colwell and other science administrators in the National Science Foundation (NSF) in 2001. However, the acronym STEM predates NSF which was used by a variety of educators including Charles E. Vela, the founder, and director of

*Figure 1. STEM (Science, Technology, Engineering, Mathematics)*

the Center for the Advancement of Hispanics in Science and Engineering Education (CAHSEE). (CAHSEE - About CAHSEE, 2018; STEM Science, Technology, Engineering, Mathematics, 2018; Group, 1996). In the early 1990s, CAHSEE started a summer program for talented under-represented students in the Washington, DC area called the STEM Institute. Based on the program's recognized success and his expertise in STEM education(National Science Foundation, 2018). Charles Vela was asked to serve on numerous NSF and Congressional panels in science, mathematics, and engineering education(The Center for the Advancement of Hispanics in Science and Engineering Education, 2018); it is through this manner that NSF was first introduced to the acronym STEM. One of the first NSF projects to use the acronym was STEMTEC, the Science, Technology, Engineering and Math Teacher Education Collaborative at the University of Massachusetts Amherst, which was founded in 1998 true to its word(Fivecolleges, 2016).

In the United States, the acronym began to be used in education and immigration debates in initiatives to begin to address the perceived lack of qualified candidates for high-tech jobs. It also addresses the concern that the subjects are often taught in isolation, instead of as an integrated curriculum(The Intermediate Unit 1 Center for STEM Education. 2008). Maintaining a citizenry that is well versed in the STEM fields is a key portion of the public education agenda of the United States (Morella, 2012). The acronym has been widely used in the immigration debate regarding access to the United States work visas for immigrants who are skilled in these fields. It has also become commonplace in education discussions as a reference to the shortage of skilled workers and inadequate education in these areas(Kakutani, 2011). The term tends not to refer to the non-professional and less visible sectors of the fields, such as electronics assembly line work.

Many organizations in the United States follow the guidelines of the National Science Foundation on what constitutes a STEM field. The NSF uses a broader definition of STEM subjects that includes subjects in the fields of chemistry, computer and information technology science, engineering, geosciences, life sciences, mathematical sciences, physics and astronomy, social sciences (anthropology, economics, psychology, and sociology), and STEM education and learning research(Kakutani, 2011). Eligibility for scholarship programs such as the CSM STEM Scholars Program uses the NSF definition(National Science Foundation).

## STEM EDUCATION AND NATIONAL SECURITY

According to the U.S. DEPARTMENT OF EDUCATION, in an ever-changing, increasingly complex world, it's more important than ever that our nation's youth are prepared to bring knowledge and skills to solve problems, make sense of information, and know-how to gather and evaluate evidence to make decisions. These are the kinds of skills that students develop in science, technology, engineering, and math—disciplines collectively known as STEM. If we want a nation where our future leaders, neighbors, and workers have the ability to understand and solve some of the complex challenges of today and tomorrow, and to meet the demands of the dynamic and evolving workforce, building students' skills, content knowledge, and fluency in STEM fields is essential. We must also make sure that no matter where children live, they have access to quality learning environments.

### Promoting Science, Technology, Engineering, or Math (STEM) Education, With a Particular Focus on Computer Science

STEM is a centerpiece of Secretary DeVos' comprehensive education agenda. The STEM priority may be used across the Departments' discretionary grant programs to further the Department's mission, which is "to promote student achievement and preparation for global competitiveness by fostering educational excellence and ensuring equal access."

### U.S. Department of Education Advances Trump Administration's STEM Investment Priorities

In November 2019, the Department announced that it invested nearly $540 million to support science, technology, engineering, and math (STEM) education, including computer science, through discretionary and research grants in Fiscal Year 2019, in accordance with President Trump's directive to foster expanded opportunities in these in-demand career fields. Of that total, there was almost $100 million in funds to support projects with a focus on Computer Science.

## Inaugural Presidential Cybersecurity Education Award

Secretary Betsy DeVos announced on October 7, 2019, the call for nominations for the Presidential Cybersecurity Education Award. This award was established on May 2, 2019, by the President's Executive Order on America's Cybersecurity Workforce. The U.S. Department of Education created the award in consultation with the Deputy Assistant to the President for Homeland Security and Counterterrorism at the National Security Council and the National Science Foundation. The nomination period opened during National Cybersecurity Awareness Month in October 2019 and closed on January 31, 2020. Nominations will be reviewed by Department staff and awardees will be recognized during Teacher Appreciation Week in May 2020.

## DOD STEM Strength Through Innovation

The Department of Defense continually seeks to increase the development of a representative, world-class STEM talent pool capable of filling our workforce needs and providing continuous access to STEM talent throughout the Nation.

## Power in Our People

The Department of Defense is the largest employer of scientists and engineers in the nation. Under the Federal STEM strategic plan, the Department is charged with developing STEM initiatives that are unique to the DoD mission and also help meet national goals of improving instruction, increasing engagement, growing the pool of STEM degree holders, broadening the participation of historically underserved groups, and improving the graduate school experience. DoD STEM represents the Department's mission to attract, inspire, and develop exceptional STEM talent across the educational continuum to sustain the Department's technological edge.

## DoD Leadership in Innovation

DoD's elite scientists and engineers have been at the cutting edge of our nation's most advanced technological breakthroughs for decades. The legacy of defense innovation includes the Internet, the Global Positioning System (GPS), virtual reality, voice recognition technology, autonomous vehicles, and cloud computing.

## INTEGRATION OF NATIONAL SECURITY WITH HIGHER EDUCATION

The following content is aimed to provide the introduction of the significant role of STEM education for National Security. We will provide an introduction to integrating the awareness training of national security into higher education with the demonstration of the practice of our education module of DHS CFATS in the chemical engineering course of Plant Safety and Security.

### Chemical Facility Anti-Terrorism Standards (CFATS)

CFATS is the Nation's first regulatory program focused specifically on security at high-risk chemical facilities. The Cybersecurity and Infrastructure Security Agency (CISA) manages the CFATS program by working with facilities to ensure they have security measures in place to reduce the risks associated with certain hazardous chemicals and prevent them from being weaponized by terrorists.

Under CFATS, a chemical facility is any establishment or individual that possesses or plans to possess any of the more than 300 chemicals of interest (COI) in Appendix A at or above the listed screening threshold quantity (STQ). These facilities must report their chemical holdings to CISA via an online survey, known as a Top-Screen. CISA uses the Top-Screen information a facility submits to determine if the facility is considered high-risk and must develop a security plan.

The CFATS regulation applies to facilities across many industries—chemical manufacturing, storage, and distribution, energy and utilities, agriculture and food, explosives, mining, electronics, plastics, universities and laboratories, paint and coatings, and healthcare and pharmaceuticals, among others.

Chemical security is not a temporary issue. As threats evolve, the Agency is committed to working with stakeholders to protect the nation's highest-risk chemical infrastructure.

On August 1, 2013, the Executive Order on Improving Chemical Facility Safety and Security (EO 13650) directed the federal government to improve the safety and security of chemical facilities and reduce the risks of hazardous chemicals to workers and communities. The EO established the Chemical Facility Safety and Security Working Group (Working Group)—tri-chaired by CISA, the Environmental Protection Agency (EPA), and the Secretary of Labor—to oversee this effort.

In response, CISA created the Infrastructure Protection (IP) Gateway—a repository of critical infrastructure tools and information—to improve coordination between federal, state, and local governments, and community stakeholders and to strengthen the CFATS program.

*Figure 2. Fact sheet (Page 1 of 2) of DHS CFATS program (https://www.cisa.gov/sites/default/files/publications/fs-cfats-overview-508.pdf)*

CISA
CYBER+INFRASTRUCTURE

DEFEND TODAY. SECURE TOMORROW.

# Chemical Facility Anti-Terrorism Standards: Overview

**Chemicals are vital to our economy. They are used to develop medicines that maintain our health, provide refrigeration for our food supply, manufacture fuel for our vehicles and build the microchip that runs our smartphones. But in the hands of a terrorist, some chemicals could potentially be weaponized.**

## What Is CFATS?

In 2006, Congress authorized the Department of Homeland Security (DHS) to establish the Chemical Facility Anti-Terrorism Standards (CFATS) program. Managed by the Cybersecurity and Infrastructure Security Agency (CISA), the CFATS program identifies and regulates high-risk chemical facilities to ensure they have security measures in place that reduce the risk of certain hazardous chemicals from being weaponized. In 2014, Congress reauthorized and amended the program through the Protecting and Securing Chemical Facilities from Terrorist Attacks Act of 2014 (6 U.S.C. § 621, et seq.). In 2019, Congress extended the four-year authorization through April 2020 via the Chemical Facility Anti-Terrorism Standards Program Extension Act.

The CFATS regulation applies to facilities across many industries, including, but not limited to:

- Chemical manufacturing, storage, and distribution
- Energy utilities
- Agriculture and food
- Explosives
- Pulp and paper
- Electronics
- Plastics
- Universities and laboratories
- Paint and coatings
- Healthcare and pharmaceuticals
- Metal production and finishing

## Appendix A and Chemicals of Interest (COI)

Appendix A of the CFATS regulation lists more than 300 COI and their respective screening threshold quantities (STQ) and concentrations. The COI are categorized into three main security issues:

- Release: Toxic, flammable, or explosive chemicals or materials that can be released at a facility.
- Theft or Diversion: Chemicals or materials that, if stolen or diverted, can be converted into weapons using simple chemistry, equipment, or techniques.
- Sabotage: Chemicals or materials that can be mixed with readily available materials.

Any facility that manufactures, stores, or distributes COI at or above the STQ and/or concentration is required to report their holdings to CISA via an online survey called a Top-Screen. Facilities must submit a Top-Screen within 60 days of coming into possession of the COI.

*Figure 3. Fact sheet (Page 2 of 2) of DHS CFATS program (https://www.cisa.gov/sites/default/files/publications/fs-cfats-overview-508.pdf)*

## CFATS Process

1. If not statutorily excluded from CFATS,[1] read the Appendix A COI List: www.cisa.gov/publication/cfats-coi-list.
2. If your facility possesses COI at or above the STQ and concentration, submit a Top-Screen via the Chemical Security Assessment Tool (CSAT): www.cisa.gov/csat-top-screen.
    - To access CSAT, complete the Chemical-terrorism Vulnerability Information (CVI) training: www.cisa.gov/cvi-authorized-user-training.
    - Register yourself and your facility in CSAT to get access to the Top-Screen survey: csat-registration.dhs.gov/.
3. CISA reviews Top-Screens using a risk-based methodology. Facilities are notified if they are:
    - Determined to be a high-risk facility and ranked into Tiers 1, 2, 3, and 4, with Tier 1 being the highest risk.
    - Determined not to be a high-risk facility and not regulated under CFATS.
4. Tiered facilities must submit a Security Vulnerability Assessment (SVA) and a Site Security Plan (SSP)—or an Alternative Security Program (ASP)—that meets the risk-based performance standards (RBPS): www.cisa.gov/risk-based-performance-standards.
    - The 18 RBPS address security issues such as perimeter security, access control, personnel security, cybersecurity, etc.
    - Your facility's security plan is tailored to its tier level, risk, and unique circumstances.
5. CISA Chemical Security Inspectors perform an authorization inspection at your facility prior to approving the SSP or ASP.
    - Once the plan is approved, inspectors conduct regular compliance inspections to verify your facility implements the agreed-upon security measures.

## CFATS Enforcement Actions

CISA is committed to helping facility personnel understand and comply with CFATS by providing technical assistance or onsite consultation. However, CISA is authorized to pursue civil enforcement action against any facility found in violation of CFATS, which could result in the imposition of a civil fine and/or the issuance of an order to cease operations. Violations vary from a facility refusing to report its COI holdings, failing to implement certain security measures, or knowingly providing false information.

## Tools and Resources

- CFATS Resources: www.cisa.gov/cfats-resources
- CFATS Process: www.cisa.gov/cfats-process
- Request a CFATS Presentation: www.cisa.gov/request-cfats-presentation
- Request a Compliance Assistance Visit: www.cisa.gov/request-compliance-assistance-visit
- CFATS Knowledge Center: csat-help.dhs.gov
- CSAT Help Desk (technical assistance): Call 1-866-323-2957 or email csat@hq.dhs.gov

## Contact Information

For any questions or comments, email CFATS@hq.dhs.gov or visit www.cisa.gov/cfats.

[1] Section 2101 of the CFATS Act of 2014 defined excluded facility as: a facility regulated under the Maritime Transportation Security Act of 2002; a public water systems as defined in the Safe Drinking Water Act; a Treatment Works as defined in the Federal Water Pollution Control Act; a facility owned or operated by the Department of Defense or the Department of Energy; and a facility subject to regulation by the Nuclear Regulatory Commission.

2019-11-05

## COURSE MODULE EXAMPLE

Below is the course syllabus which can be used to provide the introduction of the significant role of STEM education for National Security. The awareness training of national security has been integrated into higher education with the practice of education module of DHS CFATS in the chemical engineering course of Plant Safety and Security. The course syllabus has been given below.

Fall/Spring XXXX
PLANT SAFETY AND SECURITY
(Course No: XXXX XXXX-)
Instructor: XXXXXXXXXX
Office: XXXXXXXXXX
CONTACT INFORMATION
Phone: (XXX) XXX-XXXX
e-mail: XXXXX@XXXXX.edu
CLASS TIME & LOCATION
Class Time: XXXXXXXXXX
Classroom: XXXXXXXXXX
OFFICE HOURS
Office Hour: XXXXXXXXXX or by Appointment
COURSE OBJECTIVES

In the chemical process industry, plant operation safety and security are important. The knowledge, skill, and ability of plant operation safety and security are essential to the management of accident prevention and control of potential hazards and hazardous conditions in the processes with the comprehensive integrated system of human beings, the equipment, the materials, the methods, the measurements, and the environment. Process safety is part of safety management and focuses on the concerns of major hazards impacting, safety, environmental damage, and business losses. The goal of process safety management is to develop plant systems and procedures to prevent unwanted releases that may ignite and cause toxic impacts, local fires, or explosions. The safety management should cover all of the plant operations including plant commissioning and inspection, plant operations and work permit systems, plant maintenance, modification, and emergency planning and plant storage.

For the above purpose, laws and regulations are major tools for protecting people and the environment. Congress is responsible for passing laws that govern the United States. To put these laws into effect, Congress authorizes certain government organizations, including the Environmental Protection Agency (EPA), Occupational

Safety and Health Administration (OSHA), and the Department of Homeland Security (DHS) to create and enforce regulations. The applicable safety and health laws and regulations should be used for regulatory compliance and to help the development of appropriate controls to eliminate or reduce the risk for injury and illness of workers, or damage to property and/or the environment.

The students are required to conduct an advanced study on plant safety and security/abnormality management on national and global challenges for the chemical industry. This course will give the students the knowledge, skills, and abilities of the complex regulatory and legal settings surrounding process safety management, occupational safety, health and environmental regulations and how they affect the industry, legal responsibility, and accountability; ethical consideration in and external to the industrial organization. It will also provide the doctoral students an overview of risk management principles and techniques, accident analysis, safety regulations and practices, plant hazards, and their control. The class will present the combination of the synergies between performance improvement systems to help ensure safe and reliable operations, streamline procedures and cross-system auditing, and supporting regulatory and corporate compliance requirements.

The students in the class should learn how to engage in advocacy, education, and awareness as it relates to EPA(the United States Environmental Protection Agency), OSHA(Occupational Safety and Health Administration), and DHS(United States Department of Homeland Security) regulations, as well as regulations at the state and local levels. They should also be able to know how to engage with other government agencies and professional organizations, such as the U.S. Chemical Safety Board, the American Institute of Chemical Engineers, the American Petroleum Institute, the American Chemistry Council, American Fuel & Petrochemical Manufacturers, and National Fire Protection Association on advocacy, standards, common programs, etc. to support the overall mission of safety.

## Student Learning Outcomes

1. The students are required to conduct an advanced study on plant safety and security/abnormality management on national and global challenges for the chemical industry.
2. The students will be able to apply fundamental knowledge of STEM subjects (Science, Technology, Engineering, and Mathematics) in the practice of plant safety operations.
3. The students will be able to work as a member of multidisciplinary TFT (Task Forced Teams) and have an understanding of team leadership.
4. The students will be able to identify and solve chemical process safety problems.
5. The students will be able to understand professional and ethical responsibility.

6. The students will be able to have the essential skills of communication, professional writing, and oral presentation.
7. The students will be able to engage in lifelong learning through the application of ICT(Information and Communication Technology) tools.
8. The students will be able to use the techniques, skills, and modern engineering tools necessary for comprehensive engineering practice.
9. The students should be able to conduct business in a manner that protects the safety and health of their employees, others involved in their operations, customers, and the public.
10. The students should be able to use the applicable safety, health, and industrial laws and regulations for regulatory compliance and continuous improvement of appropriate controls to eliminate or reduce the risk for injury and illness of workers, or damage to property and/or the environment.
11. The students should learn how to engage in the regulatory safety programs instituted by EPA, OSHA, DHS, and other regulatory government agencies as it relates to regulations, as well as regulations at the state and local levels that are specific to the processing industry. They should also be able to engage with other agencies and professional organizations, such as the U.S. CSB(U.S. Chemical Safety and Hazard Investigation Board), AIChE(The American Institute of Chemical Engineers), API(the American Petroleum Institute), AFPM(American Fuel and Petrochemical Manufacturers) and NFPA(The National Fire Protection Association) on advocacy, standards, common programs, etc. to support the overall mission of safety.
12. The student should be familiar with the plant operations (including plant commissioning and inspection, plant operations and work permit systems, plant maintenance, modification, and emergency planning and plant storage) and the related safety management practice.
13. The student should have a good understanding of the great contribution of human factors to the success of process safety programs in the process industries.

## Course Materials

Textbook:

Crowl, D. A., & Louvar, J. F. (2019). *Chemical Process Safety: Fundamentals with Applications* (4th Edition). Prentice-Hall.

Reference:

AIChE CCPS. (2008). *CCPS Process Safety Metrics: You Don't Improve What you Don't Measure*. Access from http://www.aiche.org

AIChE CCPS. (2009). Guideline for Process Safety Metrics. Wiley.

AIChE CCPS. (2008). Guideline for Hazard Evaluation Procedure. Wiley.

AIChE CCPS. (2007). Guideline for Risk-Based Process Safety. Wiley.

AIChE CCPS. (1996). Guidelines for Integrating Process Safety Management, Environment, Safety, Health, and Quality. Wiley.

Course Subject Outline

- Syllabus and Course Overview
- Accident Investigations and Lesson Learning from Historical Cases
- Plant Commissioning and Inspection
- Plant Operations and Work Permit Systems
- Plant Maintenance, Modification, and Emergency Planning
- Plant Storage
- OSHA Process Safety Management (PSM)
- EPA Risk Management Program (RMP)
- DHS Chemical Facility Anti-Terrorism Standards (CFATS)
- Process Safety Metrics
- Aging Process Facilities and Infrastructures
- Facility Siting and Layout
- Combustible Dust Hazard Analysis
- Safe Automation of Chemical Processes
- Source Models
- Toxic and Hazardous Material Release and Dispersion • Relief Sizing • Static Discharge
- Chemical Reactivity
- Human Factors and Ergonomics
- DOT Chemical Transportation Safety and Security
- Computer Simulation for Plant Safety and Security

## CONCLUSION

It is expected that this chapter is written to give the introduction of the significant role of STEM education for National Security. The integration of the awareness training of national security into higher education has been introduced. The demonstration of the practice of education module of DHS CFATS is also given and it can be adopted in the chemical engineering course of Plant Safety and Security.

## REFERENCES

CAHSEE. (n.d.). *Founder's Biography*. The Center for the Advancement of Hispanics in Science and Engineering Education.

Career Communications. (1996). *Hispanic Engineer & IT*. Career Communications Group.

CRU. (n.d.). http://www.cru.uea.ac.uk/cru/data/temperature

Fifth Assessment ReportIPCC. (n.d.). *Summary for Policymakers*. IPCC.

Gabriele, C. (1996). Detecting Greenhouse-Gas-Induced Climate Change with an Optimal Fingerprint Method. *Journal of Climate*, *9*(October), 2281–2306.

Graduate Research Fellowship Program. (n.d.). http://www.nsf.gov

Hallinen, J. (2015). STEM Education Curriculum. *Encyclopedia Britannica*.

Kakutani, M. (2011). Bill Clinton Lays Out His Prescription for America's Future. *The New York Times*.

Morella, M. (2012). U.S. News Inducts Five to STEM Leadership Hall of Fame. *U.S. News & World Report*.

National Research Council (NRC). (2006). *Surface Temperature Reconstructions For the Last 2,000 Years*. National Academy Press.

NOAA. (n.d.). https://www.ncdc.noaa.gov/monitoring-references/faq/indicators.php

ObamaWhiteHouse.archives.gov. (n.d.). https://obamawhitehouse.archives.gov/administration/ eop/ostp/divisions/natsecintaff

Ramaswamy, V. (2006, February 24). Anthropogenic and Natural Influences in the Evolution of Lower Stratospheric Cooling. *Science*, *311*, 1138–1141.

Sabine, C. L. (2004, July 16). The Oceanic Sink for Anthropogenic CO2. *Science*, *305*, 367–371.

Santer, B. D. (1996, July). A search for human influences on the thermal structure of the atmosphere. *Nature*, *382*(4), 39–46.

Santer, B. D. (2003, July 25). Contributions of Anthropogenic and Natural Forcing to Recent Tropopause Height Changes. *Science*, *301*, 479–483.

ScienceT.EngineeringM. (n.d.). stem.ccny.cuny.edu

*STEM Education in Southwestern Pennsylvania*. (2008). The Intermediate Unit 1 Center for STEM Education.

U.S. Department of Education. (n.d.). https://www.ed.gov/stem

U.S. Department of Homeland Security. (n.d.). *Chemical facility anti-terrorism standards (CFATS)*. https://www.cisa.gov/chemical-facility-anti-terrorism-standards

## ADDITIONAL READING

Nerem, R. S., Beckley, B. D., Fasullo, J. T., Hamlington, B. D., Masters, D., & Mitchum, G. T. (2018). Climate-change–driven accelerated sea-level rise detected in the altimeter era. *Proceedings of the National Academy of Sciences of the United States of America*. Advance online publication. doi:10.1073/pnas.1717312115

## KEY TERMS AND DEFINITIONS

**AFPM (American Fuel and Petrochemical Manufacturers):** American Fuel and Petrochemical Manufacturers is an American trade association. AFPM is a trade association representing high-tech American manufacturers of virtually the entire U.S. supply of gasoline, diesel, jet fuel, other fuels, and home heating oil, as well as the petrochemicals used as building blocks for thousands of vital products in daily life.

**AIChE (The American Institute of Chemical Engineers):** The American Institute of Chemical Engineers (AIChE) is a professional organization for chemical engineers. AIChE was established in 1908 to distinguish chemical engineers as a profession independent of chemists and mechanical engineers.

**API (American Petroleum Institute):** API represents all segments of America's oil and natural gas industry. Our more than 600 members produce, process, and distribute most of the nation's energy. The industry supports more than ten million U.S. jobs and is backed by a growing grassroots movement of millions of Americans. In our first 100 years, API has developed more than 700 standards to enhance operational and environmental safety, efficiency, and sustainability. API's mission is to promote safety across the industry globally and to influence public policy in support of a strong, viable U.S. oil and natural gas industry.

**CFATS:** Chemical facility anti-terrorism standards.

**CSB (The U.S. Chemical Safety and Hazard Investigation Board):** The U.S. Chemical Safety and Hazard Investigation Board, generally referred to as the

Chemical Safety Board or CSB is an independent U.S. federal agency charged with investigating industrial chemical accidents. Headquartered in Washington, D.C., the agency's board members are appointed by the president and confirmed by the United States Senate. The CSB conducts root cause investigations of chemical accidents at fixed industrial facilities.

**Cybersecurity:** Cybersecurity is the protection of internet-connected systems such as hardware, software, and data from cyber threats. The practice is used by individuals and enterprises to protect against unauthorized access to data centers and other computerized systems.

**DHS (United States Department of Homeland Security):** The United States Department of Homeland Security (DHS) is the U.S. federal executive department responsible for public security, roughly comparable to the interior or home ministries of other countries. Its stated missions involve anti-terrorism, border security, immigration and customs, cybersecurity, and disaster prevention and management.

**EPA (The United States Environmental Protection Agency):** The Environmental Protection Agency (EPA) is an independent executive agency of the United States federal government tasked with environmental protection matters. The agency conducts environmental assessment, research, and education. It has the responsibility of maintaining and enforcing national standards under a variety of environmental laws, in consultation with state, tribal, and local governments. It delegates some permitting, monitoring, and enforcement responsibility to U.S. states and the federally recognized tribes. EPA enforcement powers include fines, sanctions, and other measures. The agency also works with industries and all levels of government in a wide variety of voluntary pollution prevention programs and energy conservation efforts.

**Higher Education:** Higher education is tertiary education leading to the award of an academic degree. Higher education, also called post-secondary education, third-level or tertiary education, is an optional final stage of formal learning that occurs after completion of secondary education.

**International S&T Cooperation:** Enhance international S&T initiatives and strengthen global S&T cooperation in priority areas such as energy, environment, health, cybersecurity, and advanced manufacturing.

**National Security:** National security or national defense is the security and defense of a nation-state, including its citizens, economy, and institutions, which is regarded as a duty of government.

**National Security and Emergency Preparedness:** Leverage technology and innovation to improve the Nation's resilience to both man-made and natural disasters, especially with respect to communication systems.

**National Security R&D Enterprise:** Strengthen the health and sufficiency of the national security R&D enterprise, including its workforce, infrastructure, and other resources.

**NFPA (The National Fire Protection Association):** The National Fire Protection Association (NFPA) is an international nonprofit organization devoted to eliminating death, injury, property, and economic loss due to fire, electrical and related hazards. In 2018, the NFPA claims to have 50,000 members and 9,000 volunteers working with the organization through its 250 technical committees.

**OSHA (Occupational Safety and Health Administration):** The Occupational Safety and Health Administration is a large regulatory agency of the United States Department of Labor that originally had federal visitorial powers to inspect and examine workplaces. OSHA's mission is to "assure safe and healthy working conditions for working men and women by setting and enforcing standards and by providing training, outreach, education, and assistance". The agency is also charged with enforcing a variety of whistleblower statutes and regulations. OSHA's workplace safety inspections have been shown to reduce injury rates and injury costs without adverse effects on employment, sales, credit ratings, or firm survival.

**STEM:** Science, technology, engineering, mathematics.

**Virtual Reality:** Virtual reality (VR) is a simulated experience that can be similar to or completely different from the real world. Applications of virtual reality can include entertainment and educational purposes

# Compilation of References

ABC. (2020, June 20). *India seeks extradition of Mumbai attacks suspected mastermind Sajid Mir.* Retrieved from ABC News: https://www.abc.net.au/news/2020-06-29/india-seeks-extradition-of-suspected-mumbai-attacker-sajid-mir/12401608

Adams v. Williams (1971) 407 U.S. 143

Adhanom, T. (2020). *WHO Director-General's speech at the Paris Peace Forum Panel: ACT-A: Covid-19 Vaccines, Tests and Therapies, the Global public good Solution - 12 November 2020.* World Health Organization. Retrieved December 05, 2020, from https://www.who.int/director-general/speeches/detail/who-director-general-s-speech-at-the-paris-peace-forum-panel-act-a-covid-19-vaccines-tests-and-therapies-the-global-public-good-solution---12-november-2020

Aftergood, S. (1996, October 9). *Secrecy and accountability in U.S. intelligence.* Federation of American Scientists. https://fas.org/sgp/cipsecr.html

Aguilar v. Texas (1964) 378 U.S. 108

Ahmad, K. (1999, July 3). *Kashmir horror insight.* Retrieved from The Lancet: https://www.thelancet.com/journals/lancet/article/PIIS0140-6736(05)75331-9/fulltext

Alderman v. United States (1967) 394 U.S. 165

Alonso, R., Bjorgo, T., Porta, D. D., Coolsaet, R., Khosrokhavar, F., Lohlker, R., Ranstorp, M., Reinares, F., Schmid, A. P., Silke, A., Taarnby, M., & De Vries, G. (2008, May 15). *Radicalisation processes leading to acts of terrorism.* European Commission Expert Group on Radicalisation. https://www.clingendael.org/sites/default/files/pdfs/20080500_cscp_report_vries.pdf

Archer, K., & Ron-Levey, I. (2020). *Trust in Government Lacking on COVID-19's Frontlines.* Accessed 01 2021. https://news.gallup.com/opinion/gallup/296594/trust-government-lacking-frontlines-covid.aspx

Arden, J., Woods, M., Hipkins, C., & Little, A. (2020). *Two new vaccines secured, enough for every New Zealander.* The Official Website of New Zealand Government. Retrieved January 12, 2021, from https://www.beehive.govt.nz/release/two-new-vaccines-secured-enough-every-new-zealander

Arizona v. Hicks (1987) 480 U.S. 321

Artigala, A. (2021). *Cartoon* [post update]. Facebook. Retrieved January 26, 2021, from https://www.facebook.com/photo.php?fbid=263055201834012&set=pb.100043886031837.-2207520000.&type=3

Bar-Joseph, U. (2013). The Politicization of Intelligence: A Comparative Study. *International Journal of Intelligence and CounterIntelligence*, *26*(2), 347–369. doi:10.1080/08850607.2013.758000

BBC. (2019a, February 27). *India Pakistan: Kashmir fighting sees Indian aircraft downed.* Retrieved from BBC: News: https://www.bbc.com/news/world-asia-47383634

BBC. (2019b, February 14). *Kashmir attack: Bomb kills 40 Indian paramilitary police in convoy.* Retrieved from BBC News: India: https://www.bbc.com/news/world-asia-india-47240660

Bekerly, S. (n.d.). *The Gavi COVAX AMC Explained.* Gavi the Vaccine Alliance. Retrieved January 26, 2021 from https://www.gavi.org/vaccineswork/gavi-covax-amc-explained

Belluz, J. (2021). *Rich countries are hoarding Covid-19 vaccines.* Vox. Retrieved February 01, 2021 from https://www.vox.com/2021/1/29/22253908/rich-countries-hoarding-covid-19-vaccines

Betts, R. K. (2003). Politicization of Intelligence: Costs and Benefits. In R. K. Betts, T. G. Mahnken, & F. Cass (Eds.), Paradoxes of Strategic Intelligence: Essays in Honor of Michael I. Handel (pp. 59–79). Academic Press.

Bisson, D. (2019). *SSH keys are a known weakness even though they offer somewhat strong encryption. Everyone is so reliant that these ports are typically open (on a known port number) and give a serious attack vector.* https://www.venafi.com/blog/top-4-risks-weak-ssh-key-management

Bland, A., & Davis, N. (2021). *Will Novavax and Johnson & Johnson Covid vaccines work against variants?* The Guardian. Retrieved February 01, 2021 from https://www.theguardian.com/society/2021/jan/29/how-effective-novavax-covid-vaccine-variants

Borum, R. (2011). Radicalization into violent extremism I: A review of social science theories. *Journal of Strategic Security*, *4*(4), 7–36. doi:10.5038/1944-0472.4.4.1

Bumper v. North Carolina (1968) 391 U.S. 543

Burdeau v. McDowell (1921). 256 U.S. 465

Buzan, B. (1983). *People, States and Fear*. University of North Carolina Press.

Buzan, B., & Weaver, O. (2003). *Regions and Powers; The Structure of International Security.* Cambridge University Press. doi:10.1017/CBO9780511491252

CAHSEE. (n.d.). *Founder's Biography*. The Center for the Advancement of Hispanics in Science and Engineering Education.

California v. Carney (1985) 471 U.S. 386

Career Communications. (1996). *Hispanic Engineer & IT*. Career Communications Group.

Carhart, L. (2019). *Do renters have the right to reject smart-home technology?* Accessed March, 3rd, 2019 from https://www.marketplace.org/shows/marketplace-tech/do-renters-have-right-dumb-apartment/

Carpenter v. United States (2018) 585 U.S.

Carranza, M. E. (2016). *India-Pakistan nuclear diplomacy: constructivism and the prospects for nuclear arms control and disarmament in South Asia*. Rowman & Littlefield.

Carranza, M. E. (2018). Deterrence or taboo? Explaining the non-use of nuclear weapons during the Indo-Pakistani posttests nuclear crises. *Contemporary Security Policy*, *39*(3), 441–463. doi:10.1080/13523260.2017.1418725

Carrol v. United States (1925) 267 U.S. 132

Centre for Disease Control and Prevention. (2021). *Different COVID-19 Vaccines*. Retrieved February 02, 2021 from https://www.cdc.gov/coronavirus/2019-ncov/vaccines/different-vaccines.html

Chaudhury, R. R. (2004). *Nuclear Doctrine, Declaratory Policy, and Escalation Control*. Washington, DC: STIMSON. Retrieved from https://www.stimson.org/2004/nuclear-doctrine-declaratory-policy-and-escalation-control/

Chowdhury & Ziaus. (2019). *Populism and how it impacts democracy*. Accessed 01 2021. https://www.thedailystar.net/opinion/perspective/news/populism-and-how-it-impacts-democracy-1714120

Cimpanu. (2019). *Here's a List of 29 Different Types of USB Attacks*. https://www.bleepingcomputer.com/news/security/heres-a-list-of-29-different-types-of-usb-attacks/

Clacherty. (2019). https://www.cso.com.au/article/600538/building-management-systems-afraid-very-afraid/

Coalition for Epidemic Preparedness Innovations, Gavi the Vaccine Alliance & World Health Organization. (2021). *COVAX Global Supply Forecast*. Author. Retrieved February 03, 2021 from https://www.gavi.org/sites/default/files/covid/covax/COVAX%20Supply%20Forecast.pdf

Cohen, S. P. (2002). India, Pakistan, and Kashmir. *The Journal of Strategic Studies*, *25*(4), 32–60. doi:10.1080/01402390412331302865

Cohen, S. P. (2013). *Shooting for a Century: The India-Pakistan Conundrum*. Brookings Institution Press.

Commission. (2004, July 22). *The 9/11 commission report*. https://www.9-11commission.gov/report/911Report.pdf

Cook, S. A. (2021). *America's Vaccine Diplomacy Is AWOL in the Middle East.* Foreign Policy. Retrieved January 10, 2021 from https://foreignpolicy.com/2021/01/08/americas-vaccine-diplomacy-is-awol-in-the-middle-east/

Coolidge v. New Hampshire (1971) 403 U.S. 443

CRU. (n.d.). http://www.cru.uea.ac.uk/cru/data/temperature

Dahl, K. R. (2007, July). *New security for new threats: The case for reforming the interagency process.* The Brookings Institution. https://www.brookings.edu/wp-content/uploads/2016/06/dahl20070731.pdf

Dalton, T., & Perkovich, G. (2016). *India's Nuclear Options and Escalation Dominance.* Carnegie Endowment for International Peace, Publications Department. Washington, DC: Carnegie Endowment for International Peace. Retrieved from https://calhoun.nps.edu/bitstream/handle/10945/48706/CP_273_India_Nuclear_Final.pdf?sequence=1&isAllowed=y

Dardaman, C. (2019). *Breaking and Entering with Zipato SmartHubs.* Black Marble. Accessed from https://blackmarble.sh/zipato-smart-hub/

Davies, P. H. J. (2019). All in Good Faith? Proximity, Politicization, and Malaysia's External Intelligence Organizations. *International Journal of Intelligence and CounterIntelligence*, *32*(4), 691–716. doi:10.1080/08850607.2019.1621105

De Silva, E. (2003). Intelligence and Policy in Combating Terrorism. In Terrorism in the Asia-Pacific – Threat and Response (pp. 108 – 132). Easter University Press.

De Silva, E. (2017). *Development of a Dynamic Model to Detect and Diminish the Politicization of Intelligence Data* (Unpublished). Virginia Research Institute.

Dempsey, J. (2020). *Carnegie Europe.* Accessed 01 2021. https://carnegieeurope.eu/strategiceurope/81352

Diaz, J. (2020). *New Zealand Will Give Free Coronavirus Vaccines To Residents, Neighboring Nations.* NPR. Retrieved January 03, 2021 from https://www.npr.org/sections/coronavirus-live-updates/2020/12/17/947403839/new-zealand-will-give-free-coronavirus-vaccines-to-residents-neighboring-nations

Dunn, J. E. (2019). *Open Sesame! Zipato's smart hub hacked to open front doors.* Naked Security. Accessed July 4· 2019 from https://nakedsecurity.sophos.com/2019/07/04/open-sesame-zipatos-smart-hub-hacked-to-open-front-doors/

Dwelo. (2019). *Documentation for Dwelo hub.* Author.

Economic Times. (2020). *Scientists identify 8 strains of coronavirus.* India Times. Retrieved January 03, 2021 from https://health.economictimes.indiatimes.com/news/industry/scientists-identify-8-strains-of-coronavirus/74931204

Eisenfeld, B. (2016). The Intelligence Dilemma: Proximity and Politicization–Analysis of External Influences. *Journal of Strategic Security*, *10*(2), 77–96. doi:10.5038/1944-0472.10.2.1583

Elinux. (2019). *The GPU mounts the SD card, loads GPU firmware and brings up display/video/3d, loads a kernel image resets the SD card host and starts the ARM. You could replace the kernel image with a bootloader image, and that would work fine*. https://elinux.org/RPi_Software

Fifth Assessment ReportIPCC. (n.d.). *Summary for Policymakers*. IPCC.

Foundation of Strategic Research. (2016). *Understanding The Ballistic Missile Proliferation: Issues Of Today, Challenges For Tomorrow*. Foundation of Strategic Research.

Gabriele, C. (1996). Detecting Greenhouse-Gas-Induced Climate Change with an Optimal Fingerprint Method. *Journal of Climate*, *9*(October), 2281–2306.

Gallagher, J. (2021). *Covid vaccine update: Those that work - and the others on the way*. BBC. Retrieved February 05, 2021 from https://www.bbc.com/news/health-51665497

Gallagher, J. (2021). *Covid vaccine: Single-dose Johnson & Johnson jab is 66% effective*. BBC. Retrieved January 30, 2021 from https://www.bbc.com/news/health-55857530

Galtung, J. (1964). An editorial. *Journal of Peace Research*, *1*(1), 1–4. https://www.jstor.org/stable/422802. doi:10.1177/002234336400100101

Galtung, J. (1969). Violence, peace, and peace research. *Journal of Peace Research*, *6*(3), 167–191. https://www.jstor.org/stable/422690. doi:10.1177/002234336900600301

Ganguly, S. (1986). *The origins of war in South Asia: Indo-Pakistani conflicts since 1947*. Westview Press.

Ganguly, S. (1999). India's Pathway to Pokhran II: The Prospects and Sources of New Delhi's Nuclear. *International Security*, *23*(4), 148–177. doi:10.1162/isec.23.4.148

Gannon, J. C. (2008). Managing Analysis in the Information Age. In *Analyzing intelligence: Origins, Obstacles, and Innovation*. Georgetown University Press.

Gates, R. M. (2006). Guarding Against Politicization: A Message to Analysts. In Ethics of Spying: A Reader for the Intelligence Professional. Scarecrow Press.

Gavi the Vaccine Alliance. (n.d.). *92 low- and middle-income economies eligible to get access to COVID-19 vaccines through Gavi COVAX AMC*. Retrieved February 05, 2021 from https://www.gavi.org/news/media-room/92-low-middle-income-economies-eligible-access-covid-19-vaccines-gavi-covax-amc

Gilmore, J. (2002, December 22). *CIA-FBI cooperation - Some recent history*. PBS. https://www.pbs.org/wgbh/frontline/article/cia-fbi-cooperation-some-recent-history/

Gokhale, N. (2017). *Securing India the Modi Way: Pathankot, Surgical Strikes and More*. Bloomsbury India.

Goldin & Mariathasan. (2014). *Butterfly Defect.* Princeton Press.

Goldin, I. (2020). *Contagion: Systemic Risks of Globalisation.* Accessed 01 2021. https://www.oxfordmartin.ox.ac.uk/blog/contagion-the-systemic-risks-of-globalisation/

Goldin, I., & Muggah, R. (2020). *Terra Incognita.* Penguin.

Gozego. (2019). *Zego drives engagement and efficiency across residential real estate communities. With our mobile-centric engagement platform, communities manage their resident-facing tasks within a single app.* https://www.gozego.com/platform/zego-smart/

Graduate Research Fellowship Program. (n.d.). http://www.nsf.gov

Grewal, B. S. (2003, August 30). *Johan Galtung: Positive and negative peace.* Auckland University of Technology. http://www.activeforpeace.org/no/fred/Positive_Negative_Peace.pdf

Habibi, E. (2019). *Anatomy of an Attack on the Industrial IoT.* Dark reading. Accessed July 4, 2019 from https://www.darkreading.com/vulnerabilities---threats/anatomy-of-an-attack-on-the-industrial-iot-/a/d-id/1331097

Hallinen, J. (2015). STEM Education Curriculum. *Encyclopedia Britannica.*

Halperin, M., & Clapp, P. (2006). *Bureaucratic politics and foreign policy.* Brookings Institution Press.

Handel, M. (n.d.). The Politics of Intelligence. *Intelligence and National Security, 2*(4), 6.

Hanni, A. (2016). When Casey's Blood Pressure Rose: A Case Study of Intelligence Politicization in the United States. *Intelligence and National Security, 31*(7), 963–977. doi:10.1080/02684527.2016.1162401

Hassan, M. (2012). Understanding drivers of violent extremism: The case of al-Shabab and Somali youth. *CTC Sentinel, 5*(8), 1-24. https://ctc.usma.edu/wp-content/uploads/2012/08/CTCSentinel-Vol5Iss84.pdf

Hastedt, G. (2013). The Politics of Intelligence and the Politicization of Intelligence: The American Experience. *Intelligence and National Security, 28*(1), 1, 5–31. doi:10.1080/02684527.2012.749062

Hegemann, H. (2018). Toward 'normal' politics? Security, parliaments and the politicization of intelligence oversight in the German Bundestag. *British Journal of Politics and International Relations, 20*(1), 175–190. doi:10.1177/1369148117745683

Henderson. (2019). https://www.nytimes.com/2019/01/22/business/smart-home-buyers-security-risks.html

Hersh, S. M. (1993, March 22). *A Reporter at large.* Retrieved from The New Yorker: https://www.newyorker.com/magazine/1993/03/29/on-the-nuclear-edge

Hertz, F. (1944). *Nationality in History and Politics.* Oxford University Press.

Higgins, D. R. (2016). *M48 Patton vs Centurion: Indo-Pakistani War 1965.* Osprey Publishing Ltd.

Hindustan Times. (2016, September 29). *India's surgical strikes across LoC: Full statement by DGMO Lt Gen Ranbir Singh*. Retrieved from Hindustan times: https://www.hindustantimes.com/india-news/india-s-surgical-strikes-across-loc-full-statement-by-dgmo-lt-gen-ranbir-singh/story-Q5yrp0gjvxKPGazDzAnVsM.html

Hulnick, A. S. (2013). Intelligence Theory – Seeking Better Models. In M. Phythian (Ed.), *Understanding the Intelligence Cycle*. Routledge.

Hussein, H., Chams, N., Chams, S., Sayegh, S., Badran, R., & Raad, M. (2015). Vaccines through Centuries: Major Cornerstones of Global Health. *Frontiers in Public Health, 3*. Advance online publication. doi:10.3389/fpubh.2015.00269 PMID:26636066

Ilardo, G. J. (2009). The 9/11 attacks—A study of Al Qaeda's use of intelligence and counterintelligence. *Studies in Conflict and Terrorism, 32*(3), 171–187. doi:10.1080/10576100802670803

Illinois v. Gates (1983) 462 U.S. 213

Index, C. P. (2019). Accessed 01 2021. https://www.transparency.org/en/cpi#

India-Pakistan Non-Attack Agreement (1988).

Jaishankar, S. (2021). *Opening Remarks by External Affairs Minister at the Joint Press Conference with Foreign Minister of Sri Lanka*. Ministry of External Affairs: Government of India. Retrieved February 05, 2021 from https://mea.gov.in/SpeechesStatements.htm?dtl/33368/Opening_Remarks_by_External_Affairs_Minister_at_the_Joint_Press_Conference_with_Foreign_Minister_of_Sri_Lanka

Jauhari, A. (2013). India-Pakistan Relations: International Implications. *Asian Social Science, 9*(1), 42–51. doi:10.5539/ass.v9n1p42

Joeck, N. (2008). *The Indo-Pakistani Nuclear Confrontation: Lessons From The Past, Contingencies For The Future*. Center for Global Security Research. Retrieved from http://www.npolicy.org/article_file/The_Indo-Pakistani_Nuclear_Confrontation.pdf

Joeck, N. (2009). The Kargil War and Nuclear Deterrence. In S. Ganguly & S. P. Kapur (Eds.), *Nuclear Proliferation in South Asia: Crisis Behaviour and the Bomb* (p. 251). Routledge.

Johnson v. United States (1948) 333 U.S. 10

Johnson, L. (2003). Bricks and mortar for a theory of intelligence. *Comparative Strategy, 22*(1), 1–28. Advance online publication. doi:10.1080/01495930390130481

Kakutani, M. (2011). Bill Clinton Lays Out His Prescription for America's Future. *The New York Times*.

Kapur, A. P. (2009). South Asia's Unstable Nuclear Decade. *Strategic Analysis, 33*(3), 393–403. doi:10.1080/09700160902790068

Katz v. United States (1967) 389 U.S. 347

Kecmanovic. (1960). *The Mass Psychology of Ethnonationalism.* Plenum Press.

Kent, S. (1949) Strategic Intelligence for American World Policy. Princeton University Press.

Kent, S. (1949). *Strategic Intelligence for American World Policy.* Princeton University.

KhanM. A.KhanA. Q. (2018). Retrieved from https://www.atomicheritage.org/history/pakistani-nuclear-program

Kretchmer, H. (2021). *Vaccine nationalism – and how it could affect us all.* World Economic Forum. Retrieved January 08, 2021 from https://www.weforum.org/agenda/2021/01/what-is-vaccine-nationalism-coronavirus-its-affects-covid-19-pandemic/

Lalwani, S., & Tallo, E. (2019, April 17). *Did India shoot down a Pakistani F-16 in February? This just became a big deal.* Retrieved from The Washington Post: https://www.washingtonpost.com/politics/2019/04/17/did-india-shoot-down-pakistani-f-back-february-this-just-became-big-deal/

Lantis, J. (2009). Strategic Culture and Tailored Deterrence: Bridging the Gap between Theory and Practice. *Contemporary Security Policy, 30*(3), 467–485. doi:10.1080/13523260903326677

Larson, S. (2019). *A smart fish tank left a casino vulnerable to hackers.* https://money.cnn.com/2017/07/19/technology/fish-tank-hack-darktrace/index.html

Lavoy, P. (2007). *Pakistan's Nuclear Posture: Security and Survivability.* Arlington: The Nonproliferation Policy Education Center (NPEC). Retrieved from http://npolicy.org/article.php?aid=291&tid=30

Lipton, D. (2018). *IMF.* Accessed 01 2021. https://www.imf.org/en/News/Articles/2018/04/30/sp042618-trust-and-the-future-of-multilateralism

Lorenz, E. (1963). Deterministic Nonperiodic Flow. *Journal of the Atmospheric Sciences, 20*(2), 130–141. doi:10.1175/1520-0469(1963)020<0130:DNF>2.0.CO;2

Louis, L. (1964). *The Dynamics of Nationalism: Readings in Its Meaning and Development.* D. Van Nostrand Company.

Lynch, L. E., Mason, K. V., & Rodriguez, N. (2015). Radicalization and violent extremism: Lessons learned from Canada, the U.K. and the U.S. *National Institute of Justice.* Retrieved October 21, 2020, from https://www.ncjrs.gov/pdffiles1/nij/249947.pdf

Maher, J. E. (2006). *Interagency unity of effort. The strategic interagency coordination center (STRIACC).* Air War College. Retrieved October 25, 2020 from https://pdfs.semanticscholar.org/c471/7c533d8e9bd469847450f1d8b08d90040d84.pdf

Malik, V. P. (2006). *Kargil from Surprise to Victory.* HarperCollins Publishers India, a joint venture with the India Today Group.

Marcus, B. M. (2021). *Ensuring Everyone in the World Gets a COVID Vaccine.* Duke Global Health Institute. Retrieved January 25, 2021 from https://globalhealth.duke.edu/news/ensuring-everyone-world-gets-covid-vaccine

Marrin, S. (2007). At Arm's Length or At the Elbow? Explaining the Distance between Analysis and Decision Makers. *International Journal of Intelligence and CounterIntelligence*, *20*(3), 401–414. doi:10.1080/08850600701249733

Mauser, D. P. (2013). *U.S. government interagency reform needed in support of national security.* United States Army War College. Retrieved October 31, 2020 from https://apps.dtic.mil/dtic/tr/fulltext/u2/a589428.pdf

McCarthy, K. (2019). *Here's a great idea: Why don't we hardcode the same private key into all our smart home hubs?* The Register. Accessed July 3, 2019. from https://www.theregister.co.uk/2019/07/03/zipato_hardcoded_key/

McCauley, C., & Moskalenko, S. (2008). Mechanisms of political radicalization: Pathways toward terrorism. *Terrorism and Political Violence*, *20*(3), 415–433. doi:10.1080/09546550802073367

McConnell, M. (2007). Overhauling intelligence. *Foreign Affairs*, *86*(4), 49–58. https://www.jstor.org/stable/20032414 9/11

Meer, T. W. G. van der. (2017). *Political Trust and the "Crisis of Democracy"*. Accessed 01 2021. https://oxfordre.com/politics/view/10.1093/acrefore/9780190228637.001.0001/acrefore-9780190228637-e-77

Microsoft. (2019). *MS16-072: Security update for Group Policy: June 14, 2016.* Microsoft. Accessed July 12, 2019 from https://support.microsoft.com/en-us/topic/ms16-072-security-update-for-group-policy-june-14-2016-7570425d-d460-3003-b2ac-a464c874725d

Miglani, S., & Karunatilake, W. (2021). *India sends free AstraZeneca vaccines to Sri Lanka for Friday roll-out.* Reuters. Retrieved January 30, 2021 from https://www.reuters.com/article/health-coronavirus-sri-lanka-vaccine-idUSKBN29X1M6

Miller, L. S., Hess, K. M., & Orthmann, C. H. (2017). *Community Policing: Partnerships for Problem Solving* (8th ed.). Cengage.

Minnesota v. Dickerson (1993) 508 U.S. 366

Modi, N. (2019, February 15). *@narendramodi.* Retrieved from Tweet: https://twitter.com/narendramodi/status/1096035566670565376?ref_src=twsrc%5Etfw%7Ctwcamp%5Etweetembed%7Ctwterm%5E1096035566670565376%7Ctwgr%5E&ref_url=https%3A%2F%2Fwww.india.com%2Fnews%2Fsacrifices-of-our-security-personnel-wont-go-in-vain-assures-prime-

Moghaddam, F. M. (2005). The staircase to terrorism. A psychological exploration. *The American Psychologist*, *60*(2), 161–169. doi:10.1037/0003-066X.60.2.161 PMID:15740448

Morella, M. (2012). U.S. News Inducts Five to STEM Leadership Hall of Fame. *U.S. News & World Report.*

Motley, J. (1987). Coping with the Terrorist Threat: The U.S. Intelligence Dilemma. In S. Cimbala (Ed.), *Intelligence and Intelligence Policy in a Democratic Society* (pp. 169–248). Transnational Publishers, Inc.

Muravitsky A. (2019). *IoT Hack: How to break into a smart home again.* Securelist by Kaspersky. Accessed July 2 2019 from https://securelist.com/iot-hack-how-to-break-a-smart-home-again/84092/

Nardone v. United States (1939) 308 U.S. 338

Nath, J. A. (2016, September 24). *Prime Minister Narendra Modi Hits Out At Pakistan After Uri Terror Attack. The Top-10 Quotes.* Retrieved from News: https://www.indiatimes.com/news/india/prime-minister-narendra-modi-hits-out-at-pakistan-after-uri-terror-attack-the-top-10-quotes-262330.html

National Research Council (NRC). (2006). *Surface Temperature Reconstructions For the Last 2,000 Years.* National Academy Press.

Nayak, P., & Krepon, M. (2012). *The Unfinished Crisis: US Crisis Management after the 2008 Mumbai Attacks.* The Henry L. Stimson Center. Retrieved from https://www.stimson.org/wp-content/files/file-attachments/Mumbai-Final_1_1.pdf

New Straits Times. (2019, August 8). *Pakistan to expel Indian envoy, suspend trade over Kashmir.* Retrieved August 11, 2020, from New Straits Times: https://www.nst.com.my/world/2019/08/510959/pakistan-expel-indian-envoy-suspend-trade-over-kashmir

New York v. Class (1986) 475 U.S. 106

NIST. (2019). *Cyber Security Framework 2014 version.* National Institute of Standards and Technology. https://www.nist.gov/cyberframework

NOAA. (n.d.). https://www.ncdc.noaa.gov/monitoring-references/faq/indicators.php

Nuclear Security Index, N. T. I. (2011). *India-Pakistan Non-Attack Agreement.* Retrieved from https://www.nti.org/learn/treaties-and-regimes/india-pakistan-non-attack-agreement/

Nuclear Security Index, N. T. I. (2019, November). *Pakistan.* Retrieved from NTI Nuclear Security Index: https://www.nti.org/learn/countries/pakistan/nuclear/

Nye, J., & Keohane, R. (2011). *Power & Interdependence.* Pearson.

ObamaWhiteHouse.archives.gov. (n.d.). https://obamawhitehouse.archives.gov/ administration/eop/ostp/divisions/natsecintaff

Office of the Director of National Intelligence. (n.d.). *Mission.* https://www.intelligence.gov/mission

Olmstead v. United States (1928) 277 U.S. 438

Olson, W. J. (2008). Interagency coordination: The normal accident or the essence of indecision. In G. Marcella (Ed.), *Affairs Of State: The Interagency And National Security* (pp. 215–254)., https://www.jstor.org/stable/resrep11925.8

Orthmann, C. H., & Hess, K. M. (2013). *Criminal Investigations.* Cengage.

Our World In Data. (2021). *Statistics and Research Coronavirus (COVID-19) Vaccinations.* Retrieved January 29, 2021 from https://ourworldindata.org/covid-vaccinations

Outlook Web Bureau. (2019, February 26). *Pakistan Army Confirms Indian Jets Dropped 'Four Bombs'.* Retrieved from Outlook: https://www.outlookindia.com/website/story/india-news-pakistan-army-confirms-indian-jets-dropped-four-bombs/326185

Pendleton, J. H. (2010, June 9). *Key challenges and solutions to strengthen interagency collaboration.* Government Accountability Office. https://www.gao.gov/new.items/d10822t.pdf

Pew Research Center. (2019). *Public Trust in Government: 1958-2019.* Accessed 01 2021. https://www.people-press.org/2019/04/11/public-trust-in-government-1958-2019/

Pillar, P. R. (2010). The Perils of Politicization. In L. K. Johnson (Ed.), *The Oxford Handbook of National Security Intelligence* (pp. 472–484). Oxford University Press.

Porta, D. D., & LaFree, G. (2011). Guest editorial: Processes of radicalization and de-radicalization. *International Journal of Conflict and Violence*, *6*(1), 4–10. doi:10.4119/ijcv-2926

Prados, J. (1986). *Presidents' Secret Wars: CIA and Pentagon Covert Operations Since World War II.* William Morrow.

Radicalisation Awareness Network. (2020, January 14). *The role of restorative justice in preventing and responding to violent extremism.* https://ec.europa.eu/home-affairs/sites/homeaffairs/files/what-we-do/networks/radicalisation_awareness_network/ran-papers/docs/ran_rvt-exit_role_of_restorative_justice_dublin_3-4_122019_en.pdf

Raghavan, S., & Chaudhuri, R. (2008, December 30). *Unlimited damage.* Retrieved August from DNA: https://www.dnaindia.com/analysis/main-article-unlimited-damage-1217693

Ramaswamy, V. (2006, February 24). Anthropogenic and Natural Influences in the Evolution of Lower Stratospheric Cooling. *Science*, *311*, 1138–1141.

Ransom, H. H. (1987). The Politicization of Intelligence. In Intelligence and the Intelligence Policy in a Democratic Society. Transnational Publishers, Inc.

Rashid, A. (2010, April 27). *Afghan crunch time: Obama must decide whether to talk to the Taliban.* Retrieved from The Washington Post: https://www.washingtonpost.com/wp-dyn/content/article/2010/04/26/AR2010042603020.html

Rashid, A. (2016, June 14). *World Asia.* BBC News.

Rassweiler, A. (2019). *Teardown: Raspberry Pi B.* https://electronics360.globalspec.com/article/4013/teardown-raspberry-pi-b

Rawlings v. Kentucky (1980) 448 U.S. 98

Reuters. (2019). *Sri Lankan Central Bank Bond Scam.* Accessed 01 2021. https://www.reuters.com/article/us-sri-lanka-bond-arrests/sri-lanka-arrests-ex-central-bank-deputy-governor-four-other-over-alleged-bond-scam-idUSKCN1R62D8

Riebling, M. (2010). *Wedge: From Pearl Harbor to 9/11: How the secret war between the FBI and CIA has endangered national security*. Simon and Schuster.

Riley v. California (2013) 573 U.S. 373

Riya, S., & Sareen, N. (2020). *Brookings*. Accessed 01 2021. https://www.brookings.edu/research/indias-limited-trade-connectivity-with-south-asia/

Riya, S., & Sareen, N. (2020). *India's limited trade connectivity in South Asia*. Accessed 01 2021. https://www.brookings.edu/research/indias-limited-trade-connectivity-with-south-asia/

Rosenbach, E., & Peritz, A. J. (2009). *Confrontation or collaboration? Congress and the Intelligence community*. Belfer Center for Science and International Affairs. https://www.belfercenter.org/sites/default/files/files/publication/IC-book-finalasof12JUNE.pdf

Rovner, J. (2011). *Fixing the Facts: National Security and the Politics of Intelligence*. Cornell University Press. doi:10.7591/cornell/9780801448294.001.0001

Rublee, M. R. (2017). India-Pakistan nuclear diplomacy: Constructivism and the prospects for nuclear arms control and disarmament in South Asia. *Contemporary Security Policy*, *38*(3), 483–490. doi:10.1080/13523260.2017.1312075

Sabine, C. L. (2004, July 16). The Oceanic Sink for Anthropogenic CO2. *Science*, *305*, 367–371.

Sally, R. (2020). *LKYSPP*. Accessed 01 2021. https://lkyspp.nus.edu.sg/news-events/events/details/the-future-of-asian-trade-and-globalisation-after-covid-19

Sanjay, K., & Mathur, P. (2018). *A glass half full: The promise of regional trade in South Asia*. World Bank Publication.

Santer, B. D. (1996, July). A search for human influences on the thermal structure of the atmosphere. *Nature*, *382*(4), 39–46.

Santer, B. D. (2003, July 25). Contributions of Anthropogenic and Natural Forcing to Recent Tropopause Height Changes. *Science*, *301*, 479–483.

Sasikumar, K. (2019). India-Pakistan Crises under the Nuclear Shadow: The Role of Reassurance. *Journal for Peace and Nuclear Disarmament*, 151-169. doi:10.1080/25751654.2019.1619229

Schmid, A. P. (2013). Radicalisation, de-radicalisation, counter-radicalisation: A conceptual discussion and literature review. *International Centre for Counter-Terrorism – The Hague*. Retrieved October 19, 2020, from https://www.icct.nl/download/file/ICCT-Schmid-Radicalisation-De-Radicalisation-Counter-Radicalisation-March-2013.pdf

Schneckloth v. Bustamonte (1973) 412 U.S. 218

Schwab, K. (2016). *WEF*. Accessed 2021 01. https://www.weforum.org/about/the-fourth-industrial-revolution-by-klaus-schwab

ScienceT.EngineeringM. (n.d.). stem.ccny.cuny.edu

Security Service MI5. (2008). *Behavioural science unit operational briefing note: Understanding radicalisation and violent extremism in the UK.* http://image.guardian.co.uk/sys-files/Guardian/documents/2008/08/20/mi5.pdf

Segall, R. (2010). The Intelligence Community: Resolving conflicts between agencies for national security. *American Intelligence Journal, 28*(1), 67-77. https://www.jstor.org/stable/44327131

Seligman, L. (2019, April 4). *Did India Shoot Down a Pakistani Jet? U.S. Count Says No.* Retrieved from Foreign Policy: https://foreignpolicy.com/2019/04/04/did-india-shoot-down-a-pakistani-jet-u-s-count-says-no/

Senate Select Committee on Intelligence. (2010). *Attempted terrorist attack on Northwest Airlines flight 253.* https://www.congress.gov/111/crpt/srpt199/CRPT-111srpt199.pdf

Seo, H. (2018). Intelligence Politicization in the Republic of Korea: Implications for Reform. *International Journal of Intelligence and Counterintelligence. Taylor Francis., 31*(3), 451–478. doi:10.1080/08850607.2018.1466566

Sharma, V. (2016, September 25). *Mann ki Baat on, to Pak.* Retrieved from The Tribune: https://www.tribuneindia.com/news/archive/nation/sacrifice-of-18-soldiers-won-t-go-in-vain-will-isolate-pak-pm-300160

Silverthorne Lumber Company v. United States (1920) 251 U.S. 385

Singh, R., & Chaudhuri, P. P. (2011, May 6). *Can India pull off a covert strike?* Retrieved from Hindustan Times: https://www.hindustantimes.com/delhi/can-india-pull-off-a-covert-strike/story-yeeFCRlawj1KUPugz6b05K.html

Singh, U. V. (2012). *Indo-Pak Relations Glamour, Drama or Diplomacy.* Pentagon Press.

Smart Rent. (2019). *We take every precaution in protecting your data through encryption and the installed devices we use in units are also held to those same standards.* http://org.smartrent.com/data-security-privacy/

Smith, R. D. (2003). Global public goods and health. Bulletin of the World Health Organization. *The International Journal of Public Health 2003, 81*(7).

Solanki, V. (2020). *IISS.* Accessed 01 2021. https://www.iiss.org/blogs/analysis/2020/04/sasia-why-indias-response-to-covid-19-matters-to-us-all

Sood, V. K., & Sawhney, P. (2003). *Operation Parakram The War Unfinished.* SAGE Publications Pvt. Ltd.

Source: CIA failed to circulate report about bombing suspect. (2009, December 29). *CNN.* Retrieved October 28, 2020 from http://www.cnn.com/2009/CRIME/12/29/airline.terror.cia/index.html

Spade, M. (2011, December 27). *Case 33: The underwear bomber.* Ohio State University. https://politicalscience.osu.edu/faculty/jmueller/33UDWR7.pdf

Spinelli v United States (1969) 393 U.S. 410

Squall. (2019). *Security Issues in PrivateEyePi Home Alarm System: Why I would not use it!* https://h4des.org/blog/index.php?/archives/353-Security-Issues-in-PrivateEyePi-Home-Alarm-System-Why-I-would-not-use-it!.html

Srinivasan, M. (2020). Accessed 01 2021. https://www.thehindu.com/news/international/gotabaya-seeks-additional-11-billion-swap-facility-from-modi/article31662546.ece

*STEM Education in Southwestern Pennsylvania*. (2008). The Intermediate Unit 1 Center for STEM Education.

Sytas, A. (2021). *Enthusiasm over COVID-19 vaccines tempered by talk of protectionism and hoarding*. Reuters. Retrieved January 30, 2021 from https://www.reuters.com/article/health-coronavirus-vaccines-int-idUSKBN29V2B4

Tamanaha, B. Z. (2010). Are we safer from terrorism? No, but we can be. *Yale Law & Policy Review*, *28*(2). https://digitalcommons.law.yale.edu/ylpr/vol28/iss2/7

Terry v. Ohio (1968) 392 U.S.1

The Economist. (2021). *More than 85 poor countries will not have widespread access to coronavirus vaccines before 2023*. Retrieved January 30, 2021 from https://www.eiu.com/n/85-poor-countries-will-not-have-access-to-coronavirus-vaccines/

The Hindu Business Line. (2021). *Sri Lanka to procure 2 to 3 million doses of Covid-19 vaccine from India: Official*. Retrieved January 28, 2021 from https://www.thehindubusinessline.com/news/world/sri-lanka-to-procure-2-to-3-million-doses-of-covid-19-vaccine-from-india-official/article33675032.ece

The Hindu. (2010, May 13). *'Cancer' of terror, not India, a threat to Pakistan: Obama*. Retrieved from The Hindu: https://www.thehindu.com/news/international/lsquoCancer-of-terror-not-India-a-threat-to-Pakistan-Obama/article16300628.ece

The Times of India. (2019, February 16). *Jaish terrorists attack CRPF convoy in Kashmir, killing at least*. Retrieved from The Times of India: https://timesofindia.indiatimes.com/india/37-crpf-jawans-martyred-in-ied-blast-in-jks-pulwama/articleshow/67992189.cms

The World Health Organization. (2014). The immunization programme that saved millions of lives. *Bulletin of the World Health Organization*, *92*(5), 314–315. doi:10.2471/BLT.14.020514 PMID:24839319

Treverton, G. F. (2008). Intelligence Analysis: Between 'Politicization' and Irrelevance. In Analyzing intelligence: Origins, Obstacles, and Innovation. Georgetown University Press.

Trip, S., Bora, C. H., Marian, M., Halmajan, A., & Drugas, M. L. (2019). Psychological mechanisms involved in radicalization and extremism. A Rational Emotive Behavioral Conceptualization. *Frontiers in Psychology*, *10*, 1–8. doi:10.3389/fpsyg.2019.00437 PMID:30894828

U.S. Department of Education. (n.d.). https://www.ed.gov/stem

U.S. Department of Homeland Security. (n.d.). *Chemical facility anti-terrorism standards (CFATS).* https://www.cisa.gov/chemical-facility-anti-terrorism-standards

United Nations Development Program. (1994). *Human development Report 1994*. Oxford University Press.

United Nations. (2020). *Office for Disarmament Affairs*. Retrieved from The United Nations: https://www.un.org/disarmament/wmd/nuclear/npt/

United States Constitution, Amendment IV United States v. Jones (2012) 565 U.S. 400

United States v. Mendenhall (1980) 446 U.S. 544

United States v. Wurie (2014) 728 F.3d 1

Upadhyaya, S. (2013). *Country Grouping in UNIDO Statistics*. United Nations Industrial Development Organization.

Vergani, M., Iqbal, M., & Barton, G. (2018). The 3 Ps of radicalisation: Push, pull and personal. A systematic scoping review of the scientific evidence about radicalisation into violent extremism. *Studies in Conflict and Terrorism, 43*(10), 854–893. doi:10.1080/1057610X.2018.1505686

Vidino, L. (2010). Countering radicalization in America. Lessons from Europe. *United States Institute of Peace Special Report, 262,* 1-16. https://www.usip.org/sites/default/files/resources/SR262%20-%20Countering_Radicalization_in_America.pdf

Walter v. United States (1980) 477 U.S. 649

Weeks v. United States (1914) 232 U.S. 383

Wheaton, S. (2020). *Chinese vaccine would be 'global public good,' Xi says.* Retrieved January 05, 2021 from https://www.politico.eu/article/chinese-vaccine-would-be-global-public-good-xi-says/

Whitebread, C. H., & Sloboggin, C. (2015). *Criminal Procedure: An Analysis of Cases and Concepts* (6th ed.). Foundation Press.

Whittaker, Z. (2019). *Security flaws in popular smart home hub let hackers unlock front doors.* TechCrunch. Accessed July 2, 2019 from https://techcrunch.com/2019/07/02/smart-home-hub-flaws-unlock-doors/

WHO. (2020). *Pneumonia of unknown cause – China.* 01 05. Accessed 03 15, 2021. https://www.who.int/csr/don/05-january-2020-pneumonia-of-unkown-cause-china/en/

Wikipedia. (2019). *DNS Hikacking.* Wikipedia. Accessed July 7, 2019 from https://en.wikipedia.org/wiki/DNS_hijacking

Wilmoth, J. (2019). *Cryptocurrency Exchange EtherDelta Hacked in DNS Hijacking Scheme.* CNN. Accessed July 5, 2019 from https://www.ccn.com/cryptocurrency-exchange-etherdelta-hacked-in-dns-hijacking-scheme/

Wintour, P. (2021). *World's poor need action, not Covid 'vaccine nationalism', Say Experts*. The Guardian. Retrieved January 25, 2021 from https://www.theguardian.com/world/2021/jan/22/worlds-poor-need-action-not-covid-vaccine-nationalism-say-experts

World Bank. (2019). *World Bank's World Integrated Trade Solution (WITS)*. World Bank.

Worldometer. (2021). *Countries in the world by population*. Retrieved January 25, 2021 from https://www.worldometers.info/world-population/population-by-country/

Zegart, A. B. (2005). September 11 and the adaptation failure of U.S. intelligence agencies. *International Security*, *29*(4), 78–111. doi:10.1162/isec.2005.29.4.78

# Related References

To continue our tradition of advancing information science and technology research, we have compiled a list of recommended IGI Global readings. These references will provide additional information and guidance to further enrich your knowledge and assist you with your own research and future publications.

Abbas, R., Michael, K., & Michael, M. G. (2017). What Can People Do with Your Spatial Data?: Socio-Ethical Scenarios. In A. Marrington, D. Kerr, & J. Gammack (Eds.), *Managing Security Issues and the Hidden Dangers of Wearable Technologies* (pp. 206–237). Hershey, PA: IGI Global. doi:10.4018/978-1-5225-1016-1.ch009

Abulaish, M., & Haldar, N. A. (2018). Advances in Digital Forensics Frameworks and Tools: A Comparative Insight and Ranking. *International Journal of Digital Crime and Forensics*, *10*(2), 95–119. doi:10.4018/IJDCF.2018040106

Ahmad, F. A., Kumar, P., Shrivastava, G., & Bouhlel, M. S. (2018). Bitcoin: Digital Decentralized Cryptocurrency. In G. Shrivastava, P. Kumar, B. Gupta, S. Bala, & N. Dey (Eds.), *Handbook of Research on Network Forensics and Analysis Techniques* (pp. 395–415). Hershey, PA: IGI Global. doi:10.4018/978-1-5225-4100-4.ch021

Ahmed, A. A. (2017). Investigation Approach for Network Attack Intention Recognition. *International Journal of Digital Crime and Forensics*, *9*(1), 17–38. doi:10.4018/IJDCF.2017010102

Akhtar, Z. (2017). Biometric Spoofing and Anti-Spoofing. In M. Dawson, D. Kisku, P. Gupta, J. Sing, & W. Li (Eds.), Developing Next-Generation Countermeasures for Homeland Security Threat Prevention (pp. 121-139). Hershey, PA: IGI Global. doi:10.4018/978-1-5225-0703-1.ch007

Akowuah, F. E., Land, J., Yuan, X., Yang, L., Xu, J., & Wang, H. (2018). Standards and Guides for Implementing Security and Privacy for Health Information Technology. In Y. Maleh (Ed.), *Security and Privacy Management, Techniques, and Protocols* (pp. 214–236). Hershey, PA: IGI Global. doi:10.4018/978-1-5225-5583-4.ch008

Akremi, A., Sallay, H., & Rouached, M. (2018). Intrusion Detection Systems Alerts Reduction: New Approach for Forensics Readiness. In Y. Maleh (Ed.), *Security and Privacy Management, Techniques, and Protocols* (pp. 255–275). Hershey, PA: IGI Global. doi:10.4018/978-1-5225-5583-4.ch010

Aldwairi, M., Hasan, M., & Balbahaith, Z. (2017). Detection of Drive-by Download Attacks Using Machine Learning Approach. *International Journal of Information Security and Privacy*, *11*(4), 16–28. doi:10.4018/IJISP.2017100102

Alohali, B. (2017). Detection Protocol of Possible Crime Scenes Using Internet of Things (IoT). In M. Moore (Ed.), *Cybersecurity Breaches and Issues Surrounding Online Threat Protection* (pp. 175–196). Hershey, PA: IGI Global. doi:10.4018/978-1-5225-1941-6.ch008

AlShahrani, A. M., Al-Abadi, M. A., Al-Malki, A. S., Ashour, A. S., & Dey, N. (2017). Automated System for Crops Recognition and Classification. In N. Dey, A. Ashour, & S. Acharjee (Eds.), *Applied Video Processing in Surveillance and Monitoring Systems* (pp. 54–69). Hershey, PA: IGI Global. doi:10.4018/978-1-5225-1022-2.ch003

Anand, R., Shrivastava, G., Gupta, S., Peng, S., & Sindhwani, N. (2018). Audio Watermarking With Reduced Number of Random Samples. In G. Shrivastava, P. Kumar, B. Gupta, S. Bala, & N. Dey (Eds.), *Handbook of Research on Network Forensics and Analysis Techniques* (pp. 372–394). Hershey, PA: IGI Global. doi:10.4018/978-1-5225-4100-4.ch020

Anand, R., Sinha, A., Bhardwaj, A., & Sreeraj, A. (2018). Flawed Security of Social Network of Things. In G. Shrivastava, P. Kumar, B. Gupta, S. Bala, & N. Dey (Eds.), *Handbook of Research on Network Forensics and Analysis Techniques* (pp. 65–86). Hershey, PA: IGI Global. doi:10.4018/978-1-5225-4100-4.ch005

Aneja, M. J., Bhatia, T., Sharma, G., & Shrivastava, G. (2018). Artificial Intelligence Based Intrusion Detection System to Detect Flooding Attack in VANETs. In G. Shrivastava, P. Kumar, B. Gupta, S. Bala, & N. Dey (Eds.), *Handbook of Research on Network Forensics and Analysis Techniques* (pp. 87–100). Hershey, PA: IGI Global. doi:10.4018/978-1-5225-4100-4.ch006

Antunes, F., Freire, M., & Costa, J. P. (2018). From Motivation and Self-Structure to a Decision-Support Framework for Online Social Networks. In V. Ahuja & S. Rathore (Eds.), *Multidisciplinary Perspectives on Human Capital and Information Technology Professionals* (pp. 116–136). Hershey, PA: IGI Global. doi:10.4018/978-1-5225-5297-0.ch007

Atli, D. (2017). Cybercrimes via Virtual Currencies in International Business. In M. Moore (Ed.), *Cybersecurity Breaches and Issues Surrounding Online Threat Protection* (pp. 121–143). Hershey, PA: IGI Global. doi:10.4018/978-1-5225-1941-6.ch006

Baazeem, R. M. (2018). The Role of Religiosity in Technology Acceptance: The Case of Privacy in Saudi Arabia. In J. McAlaney, L. Frumkin, & V. Benson (Eds.), *Psychological and Behavioral Examinations in Cyber Security* (pp. 172–193). Hershey, PA: IGI Global. doi:10.4018/978-1-5225-4053-3.ch010

Bailey, W. J. (2017). Protection of Critical Homeland Assets: Using a Proactive, Adaptive Security Management Driven Process. In M. Dawson, D. Kisku, P. Gupta, J. Sing, & W. Li (Eds.), Developing Next-Generation Countermeasures for Homeland Security Threat Prevention (pp. 17-50). Hershey, PA: IGI Global. doi:10.4018/978-1-5225-0703-1.ch002

Bajaj, S. (2018). Current Drift in Energy Efficiency Cloud Computing: New Provocations, Workload Prediction, Consolidation, and Resource Over Commitment. In S. Aljawarneh & M. Malhotra (Eds.), *Critical Research on Scalability and Security Issues in Virtual Cloud Environments* (pp. 283–303). Hershey, PA: IGI Global. doi:10.4018/978-1-5225-3029-9.ch014

Balasubramanian, K. (2018). Hash Functions and Their Applications. In K. Balasubramanian & M. Rajakani (Eds.), *Algorithmic Strategies for Solving Complex Problems in Cryptography* (pp. 66–77). Hershey, PA: IGI Global. doi:10.4018/978-1-5225-2915-6.ch005

Balasubramanian, K. (2018). Recent Developments in Cryptography: A Survey. In K. Balasubramanian & M. Rajakani (Eds.), *Algorithmic Strategies for Solving Complex Problems in Cryptography* (pp. 1–22). Hershey, PA: IGI Global. doi:10.4018/978-1-5225-2915-6.ch001

Balasubramanian, K. (2018). Secure Two Party Computation. In K. Balasubramanian & M. Rajakani (Eds.), *Algorithmic Strategies for Solving Complex Problems in Cryptography* (pp. 145–153). Hershey, PA: IGI Global. doi:10.4018/978-1-5225-2915-6.ch012

Balasubramanian, K. (2018). Securing Public Key Encryption Against Adaptive Chosen Ciphertext Attacks. In K. Balasubramanian & M. Rajakani (Eds.), *Algorithmic Strategies for Solving Complex Problems in Cryptography* (pp. 134–144). Hershey, PA: IGI Global. doi:10.4018/978-1-5225-2915-6.ch011

Balasubramanian, K. (2018). Variants of the Diffie-Hellman Problem. In K. Balasubramanian & M. Rajakani (Eds.), *Algorithmic Strategies for Solving Complex Problems in Cryptography* (pp. 40–54). Hershey, PA: IGI Global. doi:10.4018/978-1-5225-2915-6.ch003

Balasubramanian, K., & K., M. (2018). Secure Group Key Agreement Protocols. In K. Balasubramanian, & M. Rajakani (Eds.), *Algorithmic Strategies for Solving Complex Problems in Cryptography* (pp. 55-65). Hershey, PA: IGI Global. doi:10.4018/978-1-5225-2915-6.ch004

Balasubramanian, K., & M., R. (2018). Problems in Cryptography and Cryptanalysis. In K. Balasubramanian, & M. Rajakani (Eds.), *Algorithmic Strategies for Solving Complex Problems in Cryptography* (pp. 23-39). Hershey, PA: IGI Global. doi:10.4018/978-1-5225-2915-6.ch002

Balasubramanian, K., & Abbas, A. M. (2018). Integer Factoring Algorithms. In K. Balasubramanian & M. Rajakani (Eds.), *Algorithmic Strategies for Solving Complex Problems in Cryptography* (pp. 228–240). Hershey, PA: IGI Global. doi:10.4018/978-1-5225-2915-6.ch017

Balasubramanian, K., & Abbas, A. M. (2018). Secure Bootstrapping Using the Trusted Platform Module. In K. Balasubramanian & M. Rajakani (Eds.), *Algorithmic Strategies for Solving Complex Problems in Cryptography* (pp. 167–185). Hershey, PA: IGI Global. doi:10.4018/978-1-5225-2915-6.ch014

Balasubramanian, K., & Mathanan, J. (2018). Cryptographic Voting Protocols. In K. Balasubramanian & M. Rajakani (Eds.), *Algorithmic Strategies for Solving Complex Problems in Cryptography* (pp. 124–133). Hershey, PA: IGI Global. doi:10.4018/978-1-5225-2915-6.ch010

Balasubramanian, K., & Rajakani, M. (2018). Secure Multiparty Computation. In K. Balasubramanian & M. Rajakani (Eds.), *Algorithmic Strategies for Solving Complex Problems in Cryptography* (pp. 154–166). Hershey, PA: IGI Global. doi:10.4018/978-1-5225-2915-6.ch013

Balasubramanian, K., & Rajakani, M. (2018). The Quadratic Sieve Algorithm for Integer Factoring. In K. Balasubramanian & M. Rajakani (Eds.), *Algorithmic Strategies for Solving Complex Problems in Cryptography* (pp. 241–252). Hershey, PA: IGI Global. doi:10.4018/978-1-5225-2915-6.ch018

Barone, P. A. (2017). Defining and Understanding the Development of Juvenile Delinquency from an Environmental, Sociological, and Theoretical Perspective. In S. Egharevba (Ed.), *Police Brutality, Racial Profiling, and Discrimination in the Criminal Justice System* (pp. 215–238). Hershey, PA: IGI Global. doi:10.4018/978-1-5225-1088-8.ch010

Beauchere, J. F. (2018). Encouraging Digital Civility: What Companies and Others Can Do. In R. Luppicini (Ed.), *The Changing Scope of Technoethics in Contemporary Society* (pp. 262–274). Hershey, PA: IGI Global. doi:10.4018/978-1-5225-5094-5.ch014

Behera, C. K., & Bhaskari, D. L. (2017). Malware Methodologies and Its Future: A Survey. *International Journal of Information Security and Privacy*, *11*(4), 47–64. doi:10.4018/IJISP.2017100104

Benson, V., McAlaney, J., & Frumkin, L. A. (2018). Emerging Threats for the Human Element and Countermeasures in Current Cyber Security Landscape. In J. McAlaney, L. Frumkin, & V. Benson (Eds.), *Psychological and Behavioral Examinations in Cyber Security* (pp. 266–271). Hershey, PA: IGI Global. doi:10.4018/978-1-5225-4053-3.ch016

Berbecaru, D. (2018). On Creating Digital Evidence in IP Networks With NetTrack. In G. Shrivastava, P. Kumar, B. Gupta, S. Bala, & N. Dey (Eds.), *Handbook of Research on Network Forensics and Analysis Techniques* (pp. 225–245). Hershey, PA: IGI Global. doi:10.4018/978-1-5225-4100-4.ch012

Berki, E., Valtanen, J., Chaudhary, S., & Li, L. (2018). The Need for Multi-Disciplinary Approaches and Multi-Level Knowledge for Cybersecurity Professionals. In V. Ahuja & S. Rathore (Eds.), *Multidisciplinary Perspectives on Human Capital and Information Technology Professionals* (pp. 72–94). Hershey, PA: IGI Global. doi:10.4018/978-1-5225-5297-0.ch005

Bhardwaj, A. (2017). Ransomware: A Rising Threat of new age Digital Extortion. In S. Aljawarneh (Ed.), *Online Banking Security Measures and Data Protection* (pp. 189–221). Hershey, PA: IGI Global. doi:10.4018/978-1-5225-0864-9.ch012

Bhattacharjee, J., Sengupta, A., Barik, M. S., & Mazumdar, C. (2018). An Analytical Study of Methodologies and Tools for Enterprise Information Security Risk Management. In M. Gupta, R. Sharman, J. Walp, & P. Mulgund (Eds.), *Information Technology Risk Management and Compliance in Modern Organizations* (pp. 1–20). Hershey, PA: IGI Global. doi:10.4018/978-1-5225-2604-9.ch001

Bruno, G. (2018). Handling the Dataflow in Business Process Models. In V. Ahuja & S. Rathore (Eds.), *Multidisciplinary Perspectives on Human Capital and Information Technology Professionals* (pp. 137–151). Hershey, PA: IGI Global. doi:10.4018/978-1-5225-5297-0.ch008

Carneiro, A. D. (2017). Defending Information Networks in Cyberspace: Some Notes on Security Needs. In M. Dawson, D. Kisku, P. Gupta, J. Sing, & W. Li (Eds.), Developing Next-Generation Countermeasures for Homeland Security Threat Prevention (pp. 354-375). Hershey, PA: IGI Global. doi:10.4018/978-1-5225-0703-1.ch016

Chakraborty, S., Patra, P. K., Maji, P., Ashour, A. S., & Dey, N. (2017). Image Registration Techniques and Frameworks: A Review. In N. Dey, A. Ashour, & S. Acharjee (Eds.), *Applied Video Processing in Surveillance and Monitoring Systems* (pp. 102–114). Hershey, PA: IGI Global. doi:10.4018/978-1-5225-1022-2.ch005

Chaudhari, G., & Mulgund, P. (2018). Strengthening IT Governance With COBIT 5. In M. Gupta, R. Sharman, J. Walp, & P. Mulgund (Eds.), *Information Technology Risk Management and Compliance in Modern Organizations* (pp. 48–69). Hershey, PA: IGI Global. doi:10.4018/978-1-5225-2604-9.ch003

Cheikh, M., Hacini, S., & Boufaida, Z. (2018). Visualization Technique for Intrusion Detection. In Y. Maleh (Ed.), *Security and Privacy Management, Techniques, and Protocols* (pp. 276–290). Hershey, PA: IGI Global. doi:10.4018/978-1-5225-5583-4.ch011

Chen, G., Ding, L., Du, J., Zhou, G., Qin, P., Chen, G., & Liu, Q. (2018). Trust Evaluation Strategy for Single Sign-on Solution in Cloud. *International Journal of Digital Crime and Forensics, 10*(1), 1–11. doi:10.4018/IJDCF.2018010101

Chen, J., & Peng, F. (2018). A Perceptual Encryption Scheme for HEVC Video with Lossless Compression. *International Journal of Digital Crime and Forensics, 10*(1), 67–78. doi:10.4018/IJDCF.2018010106

Chen, K., & Xu, D. (2018). An Efficient Reversible Data Hiding Scheme for Encrypted Images. *International Journal of Digital Crime and Forensics, 10*(2), 1–22. doi:10.4018/IJDCF.2018040101

Chen, Z., Lu, J., Yang, P., & Luo, X. (2017). Recognizing Substitution Steganography of Spatial Domain Based on the Characteristics of Pixels Correlation. *International Journal of Digital Crime and Forensics, 9*(4), 48–61. doi:10.4018/IJDCF.2017100105

Cherkaoui, R., Zbakh, M., Braeken, A., & Touhafi, A. (2018). Anomaly Detection in Cloud Computing and Internet of Things Environments: Latest Technologies. In K. Munir (Ed.), *Cloud Computing Technologies for Green Enterprises* (pp. 251–265). Hershey, PA: IGI Global. doi:10.4018/978-1-5225-3038-1.ch010

Chowdhury, A., Karmakar, G., & Kamruzzaman, J. (2017). Survey of Recent Cyber Security Attacks on Robotic Systems and Their Mitigation Approaches. In R. Kumar, P. Pattnaik, & P. Pandey (Eds.), *Detecting and Mitigating Robotic Cyber Security Risks* (pp. 284–299). Hershey, PA: IGI Global. doi:10.4018/978-1-5225-2154-9.ch019

Cortese, F. A. (2018). The Techoethical Ethos of Technic Self-Determination: Technological Determinism as the Ontic Fundament of Freewill. In R. Luppicini (Ed.), *The Changing Scope of Technoethics in Contemporary Society* (pp. 74–104). Hershey, PA: IGI Global. doi:10.4018/978-1-5225-5094-5.ch005

Crosston, M. D. (2017). The Fight for Cyber Thoreau: Distinguishing Virtual Disobedience from Digital Destruction. In M. Korstanje (Ed.), *Threat Mitigation and Detection of Cyber Warfare and Terrorism Activities* (pp. 198–219). Hershey, PA: IGI Global. doi:10.4018/978-1-5225-1938-6.ch009

da Costa, F., & de Sá-Soares, F. (2017). Authenticity Challenges of Wearable Technologies. In A. Marrington, D. Kerr, & J. Gammack (Eds.), *Managing Security Issues and the Hidden Dangers of Wearable Technologies* (pp. 98–130). Hershey, PA: IGI Global. doi:10.4018/978-1-5225-1016-1.ch005

Dafflon, B., Guériau, M., & Gechter, F. (2017). Using Physics Inspired Wave Agents in a Virtual Environment: Longitudinal Distance Control in Robots Platoon. *International Journal of Monitoring and Surveillance Technologies Research, 5*(2), 15–28. doi:10.4018/IJMSTR.2017040102

Dash, S. R., Sheeraz, A. S., & Samantaray, A. (2018). Filtration and Classification of ECG Signals. In C. Pradhan, H. Das, B. Naik, & N. Dey (Eds.), *Handbook of Research on Information Security in Biomedical Signal Processing* (pp. 72–94). Hershey, PA: IGI Global. doi:10.4018/978-1-5225-5152-2.ch005

Dhavale, S. V. (2018). Insider Attack Analysis in Building Effective Cyber Security for an Organization. In J. McAlaney, L. Frumkin, & V. Benson (Eds.), *Psychological and Behavioral Examinations in Cyber Security* (pp. 222–238). Hershey, PA: IGI Global. doi:10.4018/978-1-5225-4053-3.ch013

Dixit, P. (2018). Security Issues in Web Services. In G. Shrivastava, P. Kumar, B. Gupta, S. Bala, & N. Dey (Eds.), *Handbook of Research on Network Forensics and Analysis Techniques* (pp. 57–64). Hershey, PA: IGI Global. doi:10.4018/978-1-5225-4100-4.ch004

Doraikannan, S. (2018). Efficient Implementation of Digital Signature Algorithms. In K. Balasubramanian & M. Rajakani (Eds.), *Algorithmic Strategies for Solving Complex Problems in Cryptography* (pp. 78–86). Hershey, PA: IGI Global. doi:10.4018/978-1-5225-2915-6.ch006

E., J. V., Mohan, J., & K., A. (2018). Automatic Detection of Tumor and Bleed in Magnetic Resonance Brain Images. In C. Pradhan, H. Das, B. Naik, & N. Dey (Eds.), *Handbook of Research on Information Security in Biomedical Signal Processing* (pp. 291-303). Hershey, PA: IGI Global. doi:10.4018/978-1-5225-5152-2.ch015

Escamilla, I., Ruíz, M. T., Ibarra, M. M., Soto, V. L., Quintero, R., & Guzmán, G. (2018). Geocoding Tweets Based on Semantic Web and Ontologies. In M. Lytras, N. Aljohani, E. Damiani, & K. Chui (Eds.), *Innovations, Developments, and Applications of Semantic Web and Information Systems* (pp. 372–392). Hershey, PA: IGI Global. doi:10.4018/978-1-5225-5042-6.ch014

Farhadi, M., Haddad, H. M., & Shahriar, H. (2018). Compliance of Electronic Health Record Applications With HIPAA Security and Privacy Requirements. In Y. Maleh (Ed.), *Security and Privacy Management, Techniques, and Protocols* (pp. 199–213). Hershey, PA: IGI Global. doi:10.4018/978-1-5225-5583-4.ch007

Fatma, S. (2018). Use and Misuse of Technology in Marketing: Cases from India. *International Journal of Technoethics*, *9*(1), 27–36. doi:10.4018/IJT.2018010103

Fazlali, M., & Khodamoradi, P. (2018). Metamorphic Malware Detection Using Minimal Opcode Statistical Patterns. In Y. Maleh (Ed.), *Security and Privacy Management, Techniques, and Protocols* (pp. 337–359). Hershey, PA: IGI Global. doi:10.4018/978-1-5225-5583-4.ch014

Filiol, É., & Gallais, C. (2017). Optimization of Operational Large-Scale (Cyber) Attacks by a Combinational Approach. *International Journal of Cyber Warfare & Terrorism*, *7*(3), 29–43. doi:10.4018/IJCWT.2017070103

Forge, J. (2018). The Case Against Weapons Research. In R. Luppicini (Ed.), *The Changing Scope of Technoethics in Contemporary Society* (pp. 124–134). Hershey, PA: IGI Global. doi:10.4018/978-1-5225-5094-5.ch007

G., S., & Durai, M. S. (2018). Big Data Analytics: An Expedition Through Rapidly Budding Data Exhaustive Era. In D. Lopez, & M. Durai (Eds.), *HCI Challenges and Privacy Preservation in Big Data Security* (pp. 124-138). Hershey, PA: IGI Global. doi:10.4018/978-1-5225-2863-0.ch006

Gammack, J., & Marrington, A. (2017). The Promise and Perils of Wearable Technologies. In A. Marrington, D. Kerr, & J. Gammack (Eds.), *Managing Security Issues and the Hidden Dangers of Wearable Technologies* (pp. 1–17). Hershey, PA: IGI Global. doi:10.4018/978-1-5225-1016-1.ch001

Gamoura, S. C. (2018). A Cloud-Based Approach for Cross-Management of Disaster Plans: Managing Risk in Networked Enterprises. In S. Aljawarneh & M. Malhotra (Eds.), *Critical Research on Scalability and Security Issues in Virtual Cloud Environments* (pp. 240–268). Hershey, PA: IGI Global. doi:10.4018/978-1-5225-3029-9.ch012

Gao, L., Gao, T., Zhao, J., & Liu, Y. (2018). Reversible Watermarking in Digital Image Using PVO and RDWT. *International Journal of Digital Crime and Forensics, 10*(2), 40–55. doi:10.4018/IJDCF.2018040103

Geetha, S., & Sindhu, S. S. (2016). Audio Stego Intrusion Detection System through Hybrid Neural Tree Model. In B. Gupta, D. Agrawal, & S. Yamaguchi (Eds.), *Handbook of Research on Modern Cryptographic Solutions for Computer and Cyber Security* (pp. 126–144). Hershey, PA: IGI Global. doi:10.4018/978-1-5225-0105-3.ch006

Geethanjali, P. (2018). Bio-Inspired Techniques in Human-Computer Interface for Control of Assistive Devices: Bio-Inspired Techniques in Assistive Devices. In D. Lopez & M. Durai (Eds.), *HCI Challenges and Privacy Preservation in Big Data Security* (pp. 23–46). Hershey, PA: IGI Global. doi:10.4018/978-1-5225-2863-0.ch002

Ghany, K. K., & Zawbaa, H. M. (2017). Hybrid Biometrics and Watermarking Authentication. In S. Zoughbi (Ed.), *Securing Government Information and Data in Developing Countries* (pp. 37–61). Hershey, PA: IGI Global. doi:10.4018/978-1-5225-1703-0.ch003

Hacini, S., Guessoum, Z., & Cheikh, M. (2018). False Alarm Reduction: A Profiling Mechanism and New Research Directions. In Y. Maleh (Ed.), *Security and Privacy Management, Techniques, and Protocols* (pp. 291–320). Hershey, PA: IGI Global. doi:10.4018/978-1-5225-5583-4.ch012

Hadlington, L. (2018). The "Human Factor" in Cybersecurity: Exploring the Accidental Insider. In J. McAlaney, L. Frumkin, & V. Benson (Eds.), Psychological and Behavioral Examinations in Cyber Security (pp. 46-63). Hershey, PA: IGI Global. doi:10.4018/978-1-5225-4053-3.ch003

Haldorai, A., & Ramu, A. (2018). The Impact of Big Data Analytics and Challenges to Cyber Security. In G. Shrivastava, P. Kumar, B. Gupta, S. Bala, & N. Dey (Eds.), *Handbook of Research on Network Forensics and Analysis Techniques* (pp. 300–314). Hershey, PA: IGI Global. doi:10.4018/978-1-5225-4100-4.ch016

Hariharan, S., Prasanth, V. S., & Saravanan, P. (2018). Role of Bibliographical Databases in Measuring Information: A Conceptual View. In J. Jeyasekar & P. Saravanan (Eds.), *Innovations in Measuring and Evaluating Scientific Information* (pp. 61–71). Hershey, PA: IGI Global. doi:10.4018/978-1-5225-3457-0.ch005

Hore, S., Chatterjee, S., Chakraborty, S., & Shaw, R. K. (2017). Analysis of Different Feature Description Algorithm in object Recognition. In N. Dey, A. Ashour, & P. Patra (Eds.), *Feature Detectors and Motion Detection in Video Processing* (pp. 66–99). Hershey, PA: IGI Global. doi:10.4018/978-1-5225-1025-3.ch004

Hurley, J. S. (2017). Cyberspace: The New Battlefield - An Approach via the Analytics Hierarchy Process. *International Journal of Cyber Warfare & Terrorism*, *7*(3), 1–15. doi:10.4018/IJCWT.2017070101

Hussain, M., & Kaliya, N. (2018). An Improvised Framework for Privacy Preservation in IoT. *International Journal of Information Security and Privacy*, *12*(2), 46–63. doi:10.4018/IJISP.2018040104

Ilahi-Amri, M., Cheniti-Belcadhi, L., & Braham, R. (2018). Competence E-Assessment Based on Semantic Web: From Modeling to Validation. In V. Ahuja & S. Rathore (Eds.), *Multidisciplinary Perspectives on Human Capital and Information Technology Professionals* (pp. 246–267). Hershey, PA: IGI Global. doi:10.4018/978-1-5225-5297-0.ch013

Jambhekar, N., & Dhawale, C. A. (2018). Cryptography in Big Data Security. In D. Lopez & M. Durai (Eds.), *HCI Challenges and Privacy Preservation in Big Data Security* (pp. 71–94). Hershey, PA: IGI Global. doi:10.4018/978-1-5225-2863-0.ch004

Jansen van Vuuren, J., Leenen, L., Plint, G., Zaaiman, J., & Phahlamohlaka, J. (2017). Formulating the Building Blocks for National Cyberpower. *International Journal of Cyber Warfare & Terrorism*, *7*(3), 16–28. doi:10.4018/IJCWT.2017070102

Jaswal, S., & Malhotra, M. (2018). Identification of Various Privacy and Trust Issues in Cloud Computing Environment. In S. Aljawarneh & M. Malhotra (Eds.), *Critical Research on Scalability and Security Issues in Virtual Cloud Environments* (pp. 95–121). Hershey, PA: IGI Global. doi:10.4018/978-1-5225-3029-9.ch005

Jaswal, S., & Singh, G. (2018). A Comprehensive Survey on Trust Issue and Its Deployed Models in Computing Environment. In S. Aljawarneh & M. Malhotra (Eds.), *Critical Research on Scalability and Security Issues in Virtual Cloud Environments* (pp. 150–166). Hershey, PA: IGI Global. doi:10.4018/978-1-5225-3029-9.ch007

Javid, T. (2018). Secure Access to Biomedical Images. In C. Pradhan, H. Das, B. Naik, & N. Dey (Eds.), *Handbook of Research on Information Security in Biomedical Signal Processing* (pp. 38–53). Hershey, PA: IGI Global. doi:10.4018/978-1-5225-5152-2.ch003

Jeyakumar, B., Durai, M. S., & Lopez, D. (2018). Case Studies in Amalgamation of Deep Learning and Big Data. In D. Lopez & M. Durai (Eds.), *HCI Challenges and Privacy Preservation in Big Data Security* (pp. 159–174). Hershey, PA: IGI Global. doi:10.4018/978-1-5225-2863-0.ch008

Jeyaprakash, H. M. K., K., & S., G. (2018). A Comparative Review of Various Machine Learning Approaches for Improving the Performance of Stego Anomaly Detection. In G. Shrivastava, P. Kumar, B. Gupta, S. Bala, & N. Dey (Eds.), Handbook of Research on Network Forensics and Analysis Techniques (pp. 351-371). Hershey, PA: IGI Global. doi:10.4018/978-1-5225-4100-4.ch019

Jeyasekar, J. J. (2018). Dynamics of Indian Forensic Science Research. In J. Jeyasekar & P. Saravanan (Eds.), *Innovations in Measuring and Evaluating Scientific Information* (pp. 125–147). Hershey, PA: IGI Global. doi:10.4018/978-1-5225-3457-0.ch009

Jones, H. S., & Moncur, W. (2018). The Role of Psychology in Understanding Online Trust. In J. McAlaney, L. Frumkin, & V. Benson (Eds.), *Psychological and Behavioral Examinations in Cyber Security* (pp. 109–132). Hershey, PA: IGI Global. doi:10.4018/978-1-5225-4053-3.ch007

Jones, H. S., & Towse, J. (2018). Examinations of Email Fraud Susceptibility: Perspectives From Academic Research and Industry Practice. In J. McAlaney, L. Frumkin, & V. Benson (Eds.), *Psychological and Behavioral Examinations in Cyber Security* (pp. 80–97). Hershey, PA: IGI Global. doi:10.4018/978-1-5225-4053-3.ch005

Joseph, A., & Singh, K. J. (2018). Digital Forensics in Distributed Environment. In G. Shrivastava, P. Kumar, B. Gupta, S. Bala, & N. Dey (Eds.), *Handbook of Research on Network Forensics and Analysis Techniques* (pp. 246–265). Hershey, PA: IGI Global. doi:10.4018/978-1-5225-4100-4.ch013

K., I., & A, V. (2018). Monitoring and Auditing in the Cloud. In K. Munir (Ed.), *Cloud Computing Technologies for Green Enterprises* (pp. 318-350). Hershey, PA: IGI Global. doi:10.4018/978-1-5225-3038-1.ch013

Kashyap, R., & Piersson, A. D. (2018). Impact of Big Data on Security. In G. Shrivastava, P. Kumar, B. Gupta, S. Bala, & N. Dey (Eds.), *Handbook of Research on Network Forensics and Analysis Techniques* (pp. 283–299). Hershey, PA: IGI Global. doi:10.4018/978-1-5225-4100-4.ch015

Kastrati, Z., Imran, A. S., & Yayilgan, S. Y. (2018). A Hybrid Concept Learning Approach to Ontology Enrichment. In M. Lytras, N. Aljohani, E. Damiani, & K. Chui (Eds.), *Innovations, Developments, and Applications of Semantic Web and Information Systems* (pp. 85–119). Hershey, PA: IGI Global. doi:10.4018/978-1-5225-5042-6.ch004

Kaur, H., & Saxena, S. (2018). UWDBCSN Analysis During Node Replication Attack in WSN. In C. Pradhan, H. Das, B. Naik, & N. Dey (Eds.), *Handbook of Research on Information Security in Biomedical Signal Processing* (pp. 210–227). Hershey, PA: IGI Global. doi:10.4018/978-1-5225-5152-2.ch011

Kaushal, P. K., & Sobti, R. (2018). Breaching Security of Full Round Tiny Encryption Algorithm. *International Journal of Information Security and Privacy*, *12*(1), 89–98. doi:10.4018/IJISP.2018010108

Kavati, I., Prasad, M. V., & Bhagvati, C. (2017). Search Space Reduction in Biometric Databases: A Review. In M. Dawson, D. Kisku, P. Gupta, J. Sing, & W. Li (Eds.), Developing Next-Generation Countermeasures for Homeland Security Threat Prevention (pp. 236-262). Hershey, PA: IGI Global. doi:10.4018/978-1-5225-0703-1.ch011

Kaye, L. K. (2018). Online Research Methods. In J. McAlaney, L. Frumkin, & V. Benson (Eds.), *Psychological and Behavioral Examinations in Cyber Security* (pp. 253–265). Hershey, PA: IGI Global. doi:10.4018/978-1-5225-4053-3.ch015

Kenekar, T. V., & Dani, A. R. (2017). Privacy Preserving Data Mining on Unstructured Data. In S. Tamane, V. Solanki, & N. Dey (Eds.), *Privacy and Security Policies in Big Data* (pp. 167–190). Hershey, PA: IGI Global. doi:10.4018/978-1-5225-2486-1.ch008

Khaire, P. A., & Kotkondawar, R. R. (2017). Measures of Image and Video Segmentation. In N. Dey, A. Ashour, & S. Acharjee (Eds.), *Applied Video Processing in Surveillance and Monitoring Systems* (pp. 28–53). Hershey, PA: IGI Global. doi:10.4018/978-1-5225-1022-2.ch002

Knibbs, C., Goss, S., & Anthony, K. (2017). Counsellors' Phenomenological Experiences of Working with Children or Young People who have been Cyberbullied: Using Thematic Analysis of Semi Structured Interviews. *International Journal of Technoethics*, *8*(1), 68–86. doi:10.4018/IJT.2017010106

Ko, A., & Gillani, S. (2018). Ontology Maintenance Through Semantic Text Mining: An Application for IT Governance Domain. In M. Lytras, N. Aljohani, E. Damiani, & K. Chui (Eds.), *Innovations, Developments, and Applications of Semantic Web and Information Systems* (pp. 350–371). Hershey, PA: IGI Global. doi:10.4018/978-1-5225-5042-6.ch013

Kohler, J., Lorenz, C. R., Gumbel, M., Specht, T., & Simov, K. (2017). A Security-By-Distribution Approach to Manage Big Data in a Federation of Untrustworthy Clouds. In S. Tamane, V. Solanki, & N. Dey (Eds.), *Privacy and Security Policies in Big Data* (pp. 92–123). Hershey, PA: IGI Global. doi:10.4018/978-1-5225-2486-1.ch005

Korstanje, M. E. (2017). English Speaking Countries and the Culture of Fear: Understanding Technology and Terrorism. In M. Korstanje (Ed.), *Threat Mitigation and Detection of Cyber Warfare and Terrorism Activities* (pp. 92–110). Hershey, PA: IGI Global. doi:10.4018/978-1-5225-1938-6.ch005

Korstanje, M. E. (2018). How Can World Leaders Understand the Perverse Core of Terrorism?: Terror in the Global Village. In C. Akrivopoulou (Ed.), *Global Perspectives on Human Migration, Asylum, and Security* (pp. 48–67). Hershey, PA: IGI Global. doi:10.4018/978-1-5225-2817-3.ch003

Krishnamachariar, P. K., & Gupta, M. (2018). Swimming Upstream in Turbulent Waters: Auditing Agile Development. In M. Gupta, R. Sharman, J. Walp, & P. Mulgund (Eds.), *Information Technology Risk Management and Compliance in Modern Organizations* (pp. 268–300). Hershey, PA: IGI Global. doi:10.4018/978-1-5225-2604-9.ch010

Ksiazak, P., Farrelly, W., & Curran, K. (2018). A Lightweight Authentication and Encryption Protocol for Secure Communications Between Resource-Limited Devices Without Hardware Modification: Resource-Limited Device Authentication. In Y. Maleh (Ed.), *Security and Privacy Management, Techniques, and Protocols* (pp. 1–46). Hershey, PA: IGI Global. doi:10.4018/978-1-5225-5583-4.ch001

Kukkuvada, A., & Basavaraju, P. (2018). Mutual Correlation-Based Anonymization for Privacy Preserving Medical Data Publishing. In C. Pradhan, H. Das, B. Naik, & N. Dey (Eds.), *Handbook of Research on Information Security in Biomedical Signal Processing* (pp. 304–319). Hershey, PA: IGI Global. doi:10.4018/978-1-5225-5152-2.ch016

Kumar, G., & Saini, H. (2018). Secure and Robust Telemedicine using ECC on Radix-8 with Formal Verification. *International Journal of Information Security and Privacy, 12*(1), 13–28. doi:10.4018/IJISP.2018010102

Kumar, M., & Bhandari, A. (2017). Performance Evaluation of Web Server's Request Queue against AL-DDoS Attacks in NS-2. *International Journal of Information Security and Privacy*, *11*(4), 29–46. doi:10.4018/IJISP.2017100103

Kumar, M., & Vardhan, M. (2018). Privacy Preserving and Efficient Outsourcing Algorithm to Public Cloud: A Case of Statistical Analysis. *International Journal of Information Security and Privacy*, *12*(2), 1–25. doi:10.4018/IJISP.2018040101

Kumar, R. (2018). A Robust Biometrics System Using Finger Knuckle Print. In G. Shrivastava, P. Kumar, B. Gupta, S. Bala, & N. Dey (Eds.), *Handbook of Research on Network Forensics and Analysis Techniques* (pp. 416–446). Hershey, PA: IGI Global. doi:10.4018/978-1-5225-4100-4.ch022

Kumar, R. (2018). DOS Attacks on Cloud Platform: Their Solutions and Implications. In S. Aljawarneh & M. Malhotra (Eds.), *Critical Research on Scalability and Security Issues in Virtual Cloud Environments* (pp. 167–184). Hershey, PA: IGI Global. doi:10.4018/978-1-5225-3029-9.ch008

Kumari, R., & Sharma, K. (2018). Cross-Layer Based Intrusion Detection and Prevention for Network. In G. Shrivastava, P. Kumar, B. Gupta, S. Bala, & N. Dey (Eds.), *Handbook of Research on Network Forensics and Analysis Techniques* (pp. 38–56). Hershey, PA: IGI Global. doi:10.4018/978-1-5225-4100-4.ch003

Lapke, M. (2018). A Semiotic Examination of the Security Policy Lifecycle. In Y. Maleh (Ed.), *Security and Privacy Management, Techniques, and Protocols* (pp. 237–253). Hershey, PA: IGI Global. doi:10.4018/978-1-5225-5583-4.ch009

Liang, Z., Feng, B., Xu, X., Wu, X., & Yang, T. (2018). Geometrically Invariant Image Watermarking Using Histogram Adjustment. *International Journal of Digital Crime and Forensics*, *10*(1), 54–66. doi:10.4018/IJDCF.2018010105

Liu, Z. J. (2017). A Cyber Crime Investigation Model Based on Case Characteristics. *International Journal of Digital Crime and Forensics*, *9*(4), 40–47. doi:10.4018/IJDCF.2017100104

Loganathan, S. (2018). A Step-by-Step Procedural Methodology for Improving an Organization's IT Risk Management System. In M. Gupta, R. Sharman, J. Walp, & P. Mulgund (Eds.), *Information Technology Risk Management and Compliance in Modern Organizations* (pp. 21–47). Hershey, PA: IGI Global. doi:10.4018/978-1-5225-2604-9.ch002

Long, M., Peng, F., & Gong, X. (2018). A Format-Compliant Encryption for Secure HEVC Video Sharing in Multimedia Social Network. *International Journal of Digital Crime and Forensics*, *10*(2), 23–39. doi:10.4018/IJDCF.2018040102

M., S., & M., J. (2018). Biosignal Denoising Techniques. In C. Pradhan, H. Das, B. Naik, & N. Dey (Eds.), *Handbook of Research on Information Security in Biomedical Signal Processing* (pp. 26-37). Hershey, PA: IGI Global. doi:10.4018/978-1-5225-5152-2.ch002

Mahapatra, C. (2017). Pragmatic Solutions to Cyber Security Threat in Indian Context. In R. Kumar, P. Pattnaik, & P. Pandey (Eds.), *Detecting and Mitigating Robotic Cyber Security Risks* (pp. 172–176). Hershey, PA: IGI Global. doi:10.4018/978-1-5225-2154-9.ch012

Majumder, A., Nath, S., & Das, A. (2018). Data Integrity in Mobile Cloud Computing. In K. Munir (Ed.), *Cloud Computing Technologies for Green Enterprises* (pp. 166–199). Hershey, PA: IGI Global. doi:10.4018/978-1-5225-3038-1.ch007

Maleh, Y., Zaydi, M., Sahid, A., & Ezzati, A. (2018). Building a Maturity Framework for Information Security Governance Through an Empirical Study in Organizations. In Y. Maleh (Ed.), *Security and Privacy Management, Techniques, and Protocols* (pp. 96–127). Hershey, PA: IGI Global. doi:10.4018/978-1-5225-5583-4.ch004

Malhotra, M., & Singh, A. (2018). Role of Agents to Enhance the Security and Scalability in Cloud Environment. In S. Aljawarneh & M. Malhotra (Eds.), *Critical Research on Scalability and Security Issues in Virtual Cloud Environments* (pp. 19–47). Hershey, PA: IGI Global. doi:10.4018/978-1-5225-3029-9.ch002

Mali, A. D. (2017). Recent Advances in Minimally-Obtrusive Monitoring of People's Health. *International Journal of Monitoring and Surveillance Technologies Research*, *5*(2), 44–56. doi:10.4018/IJMSTR.2017040104

Mali, A. D., & Yang, N. (2017). On Automated Generation of Keyboard Layout to Reduce Finger-Travel Distance. *International Journal of Monitoring and Surveillance Technologies Research*, *5*(2), 29–43. doi:10.4018/IJMSTR.2017040103

Mali, P. (2018). Defining Cyber Weapon in Context of Technology and Law. *International Journal of Cyber Warfare & Terrorism*, *8*(1), 43–55. doi:10.4018/IJCWT.2018010104

Malik, A., & Pandey, B. (2018). CIAS: A Comprehensive Identity Authentication Scheme for Providing Security in VANET. *International Journal of Information Security and Privacy*, *12*(1), 29–41. doi:10.4018/IJISP.2018010103

Manikandakumar, M., & Ramanujam, E. (2018). Security and Privacy Challenges in Big Data Environment. In G. Shrivastava, P. Kumar, B. Gupta, S. Bala, & N. Dey (Eds.), *Handbook of Research on Network Forensics and Analysis Techniques* (pp. 315–325). Hershey, PA: IGI Global. doi:10.4018/978-1-5225-4100-4.ch017

Manogaran, G., Thota, C., & Lopez, D. (2018). Human-Computer Interaction With Big Data Analytics. In D. Lopez & M. Durai (Eds.), *HCI Challenges and Privacy Preservation in Big Data Security* (pp. 1–22). Hershey, PA: IGI Global. doi:10.4018/978-1-5225-2863-0.ch001

Mariappan, P. B. P., & Teja, T. S. (2016). Digital Forensic and Machine Learning. In S. Geetha & A. Phamila (Eds.), *Combating Security Breaches and Criminal Activity in the Digital Sphere* (pp. 141–156). Hershey, PA: IGI Global. doi:10.4018/978-1-5225-0193-0.ch009

Marques, R., Mota, A., & Mota, L. (2016). Understanding Anti-Forensics Techniques for Combating Digital Security Breaches and Criminal Activity. In S. Geetha & A. Phamila (Eds.), *Combating Security Breaches and Criminal Activity in the Digital Sphere* (pp. 233–241). Hershey, PA: IGI Global. doi:10.4018/978-1-5225-0193-0.ch014

Mbale, J. (2018). Computer Centres Resource Cloud Elasticity-Scalability (CRECES): Copperbelt University Case Study. In S. Aljawarneh & M. Malhotra (Eds.), *Critical Research on Scalability and Security Issues in Virtual Cloud Environments* (pp. 48–70). Hershey, PA: IGI Global. doi:10.4018/978-1-5225-3029-9.ch003

McAvoy, D. (2017). Institutional Entrepreneurship in Defence Acquisition: What Don't We Understand? In K. Burgess & P. Antill (Eds.), *Emerging Strategies in Defense Acquisitions and Military Procurement* (pp. 222–241). Hershey, PA: IGI Global. doi:10.4018/978-1-5225-0599-0.ch013

McKeague, J., & Curran, K. (2018). Detecting the Use of Anonymous Proxies. *International Journal of Digital Crime and Forensics*, *10*(2), 74–94. doi:10.4018/IJDCF.2018040105

Meitei, T. G., Singh, S. A., & Majumder, S. (2018). PCG-Based Biometrics. In C. Pradhan, H. Das, B. Naik, & N. Dey (Eds.), *Handbook of Research on Information Security in Biomedical Signal Processing* (pp. 1–25). Hershey, PA: IGI Global. doi:10.4018/978-1-5225-5152-2.ch001

Menemencioğlu, O., & Orak, İ. M. (2017). A Simple Solution to Prevent Parameter Tampering in Web Applications. In M. Korstanje (Ed.), *Threat Mitigation and Detection of Cyber Warfare and Terrorism Activities* (pp. 1–20). Hershey, PA: IGI Global. doi:10.4018/978-1-5225-1938-6.ch001

Minto-Coy, I. D., & Henlin, M. G. (2017). The Development of Cybersecurity Policy and Legislative Landscape in Latin America and Caribbean States. In M. Moore (Ed.), *Cybersecurity Breaches and Issues Surrounding Online Threat Protection* (pp. 24–53). Hershey, PA: IGI Global. doi:10.4018/978-1-5225-1941-6.ch002

Mire, A. V., Dhok, S. B., Mistry, N. J., & Porey, P. D. (2016). Tampering Localization in Double Compressed Images by Investigating Noise Quantization. *International Journal of Digital Crime and Forensics*, *8*(3), 46–62. doi:10.4018/IJDCF.2016070104

Mohamed, J. H. (2018). Scientograph-Based Visualization of Computer Forensics Research Literature. In J. Jeyasekar & P. Saravanan (Eds.), *Innovations in Measuring and Evaluating Scientific Information* (pp. 148–162). Hershey, PA: IGI Global. doi:10.4018/978-1-5225-3457-0.ch010

Mohan Murthy, M. K., & Sanjay, H. A. (2018). Scalability for Cloud. In S. Aljawarneh & M. Malhotra (Eds.), *Critical Research on Scalability and Security Issues in Virtual Cloud Environments* (pp. 1–18). Hershey, PA: IGI Global. doi:10.4018/978-1-5225-3029-9.ch001

Moorthy, U., & Gandhi, U. D. (2018). A Survey of Big Data Analytics Using Machine Learning Algorithms. In D. Lopez & M. Durai (Eds.), *HCI Challenges and Privacy Preservation in Big Data Security* (pp. 95–123). Hershey, PA: IGI Global. doi:10.4018/978-1-5225-2863-0.ch005

Mountantonakis, M., Minadakis, N., Marketakis, Y., Fafalios, P., & Tzitzikas, Y. (2018). Connectivity, Value, and Evolution of a Semantic Warehouse. In M. Lytras, N. Aljohani, E. Damiani, & K. Chui (Eds.), *Innovations, Developments, and Applications of Semantic Web and Information Systems* (pp. 1–31). Hershey, PA: IGI Global. doi:10.4018/978-1-5225-5042-6.ch001

Moussa, M., & Demurjian, S. A. (2017). Differential Privacy Approach for Big Data Privacy in Healthcare. In S. Tamane, V. Solanki, & N. Dey (Eds.), *Privacy and Security Policies in Big Data* (pp. 191–213). Hershey, PA: IGI Global. doi:10.4018/978-1-5225-2486-1.ch009

Mugisha, E., Zhang, G., El Abidine, M. Z., & Eugene, M. (2017). A TPM-based Secure Multi-Cloud Storage Architecture grounded on Erasure Codes. *International Journal of Information Security and Privacy*, *11*(1), 52–64. doi:10.4018/IJISP.2017010104

Nachtigall, L. G., Araujo, R. M., & Nachtigall, G. R. (2017). Use of Images of Leaves and Fruits of Apple Trees for Automatic Identification of Symptoms of Diseases and Nutritional Disorders. *International Journal of Monitoring and Surveillance Technologies Research*, *5*(2), 1–14. doi:10.4018/IJMSTR.2017040101

Nagesh, K., Sumathy, R., Devakumar, P., & Sathiyamurthy, K. (2017). A Survey on Denial of Service Attacks and Preclusions. *International Journal of Information Security and Privacy*, *11*(4), 1–15. doi:10.4018/IJISP.2017100101

Nanda, A., Popat, P., & Vimalkumar, D. (2018). Navigating Through Choppy Waters of PCI DSS Compliance. In M. Gupta, R. Sharman, J. Walp, & P. Mulgund (Eds.), *Information Technology Risk Management and Compliance in Modern Organizations* (pp. 99–140). Hershey, PA: IGI Global. doi:10.4018/978-1-5225-2604-9.ch005

Newton, S. (2017). The Determinants of Stock Market Development in Emerging Economies: Examining the Impact of Corporate Governance and Regulatory Reforms (I). In M. Ojo & J. Van Akkeren (Eds.), *Value Relevance of Accounting Information in Capital Markets* (pp. 114–125). Hershey, PA: IGI Global. doi:10.4018/978-1-5225-1900-3.ch008

Nidhyananthan, S. S. A., J. V., & R., S. S. (2018). Wireless Enhanced Security Based on Speech Recognition. In C. Pradhan, H. Das, B. Naik, & N. Dey (Eds.), Handbook of Research on Information Security in Biomedical Signal Processing (pp. 228-253). Hershey, PA: IGI Global. doi:10.4018/978-1-5225-5152-2.ch012

Norri-Sederholm, T., Huhtinen, A., & Paakkonen, H. (2018). Ensuring Public Safety Organisations' Information Flow and Situation Picture in Hybrid Environments. *International Journal of Cyber Warfare & Terrorism*, *8*(1), 12–24. doi:10.4018/IJCWT.2018010102

Nunez, S., & Castaño, R. (2017). Building Brands in Emerging Economies: A Consumer-Oriented Approach. In Rajagopal, & R. Behl (Eds.), Business Analytics and Cyber Security Management in Organizations (pp. 183-194). Hershey, PA: IGI Global. doi:10.4018/978-1-5225-0902-8.ch013

Odella, F. (2018). Privacy Awareness and the Networking Generation. *International Journal of Technoethics*, *9*(1), 51–70. doi:10.4018/IJT.2018010105

Ojo, M., & DiGabriele, J. A. (2017). Fundamental or Enhancing Roles?: The Dual Roles of External Auditors and Forensic Accountants. In M. Ojo & J. Van Akkeren (Eds.), *Value Relevance of Accounting Information in Capital Markets* (pp. 59–78). Hershey, PA: IGI Global. doi:10.4018/978-1-5225-1900-3.ch004

P, P., & Subbiah, G. (2016). Visual Cryptography for Securing Images in Cloud. In S. Geetha, & A. Phamila (Eds.), *Combating Security Breaches and Criminal Activity in the Digital Sphere* (pp. 242-262). Hershey, PA: IGI Global. doi:10.4018/978-1-5225-0193-0.ch015

Pandey, S. (2018). An Empirical Study of the Indian IT Sector on Typologies of Workaholism as Predictors of HR Crisis. In V. Ahuja & S. Rathore (Eds.), *Multidisciplinary Perspectives on Human Capital and Information Technology Professionals* (pp. 202–224). Hershey, PA: IGI Global. doi:10.4018/978-1-5225-5297-0.ch011

Pattabiraman, A., Srinivasan, S., Swaminathan, K., & Gupta, M. (2018). Fortifying Corporate Human Wall: A Literature Review of Security Awareness and Training. In M. Gupta, R. Sharman, J. Walp, & P. Mulgund (Eds.), *Information Technology Risk Management and Compliance in Modern Organizations* (pp. 142–175). Hershey, PA: IGI Global. doi:10.4018/978-1-5225-2604-9.ch006

Prachi. (2018). Detection of Botnet Based Attacks on Network: Using Machine Learning Techniques. In G. Shrivastava, P. Kumar, B. Gupta, S. Bala, & N. Dey (Eds.), *Handbook of Research on Network Forensics and Analysis Techniques* (pp. 101-116). Hershey, PA: IGI Global. doi:10.4018/978-1-5225-4100-4.ch007

Pradhan, P. L. (2017). Proposed Round Robin CIA Pattern on RTS for Risk Assessment. *International Journal of Digital Crime and Forensics*, *9*(1), 71–85. doi:10.4018/IJDCF.2017010105

Prentice, S., & Taylor, P. J. (2018). Psychological and Behavioral Examinations of Online Terrorism. In J. McAlaney, L. Frumkin, & V. Benson (Eds.), *Psychological and Behavioral Examinations in Cyber Security* (pp. 151–171). Hershey, PA: IGI Global. doi:10.4018/978-1-5225-4053-3.ch009

Priyadarshini, I. (2017). Cyber Security Risks in Robotics. In R. Kumar, P. Pattnaik, & P. Pandey (Eds.), *Detecting and Mitigating Robotic Cyber Security Risks* (pp. 333–348). Hershey, PA: IGI Global. doi:10.4018/978-1-5225-2154-9.ch022

R., A., & D., E. (2018). Cyber Crime Toolkit Development. In G. Shrivastava, P. Kumar, B. Gupta, S. Bala, & N. Dey (Eds.), *Handbook of Research on Network Forensics and Analysis Techniques* (pp. 184-224). Hershey, PA: IGI Global. doi:10.4018/978-1-5225-4100-4.ch011

Raghunath, R. (2018). Research Trends in Forensic Sciences: A Scientometric Approach. In J. Jeyasekar & P. Saravanan (Eds.), *Innovations in Measuring and Evaluating Scientific Information* (pp. 108–124). Hershey, PA: IGI Global. doi:10.4018/978-1-5225-3457-0.ch008

Ramadhas, G., Sankar, A. S., & Sugathan, N. (2018). The Scientific Communication Process in Homoeopathic Toxicology: An Evaluative Study. In J. Jeyasekar & P. Saravanan (Eds.), *Innovations in Measuring and Evaluating Scientific Information* (pp. 163–179). Hershey, PA: IGI Global. doi:10.4018/978-1-5225-3457-0.ch011

Ramani, K. (2018). Impact of Big Data on Security: Big Data Security Issues and Defense Schemes. In G. Shrivastava, P. Kumar, B. Gupta, S. Bala, & N. Dey (Eds.), *Handbook of Research on Network Forensics and Analysis Techniques* (pp. 326–350). Hershey, PA: IGI Global. doi:10.4018/978-1-5225-4100-4.ch018

Ramos, P., Funderburk, P., & Gebelein, J. (2018). Social Media and Online Gaming: A Masquerading Funding Source. *International Journal of Cyber Warfare & Terrorism, 8*(1), 25–42. doi:10.4018/IJCWT.2018010103

Rao, N., & Srivastava, S., & K.S., S. (2017). PKI Deployment Challenges and Recommendations for ICS Networks. *International Journal of Information Security and Privacy, 11*(2), 38–48. doi:10.4018/IJISP.2017040104

Rath, M., Swain, J., Pati, B., & Pattanayak, B. K. (2018). Network Security: Attacks and Control in MANET. In G. Shrivastava, P. Kumar, B. Gupta, S. Bala, & N. Dey (Eds.), *Handbook of Research on Network Forensics and Analysis Techniques* (pp. 19–37). Hershey, PA: IGI Global. doi:10.4018/978-1-5225-4100-4.ch002

Ricci, J., Baggili, I., & Breitinger, F. (2017). Watch What You Wear: Smartwatches and Sluggish Security. In A. Marrington, D. Kerr, & J. Gammack (Eds.), *Managing Security Issues and the Hidden Dangers of Wearable Technologies* (pp. 47–73). Hershey, PA: IGI Global. doi:10.4018/978-1-5225-1016-1.ch003

Rossi, J. A. (2017). Revisiting the Value Relevance of Accounting Information in the Italian and UK Stock Markets. In M. Ojo & J. Van Akkeren (Eds.), *Value Relevance of Accounting Information in Capital Markets* (pp. 102–113). Hershey, PA: IGI Global. doi:10.4018/978-1-5225-1900-3.ch007

Rowe, N. C. (2016). Privacy Concerns with Digital Forensics. In R. Cropf & T. Bagwell (Eds.), *Ethical Issues and Citizen Rights in the Era of Digital Government Surveillance* (pp. 145–162). Hershey, PA: IGI Global. doi:10.4018/978-1-4666-9905-2.ch008

Sabillon, R., Serra-Ruiz, J., Cavaller, V., & Cano, J. J. (2017). Digital Forensic Analysis of Cybercrimes: Best Practices and Methodologies. *International Journal of Information Security and Privacy, 11*(2), 25–37. doi:10.4018/IJISP.2017040103

Sample, C., Cowley, J., & Bakdash, J. Z. (2018). Cyber + Culture: Exploring the Relationship. In J. McAlaney, L. Frumkin, & V. Benson (Eds.), *Psychological and Behavioral Examinations in Cyber Security* (pp. 64–79). Hershey, PA: IGI Global. doi:10.4018/978-1-5225-4053-3.ch004

Sarıgöllü, S. C., Aksakal, E., Koca, M. G., Akten, E., & Aslanbay, Y. (2018). Volunteered Surveillance. In J. McAlaney, L. Frumkin, & V. Benson (Eds.), *Psychological and Behavioral Examinations in Cyber Security* (pp. 133–150). Hershey, PA: IGI Global. doi:10.4018/978-1-5225-4053-3.ch008

Shahriar, H., Clincy, V., & Bond, W. (2018). Classification of Web-Service-Based Attacks and Mitigation Techniques. In Y. Maleh (Ed.), *Security and Privacy Management, Techniques, and Protocols* (pp. 360–378). Hershey, PA: IGI Global. doi:10.4018/978-1-5225-5583-4.ch015

Shet, S., Aswath, A. R., Hanumantharaju, M. C., & Gao, X. (2017). Design of Reconfigurable Architectures for Steganography System. In N. Dey, A. Ashour, & S. Acharjee (Eds.), *Applied Video Processing in Surveillance and Monitoring Systems* (pp. 145–168). Hershey, PA: IGI Global. doi:10.4018/978-1-5225-1022-2.ch007

Shrivastava, G., Sharma, K., Khari, M., & Zohora, S. E. (2018). Role of Cyber Security and Cyber Forensics in India. In G. Shrivastava, P. Kumar, B. Gupta, S. Bala, & N. Dey (Eds.), *Handbook of Research on Network Forensics and Analysis Techniques* (pp. 143–161). Hershey, PA: IGI Global. doi:10.4018/978-1-5225-4100-4.ch009

Singh, N. (2016). Cloud Crime and Fraud: A Study of Challenges for Cloud Security and Forensics. In S. Geetha & A. Phamila (Eds.), *Combating Security Breaches and Criminal Activity in the Digital Sphere* (pp. 68–84). Hershey, PA: IGI Global. doi:10.4018/978-1-5225-0193-0.ch005

Singh, N., Mittal, T., & Gupta, M. (2018). A Tale of Policies and Breaches: Analytical Approach to Construct Social Media Policy. In M. Gupta, R. Sharman, J. Walp, & P. Mulgund (Eds.), *Information Technology Risk Management and Compliance in Modern Organizations* (pp. 176–212). Hershey, PA: IGI Global. doi:10.4018/978-1-5225-2604-9.ch007

Singh, R., & Jalota, H. (2018). A Study of Good-Enough Security in the Context of Rural Business Process Outsourcing. In J. McAlaney, L. Frumkin, & V. Benson (Eds.), *Psychological and Behavioral Examinations in Cyber Security* (pp. 239–252). Hershey, PA: IGI Global. doi:10.4018/978-1-5225-4053-3.ch014

Sivasubramanian, K. E. (2018). Authorship Pattern and Collaborative Research Productivity of Asian Journal of Dairy and Food Research During the Year 2011 to 2015. In J. Jeyasekar & P. Saravanan (Eds.), *Innovations in Measuring and Evaluating Scientific Information* (pp. 213–222). Hershey, PA: IGI Global. doi:10.4018/978-1-5225-3457-0.ch014

Somasundaram, R., & Thirugnanam, M. (2017). IoT in Healthcare: Breaching Security Issues. In N. Jeyanthi & R. Thandeeswaran (Eds.), *Security Breaches and Threat Prevention in the Internet of Things* (pp. 174–188). Hershey, PA: IGI Global. doi:10.4018/978-1-5225-2296-6.ch008

Sonam, & Khari, M. (2018). Wireless Sensor Networks: A Technical Survey. In G. Shrivastava, P. Kumar, B. Gupta, S. Bala, & N. Dey (Eds.), *Handbook of Research on Network Forensics and Analysis Techniques* (pp. 1-18). Hershey, PA: IGI Global. doi:10.4018/978-1-5225-4100-4.ch001

Soni, P. (2018). Implications of HIPAA and Subsequent Regulations on Information Technology. In M. Gupta, R. Sharman, J. Walp, & P. Mulgund (Eds.), *Information Technology Risk Management and Compliance in Modern Organizations* (pp. 71–98). Hershey, PA: IGI Global. doi:10.4018/978-1-5225-2604-9.ch004

Sönmez, F. Ö., & Günel, B. (2018). Security Visualization Extended Review Issues, Classifications, Validation Methods, Trends, Extensions. In Y. Maleh (Ed.), *Security and Privacy Management, Techniques, and Protocols* (pp. 152–197). Hershey, PA: IGI Global. doi:10.4018/978-1-5225-5583-4.ch006

Srivastava, S. R., & Dube, S. (2018). Cyberattacks, Cybercrime and Cyberterrorism. In G. Shrivastava, P. Kumar, B. Gupta, S. Bala, & N. Dey (Eds.), *Handbook of Research on Network Forensics and Analysis Techniques* (pp. 162–183). Hershey, PA: IGI Global. doi:10.4018/978-1-5225-4100-4.ch010

Stacey, E. (2017). Contemporary Terror on the Net. In *Combating Internet-Enabled Terrorism: Emerging Research and Opportunities* (pp. 16–44). Hershey, PA: IGI Global. doi:10.4018/978-1-5225-2190-7.ch002

Sumana, M., Hareesha, K. S., & Kumar, S. (2018). Semantically Secure Classifiers for Privacy Preserving Data Mining. In Y. Maleh (Ed.), *Security and Privacy Management, Techniques, and Protocols* (pp. 66–95). Hershey, PA: IGI Global. doi:10.4018/978-1-5225-5583-4.ch003

Suresh, N., & Gupta, M. (2018). Impact of Technology Innovation: A Study on Cloud Risk Mitigation. In M. Gupta, R. Sharman, J. Walp, & P. Mulgund (Eds.), *Information Technology Risk Management and Compliance in Modern Organizations* (pp. 229–267). Hershey, PA: IGI Global. doi:10.4018/978-1-5225-2604-9.ch009

Survey, A. K. Balasubramanian & M. Rajakani (Eds.), *Algorithmic Strategies for Solving Complex Problems in Cryptography* (pp. 111–123). Hershey, PA: IGI Global. doi:10.4018/978-1-5225-2915-6.ch009

Tank, D. M. (2017). Security and Privacy Issues, Solutions, and Tools for MCC. In K. Munir (Ed.), *Security Management in Mobile Cloud Computing* (pp. 121–147). Hershey, PA: IGI Global. doi:10.4018/978-1-5225-0602-7.ch006

Thackray, H., & McAlaney, J. (2018). Groups Online: Hacktivism and Social Protest. In J. McAlaney, L. Frumkin, & V. Benson (Eds.), *Psychological and Behavioral Examinations in Cyber Security* (pp. 194–209). Hershey, PA: IGI Global. doi:10.4018/978-1-5225-4053-3.ch011

Thandeeswaran, R., Pawar, R., & Rai, M. (2017). Security Threats in Autonomous Vehicles. In N. Jeyanthi & R. Thandeeswaran (Eds.), *Security Breaches and Threat Prevention in the Internet of Things* (pp. 117–141). Hershey, PA: IGI Global. doi:10.4018/978-1-5225-2296-6.ch006

Thota, C., Manogaran, G., Lopez, D., & Vijayakumar, V. (2017). Big Data Security Framework for Distributed Cloud Data Centers. In M. Moore (Ed.), *Cybersecurity Breaches and Issues Surrounding Online Threat Protection* (pp. 288–310). Hershey, PA: IGI Global. doi:10.4018/978-1-5225-1941-6.ch012

Thukral, S., & Rodriguez, T. D. (2018). Child Sexual Abuse: Intra- and Extra-Familial Risk Factors, Reactions, and Interventions. In R. Gopalan (Ed.), *Social, Psychological, and Forensic Perspectives on Sexual Abuse* (pp. 229–258). Hershey, PA: IGI Global. doi:10.4018/978-1-5225-3958-2.ch017

Tidke, S. (2017). MonogDB: Data Management in NoSQL. In S. Tamane, V. Solanki, & N. Dey (Eds.), *Privacy and Security Policies in Big Data* (pp. 64–91). Hershey, PA: IGI Global. doi:10.4018/978-1-5225-2486-1.ch004

Tierney, M. (2018). #TerroristFinancing: An Examination of Terrorism Financing via the Internet. *International Journal of Cyber Warfare & Terrorism*, *8*(1), 1–11. doi:10.4018/IJCWT.2018010101

Topal, R. (2018). A Cyber-Psychological and Behavioral Approach to Online Radicalization. In J. McAlaney, L. Frumkin, & V. Benson (Eds.), *Psychological and Behavioral Examinations in Cyber Security* (pp. 210–221). Hershey, PA: IGI Global. doi:10.4018/978-1-5225-4053-3.ch012

Tripathy, B. K., & Baktha, K. (2018). Clustering Approaches. In *Security, Privacy, and Anonymization in Social Networks: Emerging Research and Opportunities* (pp. 51–85). Hershey, PA: IGI Global. doi:10.4018/978-1-5225-5158-4.ch004

Tripathy, B. K., & Baktha, K. (2018). De-Anonymization Techniques. In *Security, Privacy, and Anonymization in Social Networks: Emerging Research and Opportunities* (pp. 137–147). Hershey, PA: IGI Global. doi:10.4018/978-1-5225-5158-4.ch007

Tripathy, B. K., & Baktha, K. (2018). Fundamentals of Social Networks. In *Security, Privacy, and Anonymization in Social Networks: Emerging Research and Opportunities* (pp. 1–22). Hershey, PA: IGI Global. doi:10.4018/978-1-5225-5158-4.ch001

Tripathy, B. K., & Baktha, K. (2018). Graph Modification Approaches. In *Security, Privacy, and Anonymization in Social Networks: Emerging Research and Opportunities* (pp. 86–115). Hershey, PA: IGI Global. doi:10.4018/978-1-5225-5158-4.ch005

Tripathy, B. K., & Baktha, K. (2018). Social Network Anonymization Techniques. In *Security, Privacy, and Anonymization in Social Networks: Emerging Research and Opportunities* (pp. 36–50). Hershey, PA: IGI Global. doi:10.4018/978-1-5225-5158-4.ch003

Tsimperidis, I., Rostami, S., & Katos, V. (2017). Age Detection Through Keystroke Dynamics from User Authentication Failures. *International Journal of Digital Crime and Forensics*, *9*(1), 1–16. doi:10.4018/IJDCF.2017010101

Wadkar, H. S., Mishra, A., & Dixit, A. M. (2017). Framework to Secure Browser Using Configuration Analysis. *International Journal of Information Security and Privacy*, *11*(2), 49–63. doi:10.4018/IJISP.2017040105

Wahlgren, G., & Kowalski, S. J. (2018). IT Security Risk Management Model for Handling IT-Related Security Incidents: The Need for a New Escalation Approach. In Y. Maleh (Ed.), *Security and Privacy Management, Techniques, and Protocols* (pp. 129–151). Hershey, PA: IGI Global. doi:10.4018/978-1-5225-5583-4.ch005

Wall, H. J., & Kaye, L. K. (2018). Online Decision Making: Online Influence and Implications for Cyber Security. In J. McAlaney, L. Frumkin, & V. Benson (Eds.), *Psychological and Behavioral Examinations in Cyber Security* (pp. 1–25). Hershey, PA: IGI Global. doi:10.4018/978-1-5225-4053-3.ch001

Xylogiannopoulos, K. F., Karampelas, P., & Alhajj, R. (2017). Advanced Network Data Analytics for Large-Scale DDoS Attack Detection. *International Journal of Cyber Warfare & Terrorism*, *7*(3), 44–54. doi:10.4018/IJCWT.2017070104

Yan, W. Q., Wu, X., & Liu, F. (2018). Progressive Scrambling for Social Media. *International Journal of Digital Crime and Forensics*, *10*(2), 56–73. doi:10.4018/IJDCF.2018040104

Yang, L., Gao, T., Xuan, Y., & Gao, H. (2016). Contrast Modification Forensics Algorithm Based on Merged Weight Histogram of Run Length. *International Journal of Digital Crime and Forensics*, *8*(2), 27–35. doi:10.4018/IJDCF.2016040103

Yassein, M. B., Mardini, W., & Al-Abdi, A. (2018). Security Issues in the Internet of Things: A Review. In S. Aljawarneh & M. Malhotra (Eds.), *Critical Research on Scalability and Security Issues in Virtual Cloud Environments* (pp. 186–200). Hershey, PA: IGI Global. doi:10.4018/978-1-5225-3029-9.ch009

Yassein, M. B., Shatnawi, M., & l-Qasem, N. (2018). A Survey of Probabilistic Broadcast Schemes in Mobile Ad Hoc Networks. In S. Aljawarneh, & M. Malhotra (Eds.), *Critical Research on Scalability and Security Issues in Virtual Cloud Environments* (pp. 269-282). Hershey, PA: IGI Global. doi:10.4018/978-1-5225-3029-9.ch013

Yue, C., Tianliang, L., Manchun, C., & Jingying, L. (2018). Evaluation of the Attack Effect Based on Improved Grey Clustering Model. *International Journal of Digital Crime and Forensics, 10*(1), 92–100. doi:10.4018/IJDCF.2018010108

Zhang, P., He, Y., & Chow, K. (2018). Fraud Track on Secure Electronic Check System. *International Journal of Digital Crime and Forensics, 10*(2), 137–144. doi:10.4018/IJDCF.2018040108

Zhao, J., Wang, Q., Guo, J., Gao, L., & Yang, F. (2016). An Overview on Passive Image Forensics Technology for Automatic Computer Forgery. *International Journal of Digital Crime and Forensics, 8*(4), 14–25. doi:10.4018/IJDCF.2016100102

Zhao, X., Zhu, J., & Yu, H. (2016). On More Paradigms of Steganalysis. *International Journal of Digital Crime and Forensics, 8*(2), 1–15. doi:10.4018/IJDCF.2016040101

Zhou, L., Yan, W. Q., Shu, Y., & Yu, J. (2018). CVSS: A Cloud-Based Visual Surveillance System. *International Journal of Digital Crime and Forensics, 10*(1), 79–91. doi:10.4018/IJDCF.2018010107

Zhu, J., Guan, Q., Zhao, X., Cao, Y., & Chen, G. (2017). A Steganalytic Scheme Based on Classifier Selection Using Joint Image Characteristics. *International Journal of Digital Crime and Forensics, 9*(4), 1–14. doi:10.4018/IJDCF.2017100101

Zoughbi, S. (2017). Major Technology Trends Affecting Government Data in Developing Countries. In S. Zoughbi (Ed.), *Securing Government Information and Data in Developing Countries* (pp. 127–135). Hershey, PA: IGI Global. doi:10.4018/978-1-5225-1703-0.ch008

Zubairu, B. (2018). Security Risks of Biomedical Data Processing in Cloud Computing Environment. In C. Pradhan, H. Das, B. Naik, & N. Dey (Eds.), *Handbook of Research on Information Security in Biomedical Signal Processing* (pp. 177–197). Hershey, PA: IGI Global. doi:10.4018/978-1-5225-5152-2.ch009

# About the Contributors

**Eugene de Silva**, as an award-winning educator with over 30 years of experience in academia and research, earned a place in the "Who's Who in the World," "Who's Who in American Education," and "Who's Who in America." He has been the President of the Tennessee Science Department Chairs Association since 2008, and held the position of Chair of the Institute of Physics UK/USA Branch from 2013 to 2019. Professor de Silva's long-standing background in the security arena can be traced back to his honorary research fellowship from 2000 to 2004 at the Centre for Defence and International Security Studies (University of Lancaster, UK) and his 2004-2006 appointment as Director of International Relations for the Institute for Democracy and Leadership in Sri Lanka. He is now the President of the Virginia Research Institute, and continues to teach natural sciences at the college-level in the United States. Professor de Silva's active engagement in multidisciplinary research ventures is supported by his proven expertise in a multitude of fields, including the natural sciences, intelligence, and business. He is a Fellow of the Royal Society of Chemistry, UK, Institute of Physics, UK, Royal Society of Arts, UK, Institute of Professional, Business, and Technical Management, UK, Institute of Manufacturing, UK, and the Institute of Management Specialists, UK. He is also recognized as a chartered chemist, chartered scientist, and chartered physicist, in addition to being inducted to the Hall of Excellence in Quality Matters for his work in online educational courses. His significant research contributions have included books and articles in physics, chemistry, research, education, security, martial arts, and quality-assurance models. Professor de Silva's newly proposed models have been used within security settings to investigate and inquire about the politicization of intelligence and other similar issues in the security field. His educational model pertaining to the teaching of science, known as "START," has even been integrated within college settings in the United States.

**Asanga Abeyagoonasekera** is an International Security and Geopolitics Analyst and Strategic Advisor from Sri Lanka. His new book is on Sri Lanka's Geopolitical challenges 'Conundrum of an Island' (2021, Published by World Scientific, Singapore) endorsed by Walter Russell Mead as a "Useful text to understand emerging dynamics of the Indo-Pacific". He is the author of 'Sri Lanka at Crossroads' (2019) and 'Towards A Better World Order' (2015). He is a keen commentator on Geo-politics, Intranational Relations and South Asian Security matters and has written extensively and published on international journals and think tanks. He has provided consultancy to multiple development partners, private firms, and government. He is a Senior Researcher for Social Impact (USA). He serves as the Senior Advisor for Security and Geopolitics to Leader of the Opposition in Parliament of Sri Lanka. He has led two Government think tanks providing strategic advocacy on Foreign Policy and Defence in Sri Lanka. He was the Founding Director-General of the National Security Think Tank under the Ministry of Defence (INSSSL) until January 2020. Before this, he has served as the Executive Director at the Foreign Policy think tank ((Kadirgamar Institute LKIIRSS). He was the advisor to Minister of External Affairs from 2011-2015. Asanga served as a Visiting Professor for Geopolitics and Global Leadership (NKU, USA), Visiting Lecturer for International Security (Colombo University, Sri Lanka), International Political Economy (University of London in Colombo RIC). He is an Alumnus of the US State Department IVLP, Fellow at National Defense University (NESA, NDU) in Washington DC, Fellow at APCSS (Hawaii) and Young Global Leader World Economic Forum (Geneva). For his academic contribution, he was awarded the accolade Ambassador of Knowledge in 2015 from Life Learning Academia, Slovenia. In 2021 he was appointed to the Global Advisory Council along with former New Zealand Prime Minister Helen Clark and several other distinguished individuals to the Apolitical Global Academy.

* * *

**Joey Budd**, Associate Professor of Criminal Justice originally from Pittsburgh, Pennsylvania, teaches at the Louisville Education Center of Campbellsville University. Dr. Budd is also the Program Coordinator for the Master's in justice Studies program. Dr. Budd was a law enforcement officer in Georgia after serving 11 years in the United States Air Force and is a veteran of the first Gulf War. Dr. Budd's first policing job was in a small town of fewer than 1000 people; there he had the opportunity to meet people and practice community policing. He then transferred to a larger department where he was an investigator working many types of cases and meeting diverse individuals. Dr. Budd's last law enforcement job was at a sheriff's office working as a deputy sheriff with a focus on traffic offenses, especially DUI's. Dr. Budd enjoys ice hockey and cycling in his spare time along with spending time with his children and grandchildren. His research interest includes law enforcement use of force, community policing, bullying, and deviant behavior.

**Tianxing Cai** is a faculty member in the Dan. F Smith Department of Chemical and Biomolecular Engineering, Lamar University. Dr. Cai is specialized in the research fields of modeling, simulation and optimization for the industrial operation, process safety, and environment protection. His major research is the development of optimization models, simulation, and optimization for the process design, environment impact reduction and safety assessment. He also serves as newsletter editor and webmaster for divisions of AIChE.

**Eugenie de Silva**, originally from Manchester, England, has been an intelligence and security researcher and educator for over eight years. With an emphasis placed on multidisciplinary research, she has published on a variety of topics, such as law, human intelligence, education, cyber security, and even the recent COVID-19 pandemic. As a scholar from the University of Cambridge and Harvard University, she has spent many years in academia with the aim of honing her expertise in multiple fields to address pressing global issues. She has been recognized for her contributions by being named a Top Thirty Thinker Under Thirty by the Pacific Standard Magazine, earning several academic world records, and being an invited speaker to international conferences on a multitude of subjects ranging from education to security. She now focuses much of her research efforts to address the violence that stems from white supremacy within the United States.

**Terrence Frost** is originally from Dublin, Ireland now residing in Los Angeles California. Terence has over 20 years' experience working in Information security, cyber terrorism research and enterprise data storage and architecture for fortune 500 companies. Holder of both Masters and Bachelors degrees in computer related disciplines from IISER Manchester U.K. Terence is President and CEO of Cyber Living and heads the SCSRIT group of experts in technology research and reporting group. With past published work on Al Queada and cyber terrorism. Terence is focused on firewall implementation, IT security and educating companies on the best security protocols available in today's ever-changing landscape.

**Michael Littrell** is a full time digital forensics examiner and detective for the Kentucky Attorney General's Office where he executes dozens of search warrants related to cyber crimes investigations and exams hundreds of mobile devices each year. He works closely with local, state, and federal prosecutors in drafting and executing search warrants. Dr. Littrell teaches criminal justice, sociology, and digital forensics part time for various academic institutions. He is a member of the Kentucky ICAC Task Force, and a member and volunteer staff instructor for the International Association of Computer Investigative Specialists. He maintains multiple computer and mobile device forensics certifications, and works with state and local agencies to improve the scope and specificity of search warrants. Dr. Littrell has more than 15 years of law enforcement experience both as a patrol officer and detective. He has more than eight years of experience teaching criminal justice and criminology classes. He specializes in cybercrime and digital forensics investigations, particularly related to child exploitation offenses. Dr. Littrell maintains active participation in both policing and academia.

**Michael Nolan**, originally from Brisbane, Australia, has worked in USA, France and in South East Asia as a developer, infrastructure designer and security researcher. Graduate in Science from University of Queensland (1991) which was the key technology center of Australia at the time. Has worked in the field deploying open source firewall technology since it emerged as a viable and superior alternative to commercial firewall software. Reverse engineering and decompiling software since he was a child Michael is a natural ethical hacker. Michael is a life long computing enthusiast and electronics engineer/maker who is interested in seeing through the outer face of software to see its latent potential including risks. He works mostly to further understanding and protect and assist non-profit and non-governmental groups and institutions.

**Kasuni Ranasinghe** is a postgraduate student at Graduate School of Education, University of Melbourne where she specialised in education leadership and policy. She was a Research Analyst at the Institute of National Security Studies Sri Lanka (INSSSL) and a visiting lecturer at the University of Colombo. Her first Masters is in International Relations at the University of Colombo. Her Bachelors is from the Department of Economics, the University of Kelaniya. Ms Ranasinghe is a "REFERENCE WINNERS" at the Ambassador of Knowledge Program in 2019. She won the best research paper award in South Asian Economics Students Meet in 2014 held in Bhutan, which is organized by World Bank. She was awarded "Friendly AIESECer" and "Best Team Member" from AIESEC Sri Lanka in the year 2012. Further, Ms Ranasinghe is a "National colour" winner for Chess in Sri Lanka. Her research interest is political economics, regional integration, globalization, South Asia, Belt Road Initiative, security studies, Education policy, leadership management and sports education.

**Savithri Sellapperumage** is from Sri Lanka. Her academic background is in International Relations. She currently works as an Assistant Lecturer at University of Colombo, Sri Lanka. She is also an Associate Research Fellow at Institute of National Security Studies where she contributes through research/ studies on security threats/ projections of the country. Her main research interests cover geopolitics of South Asia and Environmental Governance especially pertaining to international collective effort (of conventions, agreements, and principles) towards environmental governance. She is working in a diverse array of organizational settings, including research-based organizations, government bodies, non-government organizations in addressing pressing issues of environment as well as unity and coexistence within the country.

# Index

## L



## M



## N



## O



## P



## Q



## R



## S

## T



## V



## Z

www.ingramcontent.com/pod-product-compliance
Lightning Source LLC
LaVergne TN
LVHW081325300926
849161LV00008B/1877